To the memory of
Philip Brett
(1937–2002)

Contents

Acknowledgments

Some years ago, I was sitting at dinner with a number of scholars who had made names for themselves in LGBT/queer studies. I do not need to name them, but several of them have been noted throughout this study. Each one of us had written a doctoral dissertation on gothic fiction. That might be surprising until the claims I am making can register. For this one semilegitimate area of literary study allowed scholars to address questions not otherwise available in literary discourse. My own first gay studies essay concerned gothic writers, and key chapters by Eve Sedgwick, Judith Halberstam, George Rousseau, Lee Edelman, Andrew Elfenbein, Claudia Johnson, and Kristina Straub all discuss gothic fiction.[1] That is not accidental. Gothic writing addresses concerns central to anyone interested in the literary representation of sexuality.

The chapters included in this study approach these topics from a number of directions. I feel that the effect of the variety of approaches is to enrich the topic and give various perspectives on my most salient concerns. If I have written about affectional relations in earlier books, love between men and love between women, I here address various kinds of sexual violence that have very little to do with love. That does not mean I have abandoned my earlier concerns, however. The complications of family life and the torments of forced intimacy are richly connected to the material I have considered earlier. And it is no mistake that among the writers I discuss are several I discussed in earlier studies as well: Beckford, Lewis, Maturin, Radcliffe, Shelley, and Walpole, just to name a few. I view this book, in fact, as the culmination of a career in gothic fiction.

To colleagues and students who have made this work so fulfilling, I offer my thanks. To those who are reading this book, I offer thanks as well. This topic is a rich and rewarding one, and I hope that readers can see what kinds of vistas this material opens for anyone interested in sexuality studies. If readers can see that, then I know I have achieved what I hoped to achieve in *Queer Gothic*.

I would like to thank the Regents of the University of California for research support and a sabbatical leave that allowed me to finish this project. I am also grateful to the following journals for allowing me to reprint material that appeared in an earlier version: *Eighteenth-Century Culture* (chapter 1), *Eighteenth-Century Fiction* (chapter 2), *Romanticism on the Net* (chapter 4), *Theatre Research International* (chapter 5), *Eighteenth-Century: Theory and Interpretation* (chapter 6), and *Novel* (chapter 9). I could never say enough to thank Joan Catapano, editor-in-chief at the University of Illinois Press, who encouraged me in this project, and the talented people on the staff, especially Mary Giles and Paula Newcomb, who helped make it presentable.

I also extend special thanks to those friends who supported me in this project when I lost my life-partner Philip Brett and had trouble continuing with my work. They include Steven Axelrod, Jill Campbell, Sue-Ellen Case, Joseph Childers, Patricia De Camp, Jennifer Doyle, Susan Foster, Carla Frecerro, Lisa Freeman, John Ganim, Robert Glavin, Jody Greene, Albert Johns, Katherine Kinney, Susan Lanser, Molly McGarry, Chris Mounsey, David Romàn, James Schultz, James Tobias, Hans Turley, Robyn Wiegman, and Traise Yamamoto.

Students at the University of California, Riverside, have supported my work in gothic fiction in many ways. Graduate students have helped me explore specific problems and aided in my research. These include Chrissy Crockett, Richard Hishmeh, Nowell Marshall, Joshua Rodriguez, and Christy Russell. Undergraduates have supported my teaching and encouraged me to continue work in a field that fascinates them. I am grateful to them all.

I dedicate this book to the memory of Philip Brett. When I began this project, neither of us imagined that Philip would not be around for its completion.

Queer Gothic

Introduction

Gothic fiction emerged rather suddenly as a popular form of British fiction in the later years of the eighteenth century, starting with Horace Walpole's *The Castle of Ortanto* (1764) and extending at least as far as Charles Robert Maturin's *Melmoth the Wanderer* (1820) and James Hogg's *The Private Memoirs and Confessions of a Justified Sinner* (1824). In order to explain the sudden popularity of this bizarrely outrageous yet conventional form, which reached its first apex in the 1790s, literary historians have cited aesthetic history, political unrest, literary experimentation, and personal obsession. No single account has been able to establish a reason for the popularity of gothic writing, nor have critical interpretations felt at all restricted by historical circumstances or aesthetic presuppositions. Gothic fiction has given rise to a wide range of provocative readings, and it has sustained even ahistorical accounts of personality and psyche that would have been unfathomable to those writing these sensational texts.

Recent studies of gothic fiction, such as those by Emma Clery and Robert Miles and by Edward Jacobs, have usefully extended the scope of gothic writing in the eighteenth century.[1] By looking at materials earlier in the eighteenth century and reconsidering a range of writing that has often been ignored, these critics have suggested that the term *gothic* itself shifts in meaning and cultural significance throughout the period I am considering. In an earlier book I argued that the opposite of historical specificity, rather vague and often indirect historical associations, served expressive purposes that no amount of historical investigation can explain.[2] The peculiar and often uncanny power of eighteenth-century Gothic fiction still resists attempts to explain it, and as useful as this recent historicizing of gothic has been, it does not radically change the way "gothic" functions as a literary device in the period under discussion. A wide range of writers, dispersed historically and culturally, use "gothic" to evoke a queer world that attempts to transgress the binaries of sexual decorum.[3]

What does it mean to call gothic fiction "queer"? It is no mere coincidence that the cult of gothic fiction reached its apex at the very moment when gender and sexuality were beginning to be codified for modern culture. In fact, gothic fiction offered a testing ground for many unauthorized genders and sexualities, including sodomy, tribadism, romantic friendship (male and female), incest, pedophilia, sadism, masochism, necrophilia, cannibalism, masculinized females, feminized males, miscegenation, and so on. In this sense it offers a historical model of queer theory and politics: transgressive, sexually coded, and resistant to dominant ideology. While I examine gothic fiction in order to relate it to the history of sexuality, as articulated by Michel Foucault and others, I will also describe recent works of queer theory and cultural studies in order to explore the ways in which this fiction itself is codified. Joseph Bristow offers a useful summary of the emergence of the concept of sexuality in the later nineteenth century.[4] From that perspective these works predate sexuality's codification. But by predating, they also prepare the ground, as I hope these pages will show, for later developments in sexological studies.

Transgressive social-sexual relations are the most basic common denominator of gothic writing, and from the moment in the early pages of Walpole's *The Castle of Otranto* when the anti-hero Manfred presses his suit on the fiancée of his deceased son (and she flees into the "long labyrinth of darkness" in the "subterraneous" regions of the castle), a gothic trope is fixed: terror is almost always sexual terror, and fear, and flight, and incarceration, and escape are almost always colored by the exoticism of transgressive sexual aggression.[5] Like other expressions of transgressive desire throughout the eighteenth century, gothic fiction is not about homo- or heterodesire as much as it is about the fact of desire itself. And throughout these works this desire is expressed as the exercise of (or resistance to) power. But that power is itself charged with a sexual force—a sexuality—that determines the action and gives it shape. By the same token, powerlessness has a similar valence and performs a similar function. This creates an odd sexual mood in most gothic works, closer to what we might crudely label "sadomasochism" (a binary that critics too readily take for granted) than to any other model of sexual interaction. That nearly a century of fiction (or more than two centuries, depending on how broad the definition of "gothic" is) would function in this way is in itself queer, and queer, too, is the manner in which normative sexual relations are articulated and codified. No matter how tidy, no marriage at the close of a gothic novel can entirely dispel the thrilling dys- (or different) functionality at the heart of gothic.

In this study I approach the question of "queer gothic" from a number of directions. In addition to examining the representations of same-sex desire in gothic fiction, a trope that has been variously explained by critics, including myself, I attempt to show the ways in which all normative—heteronormative, if you will—configurations of human interaction are insistently challenged and in some cases significantly undermined in these fictions.[6] I cannot make too broad a claim because these fictions never significantly challenge the "dominant fiction" of the age.[7] At the same time, however, they occur in a period that had yet to construct the elaborate superstructure of sexuality that emerged in the age of sexology at the end of the nineteenth and beginning of the twentieth centuries. Gothic fiction offered the one semirespectable area of literary endeavor in which modes of sexual and social transgression were discursively addressed on a regular basis. It therefore makes sense to consider the ways in which gothic fiction itself helped shape thinking about sexual matters—theories of sexuality, as it were—and create the darker shadows of the dominant fiction, the darkness that enables culture to function as a fiction in the first place.

I have divided this study into three parts. Part 1, "Gothic Sexuality," is a discussion of a wide range of gothic works from the perspective of transgressive sexuality, loss, incest, and prohibited desire. In the first chapter, "Gothic Fiction and the History of Sexuality," I look at the three most well-known gothic writers, Matthew G. Lewis, Ann Radcliffe, and Charles Robert Maturin, and show the ways in which they offer gothic set pieces that have as much to say about the history of sexuality as anything that emerged later from nineteenth-century sexologists. Chapter 2 examines more closely a particular configuration that can be found in the work of Radcliffe and other female gothic novelists. Using the writing of Judith Butler, Julia Kristeva, and others, I articulate a theory of the erotics of loss in gothic fiction that both explains some of its more bizarre plot devices and helps to see seemingly disparate works, like those of Radcliffe and Charlotte Dacre, focusing on the same concerns. Gothic fiction is rarely about the happy ending, if there is one, or catastrophic close. Instead the novels develop a complex of emotional relations that can be understood most usefully, it seems to me, according to the figure of loss that I discuss here. In chapter 3, I examine some of the more scandalous sodomitical reports of the late eighteenth and early nineteenth centuries and explain how reports of sexual transgression use gothic motifs and how the details of sodomitical prosecution are re-represented in gothic fiction. Gothic works that are primarily concerned with male relations, like those in *Frankenstein* or *The Private Memoirs and Confessions of a Justified Sinner,* can be seen to have incorporated some of the language of the sodomy trials and newspaper reports.

In Part 2, "Gothic Culture," I move beyond these closely argued questions about sexuality and discuss some issues of larger cultural significance. Chapter 4, "The Horrors of Catholicism," reveals the ways in which gothic writers use Roman Catholicism to motivate their tales and what that means in the context of anti-Catholic, eighteenth-century England. Chapter 5 is specifically about gothic drama and the ways in which gothic materials offered themselves for theatrical spectacle. And chapter 6, "Gothic Fiction and the End of History," addresses the ways in which gothic fiction collapses history and articulates the fear of moving outside historical time. Key to this argument is Mary Shelley's little-known novel *The Last Man* (1826), but I also discuss William Godwin's *Caleb Williams* (1794) and Robert Louis Stevenson's *Dr. Jekyll and Mr. Hyde* (1886). These works all show the ways in which apocalyptic thinking focuses on male-male desire and sees it as the cause of cultural collapse.

Part 3, "Gothic Fiction and the Queering of Culture," details a selection of late-nineteenth- and twentieth-century works in order to show how these gothic effects are reimagined after an age of sexology and psychoanalysis renders so much gothic material either delusional or pathological or both. As the family romance was rewritten in the twentieth century it is interesting to look back to see how much of this psychological dynamic gothic fiction anticipated. It is also interesting to glance at how late gothic fiction addresses some of these same concerns. In chapter 7, "Queer Company," I describe two classically neurotic heroines, the governess in Henry James's "The Turn of the Screw" (1898) and Eleanor Vance in Shirley Jackson's *The Haunting of Hill House* (1959). Both works comment on earlier gothic and suggest the ways in which twentieth-century gothic fiction revises the earlier plight of the gothic heroine. Chapter 8, "Queerer Knowledge," considers Henry James again, this time his masterpiece *The Ambassadors* (1903) in relation to Patricia Highsmith's novel *The Talented Mr. Ripley* (1955) and the film that Anthony Minghella made based on that work (1999). Chapter 9, "Anne Rice and the Queering of Culture," treats the phenomenon of Rice's popularity and attempts to explain how such blatantly queer gothic material became so popular in the 1980s and 1990s.

I imagine this book as a gathering of analyses that together make an important point about the ways in which gothic fiction anticipates the history of sexuality and gives that history its most basic materials. It is no accident that Freud relied on gothic writing to help him articulate his notions of uncanny and various delusional behaviors. Gothic writers anticipated the work of Freud and other sexologists, and it seems to me that if we attend more closely to what they have written we may find that the history of sexuality is not as constricting as it has sometimes seemed. Rather than look back from the twentieth century, that is, to see how sexuality functions in gothic fiction, I prefer to look forward from the eighteenth century to understand how gothic fiction gave sexuality a history in the first place.

PART 1

Gothic Sexuality

1

Gothic Fiction and the History of Sexuality

Gothic fiction relies on a set of narrative conventions that barely change from Horace Walpole to Charles Robert Maturin and beyond.[1] Slavoj Žižek explains why such conventions might have the uncanny power that they do. For him, "the Real is the rock upon which every attempt at symbolization stumbles, the hard core which remains the same in all possible worlds."[2] This would begin to explain the common obsessions of gothic, its seemingly inexhaustible ability to return again and again to common tropes and similar situations. At the same time, however, this promising stability "is thoroughly precarious; it is something that persists only as failed, missed, in a shadow, and dissolves itself as soon as we try to grasp it in its positive nature."[3] So many critical attempts to pin down the gothic are unsuccessful because of its uncanny structure.[4] For Žižek the function of "the Real" is clear: "All its effectivity lies in the distortions it produces in the symbolic universe of the subject: the traumatic event is ultimately just a fantasy-construct filling out a certain void in a symbolic structure and, as such, the retroactive effect of this structure."[5] This shadow-presence of the real and these distortions of the symbolic are the staple of gothic fiction. These are primal scenes, not the secretive private memory of an individual but the primal reality of the culture at large. It behooves us to look more closely at the queerness of this material so as to recognize its function in the structure of the dominant fiction.

I borrow the notion of a "dominant fiction" from Kaja Silverman, for whom this concept explains how cultural prerogatives are given the ascendancy that the "ideological state apparatus" presupposes. In her attempt to analyze the function of marginalized masculinities, Silverman reexamines the Althussarian concept of "interpellation" to include the notion that the "state apparatus" is only a "dominant fiction" rather than anything "real." Conveniently for the critic of fiction, that is, she shows the ways in which culture structures itself like fiction. Like gothic fiction? Uncannily, yes. The dominant fiction has a ghostly presence. Silverman argues further that "it is only by defining what passes for 'reality' at the level of the psyche that ideology can be said to command the subject's belief."[6] Gothic fiction attempts to rewrite "psychic" reality for the purposes of extending its own erotic power. In doing so, it shifts the range and complexity of cultural control.[7] Silverman maintains that the dominant fiction is more real than any details of concrete reality. The ideological charge is always already at work for Silverman; no writer completely escapes the force of the dominant fiction within which she or he constructs imaginative fictions. In this sense, of course, gothic fiction can be read as reinscribing the status quo. Gothic resolutions repeatedly insist on order restored and (often) on reassertion of heteronormative prerogative. At the same time, a nonteleological reading of gothic—a queer reading—can begin to show the ways in which gothic works beyond the limits of its structural "meaning" to change the structure of meaning itself. Gothic fiction is about reaching into some undefinable world beyond fictional reality, and that "beyond" can never be pulled back into narrative control. That is why gothic fiction remains as queer as it is, and it also suggests why and how gothic remains to challenge the status quo and at the same time to expand its purview.

The gothic novel, emerging at the moment battle lines of cultural reorganization were being formed in the later eighteenth century, shimmers with subversive potential. If the emergence of "the novel" celebrates the codification of middle-class values, as several critics have argued, the gothic novel records the terror implicit in the increasingly dictatorial reign of those values.[8] Gothic fiction, as I have argued in *Gothic Fiction/Gothic Form,* seems particularly, if not aggressively, open to interpretation from social, political, and sexual points of view. The gothic novel achieves this interpretative license precisely because it reflects in perhaps predictable, but nonetheless often powerful, ways the anxiety that the force of culture generates. In its excess, gothic fiction thereby challenges the cultural system that commodifies desire and renders it lurid and pathological.[9]

In *The Monk: A Romance* (1796), for instance, Matthew Gregory Lewis attempts to outrage taste and scandalize propriety in as many sexually explicit ways as he can. The central plot—that of the seemingly virtuous Monk Ambrosio, who is seduced by the scheming Matilda, herself disguised as the young novice Rosario—is fraught with uncontrollable sexual desire and motivated by "perverse" sexual transgression throughout. The ambiguous sexuality of Rosario/Matilda provides a backdrop of homoeroticism against which the larger dramas of the plot are played out. When Matilda reveals herself in turn to be an agent of Satan, the catalyst of "perversity," gender recedes as the determining factor in desire. Ambrosio's "lusts" would in any case be difficult to categorize.

After Ambrosio's desire for Matilda cools, he turns his lascivious attention to the young Antonia, daughter of the proud Elvira, his confidante. Having employed occult arts by means of which to enter Antonia's bedchamber and render her defenseless against his lust, Ambrosio is interrupted by Elvira, who challenges and accuses him. He responds by murdering her in one of the most brutal scenes of gothic fiction:

> Turning round suddenly, with one hand He grasped Elvira's throat so as to prevent her continuing her clamour, and with the other, dashing her violently upon the ground, He dragged her towards the Bed. . . . The Monk, snatching the pillow from beneath her daughter's head, covering with it Elvira's face, and pressing his knee upon her stomach with all his strength, endeavoured to put an end to her existence. He succeeded but too well. . . . The Monk continued to kneel upon her breast, witnessed without mercy the convulsive trembling of her limbs beneath him, and sustained with inhuman firmness the spectacle of her agonies, when soul and body were on the point of separating.

At last he completes his task and gazes on her "a Corse, cold, senseless, and disgusting."[10] More than a hundred pages pass before the reader is informed that the woman with whom Ambrosio struggles on the bed of his proposed sexual violation is in fact his own mother. The excessive emotion of what turns out to be the only "bed scene" in the novel, a scene between a sexually confused young man and his mother, seems the emotional center of the work.

Antonia, who is therefore Ambrosio's sister, is not spared the incestuous obsession of the unfortunate friar. Toward the close of the novel he discovers her in the underground vault of the Convent of St. Claire: "Naturally addicted to the gratification of the senses, in the full vigour of manhood, and heat of blood, He had suffered his temperament to acquire such ascendancy, that his lust was become madness. . . . He longed for the possession of her [Antonia's] person; and even the gloom of the vault, the surrounding silence, and the resistance which He expected from her, seemed to give a fresh edge to his fierce and unbridled desires" (380). After Ambrosio accomplishes

Antonia's "dishonour" in the "violence of his lustful delirium," he curses her fatal charms and blames her for his fall from grace. He determines further that she must never leave the dungeon. When she tries to escape he kills her by plunging his dagger twice into her bosom—suggesting at once the murderous impulse harbored within his incestuous desire. For Stephen Bruhn, "The 'Gothic body' is that which is put on excessive display, and whose violent, vulnerable immediacy gives . . . Gothic fiction [its] beautiful barbarity, [its] troublesome power."[11] The "troublesome power" in *The Monk* remains connected to the family in this way because Lewis reserves bodily excess for such scenes of family intimacy.

These scenes are usually dismissed as merely sensational, yet however sensationalistic they seem, they are also as political as anything in late-eighteenth-century fiction. It is the nature of patriarchy to make incest, for instance, its most basic prohibition, for unless the terms of familial desire are carefully controlled, according to the logic of patriarchy, the fabric of society will break down. Studies by anthropologists such as Claude Lévi-Strauss and others have demonstrated that the distribution of power depends on the control of intrafamilial relations by means of an "exchange" of women and that the incest taboo serves as much a political as a sexual function.[12]

In another context I have argued that incest is a cultural taboo rather than a "natural" one.[13] That does not make it less deeply encoded as a personal taboo, and when Ambrosio "rapes" and murders his mother Elvira for getting in the way of his desire for his sister Antonia—and in turn rapes and murders Antonia because she comes to represent the hideousness of his desires—he transcendently violates the most basic law of patriarchal culture. After Ambrosio is informed of his incestuous crimes, during the closing pages of the novel, he is filled with the horror of self-disgust. This horror, however, comes so late that the effect of the incest is at least potentially subversive; by abusing the relations between himself and his mother and sister he is doing more than giving his villainous character an appallingly misogynist twist. The act of incest is political because it defies the attempt of society to control desire. Cultural critics have suggested that the regulation of marriage ties is a restriction that serves the purposes of the patriarchy; Ambrosio at the very least defies such a restriction in his experiments with "perversion." In raping and murdering the women in his life, moreover, Ambrosio underlines the other, the forbidden desire that Rosario at first represented. At one point in the midst of his nefarious decline, the narrator tells us that in a moment of reflection "he regretted Rosario, the fond, the gentle, and submissive" (232). If Ambrosio must be forced to fulfill the role of the male in patriarchal culture, he does so violently, with none of the subterfuge at work in the society around him. He turns the romantic fiction inside out in order to show that sexuality is always about power and that power, perhaps more important, is always about sexuality.

Foucault would argue that this attempt at subversion is not only doomed to failure but also is an aspect of the extension of cultural control that he calls "the deployment of sexuality." Foucault claims that sexuality itself becomes a mode of social knowledge and control. "[I]n a society such as ours," he says, "where the family is the most active site of sexuality, and where it is doubtless the exigencies of the latter which maintain and prolong its existence, incest . . . occupies a central place; it is constantly being solicited and refused; it is an object of obsession and attraction, a dreadful secret and an indispensable pivot." But Lewis exposes this "affective intensification of the family space" and ridicules the terms of the Oedipal "fantasy" almost as directly as Foucault does. Lewis seems to understand implicitly what it means to be trapped in a regime that makes sexuality the central, the single transgression. By turning the Oedipal "fantasy" into vivid and horrifying (fictional) reality, Lewis exposes the process of cultural control that Foucault came later to describe. What Foucault calls the pathologization of pleasure has its fictional equivalent in a novel like *The Monk* in which sexuality becomes a form of public madness that defies the culture that would attempt to control, contain, or even know it.[14]

Ann Radcliffe's evocation of female anxiety in works such as *The Mysteries of Udolpho* (1794) also pushes at the limits of the normative.[15] When Emily St. Aubert first sees the Castle of Udolpho, where she will live with her aunt and her aunt's husband, the nefarious Montoni, it has an almost human presence for her: "Emily gazed with melancholy awe upon the castle, which she understood to be Montoni's; for, though it was now lighted up by the setting sun, the gothic greatness of its features, and its mouldering walls of dark grey stone, rendered it a gloomy and sublime object. . . . Silent, lonely, and sublime, it seemed to stand the sovereign of the scene, and to frown defiance on all, who dared to invade its solitary reign."[16]

Emily's first view of the castle connects it to its owner, and there is every reason to think that the castle itself, "gloomy and sublime," is a constant reminder of the evil Montoni. Such textbook descriptions of landscape are associated with eighteenth-century concepts of the picturesque, or the sublime, inspired by the philosophy of Edmund Burke, whose *Philosophical Enquiry into the Origin of Our Ideas of the Sublime and the Beautiful* (1757) popularized the notion of pleasurable terror and outlined an entire range of techniques for engaging the emotions associated with the gothic. As Fred Botting says, "No topic of aesthetic inquiry in the eighteenth century generated greater interest than the sublime."[17] Radcliffean "sublime" always involves fascination with what is fearful. Vijay Mishra notes, "The experience of the sublime pushes the imagination to a crisis point, to a point of exhaustion and chaos."[18] This compulsive pursuit of an exhausting and chaotic encounter with the other could be equated with desire, but it is not necessarily a desire for the "owner" of the castle. For Robert Miles, "Radcliffe's picturesque appears to turn on absence—the melancholy viewer is filled with a poignant yearning for something that forever eludes her." Miles goes on to argue that the picturesque "is actually a moment of plenitude, one associated with maternal nurturing. This is because the picturesque moment is for the heroine an instance of artistic self-fulfillment."[19] That is how the picturesque should work, but a scene like this one short-circuits self-fulfillment with the dread associated with the view itself. The more precise rendering of the view makes the terror it invokes more powerful.

Later, when Emily has suffered enough mental abuse from her step-father to realize that she is in real danger, she finds the dreary castle itself more terrifying and more attractive than anyone who inhabits it. In seeking her aunt in a distant tower, for instance, she "proceeded through a passage, adjoining the vaults, the walls of which were drooping with unwholesome dews, and the vapours, that crept along the ground, made the torch burn so dimly, that Emily expected every moment to see it extinguished." She then looks through "a pair of iron gates" to see "by uncertain flashes of light, the vaults beyond, and near her, heaps of earth, that seemed to surround an open grave" (345). These descriptions are more specific than Walpole's "long labyrinth of darkness," and the details all help to draw a picture that makes understandable the critical desire to connect passages of the castle and passages of memory. Emily seems drawn into these dim, vapourous, and unwholesome spaces; she sees them uncertainly, and she fears for her own safety even as she insists on penetrating further into the gloom and secrecy of this dark interior. The spectral presence of the castle has an alarming "uncanniness," as if Emily, trapped in the passages of repressed memory, recognized in these threatening spaces something about herself that she had always known.[20] David Punter claims that "the Gothic and the sublime best encounter each other on the terrain of memory and forgetting," and that is what Radcliffe accomplishes.[21] Memory offers the heroine the opportunity to confront her deepest fears and darkest desires.

What critics such as Claire Kahane have argued so persuasively is that when the "secret" of the castle turns out to be the history of the sexually transgres-sive Madame Laurentini, this threatening maternal figure becomes, in a way, the "meaning" of the work. "As a victimizer victimized by her own desire," Kahane says, "Laurentini is presented as Emily's potential precursor, a mad mother-sister-double who mirrors Emily's own potential for transgression and madness."[22] "Female Gothic," in other words, confronts the heroine with her own desires and thrills her with the possibility of transgression. In Radcliffe's novels of course the transgression remains only a threat, a threat contained in the forced marital conclusions upon which she insists. Emily as heroine cannot transgress, and no one for a moment imagines that she will.

As heroine, however, she can—indeed, she must—suffer. Some critics have gone so far as to suggest that the attraction a heroine like Emily comes inexplicably to feel for the inward reaches of the castle is in fact the sign of a repressed masochistic desire for the shadowy gothic villain hero himself. Cynthia Griffin Wolff calls this figure the demon-lover: "Despite the fact that the man is darkly attractive, the woman generally shuns him, shrink-ing as from some invisible contamination. Too often to be insignificant, this aversion is justified when he eventually proves to be a long-lost relation: an uncle, a step-father, sometimes the biological father himself—lusting after the innocent daughter's chastity."[23] In Wolff's analysis, the demon lover, who "dominat[es] the fiction as its undeniable emotional focus," is secretly attractive to the heroine and becomes the source of a power that releases her from the confines of a sentimental world.

In imagining the possibility of female-female desire in gothic fiction, how-ever, I return to the maternal obsession that Kahane describes and reinvest it with the erotic potential that is more than merely hinted. Far more than the gothic villain, the maternal figure in "female gothic" holds out the possibil-ity of love, of self-realization, and of escape from the confines of patriarchal culture. For instance, in Radcliffe's *The Italian; or, The Confessional of the Black Penitents* (1797), which is in some ways a response to *The Monk*, doubly transgressive female-female desire resides at the heart of the novel and gives it structure. As Susan Greenfield has argued, "The Gothic can . . . emphasize the power and potential eroticism of mother-daughter relations."[24] Green-field claims that the mother can be the object of openly erotic desire only so long as the familial relation is repressed. At the same time, however, *The Italian* and other "female gothic" works are structured so as to heighten the erotics of maternal relations as vividly and aggressively as Sarah Scott does in her same-sex utopian vision in *Millenium Hall*.[25] Ellena di Rosalba, the heroine of *The Italian,* is lost until she finds her mother in the corridors of the Convent of the Santa della Pietà.[26] Susan Wolstenholme discusses the *"gendered* relationship between audience and spectacle" in Radcliffe's fiction. She also says that "For Radcliffe, writing *The Italian* as a corrective to Lewis's *The Monk,* a text not just less squeamish about rape and incest but actually relishing its own sordid details, decorum veils predatory sex."[27] But it also transforms the predatory into the nurturing, conventual love that instills an uncanny power.

Ellena's melancholic incorporation of the lost mother—her desire for the mother—is played out against her oddly muted love affair with the predictably ineffectual Vivaldi. She wants him, to be sure, but she does not know how to articulate this desire. It is her mother Olivia who teaches her what desire means. Judith Butler says that "if the assumption of femininity and the assumption of masculinity proceed through the accomplishment of an always tenuous heterosexuality, we might understand this accomplishment as mandating the abandonment of homosexual attachments or, perhaps more trenchantly, *preempting* the possibility of homosexual attachment, a foreclosure of possibility which produces a domain of homosexuality understood as unlivable passion and ungrievable loss."[28]

Ellena and her mother sigh together over the broken body of masculinity because in their love they recognize the loss that a heteronormative narrative represents. But in the end they incorporate that loss into the heterosexuality that the novel putatively celebrates. What complicates the heteronormativity here is the love they have rediscovered for one another, melancholy and muted as it is. Diane Long Hoeveler argues that "what is at stake in the female gothic novel is psychic and linguistic reconfiguration of parental figures."[29] Gothic fiction offers a range of possibilities as to what forms this "reconfiguration" takes and by what means it is inscribed on the psyches of heroes and heroines.

Melancholy is vivid in the characters in Charles Robert Maturin's *Melmoth the Wanderer* (1820) as well. These characters manage not to succumb to the nefarious skill of the infernal Melmoth, the "perverse" emissary who appears in each of the several interpolated tales of the novel to tempt them with "escape" from present difficulties. They do not need to sell their souls to the devil, however, when their bodies have already condemned them to a hell on earth.[30]

In the most famous of the interpolated tales, for instance, "The Tale of the Spaniard," Alonzo de Monçada tells the story of his incarceration at the hands of the Inquisition. The political abuses of the Inquisition are hideous and disturbing, as are the intrusions of infernal temptation, but Maturin makes the body itself the site of transgression. The body, in other words, traps the subject within an ideology that literally dismembers the body for its own purposes. Stephen Bruhm says that "in the experience of terror, the mind imagines a certain physical experience which it reproduces on the body as the experience of pain."[31]

That "experience of pain" is dramatized in gruesome terms. In a sense, Maturin reverses this process as a reminder of the relation between psychological and physical suffering, between the mind and the body. When Monçada and a guide are pushing their way through an underground passage, which is so constricted so as almost to cause suffocation, Monçada says that he "could not help recollecting and *applying*" a story about a group of travelers exploring the vaults of the Egyptian pyramids. "One of them, who was advancing, as I was, on his hands and knees, stuck in the passage, and, whether from terror, or from the natural consequences of his situation, swelled so that it was impossible for him to retreat, advance, or allow a passage for his companions." When the others realized that this companion threatens their own survival, their guide "proposed, in the selfishness to which the feeling of vital danger reduces all, to cut off the limbs of the wretched being who obstructed their passage." At this suggestion the companion manages somehow to squeeze himself out of the way. "He was suffocated, however, in the effort, and left behind a corse."[32]

What is interesting is not just the vivid portrayal of the physical effects of fear but rather that the community of travelers is beset by fear because one individual has "blocked" their passage. They have no trouble planning to free their way by dismembering the person before them. The act, a brutal and self-centered substitute for castration, helps dramatize the ways in which bourgeois culture handles the individual. Castration, figural or literal, is all there is for those who stand in the way of what the culture values most, in this case its own survival. Punter argues that "Gothic enacts an introjection of the destruction of the body, and thus it introjects death; in so doing it attains sublimity because it is necessary for there to be a circling, hovering, transcendent self which can enact the survival and supersession of physical difficulties, the 'last man,' the wanderer, the ancient mariner."[33] If introjection is a kind of internalization of parental power, in this case the parental power is writ large, a superego represented in this novel as the Catholic church and its offices of the Inquisition.

When, later in his tale, Monçada hears the story of illicit love in the confines of a monastery, the result is strikingly similar. In this case his companion tells of a novice and his growing sentimental attachment to a young monk. The narrator, a "parricide," gives the following account:

> One evening as the young monk and his darling novice were in the garden, the former plucked a peach, which he immediately offered to his favourite; the latter accepted it with a movement I thought rather awkward—it seemed like what I imagined would be the reverence of a female. The young monk divided the peach with a knife; in doing so, the knife grazed the finger of the novice, and the monk, in agitation inexpressible, tore his habit to bind up the wound. I saw it all—my mind was made up on the business—I went to the Superior that very night. The result may be conceived. They were watched. . . .

After setting a trap for the two, after he is certain that they have arranged to spend the night together, the parricide brings the superior and other monks to witness the depravity: "We burst into the cell. The wretched husband and wife were locked in each others arms. You may imagine the scene that followed" (205–7).

The convent's superior, "who had no more idea of the intercourse between the sexes, than between two beings of different species," is so horrified at this spectacle of "two human beings of different sexes, who dared to love one another" (207) that his own sexual proclivities may be called into question. If they are—if, that is, he represents the male-male desire implicit in monastic life—he also helps explain how what is transgressive in one context becomes the agent of cultural control in another. The kind of surveillance that comes "naturally" in a convent—religious life builds surveillance into its communal system—has had the salubrious effect of ferreting out male-female desire and extirpating it from the society in question. This transaction succeeds by employing those who would otherwise find themselves in violation of the law they are so desperate to serve.

What does happen is that these lovers are lured, in the hope of "escape," into the underground passages of the convent and there trapped by the parricide in a chamber that is nailed shut and from which they can never escape. Soon they turn on one another, and before the narration ceases the husband sinks his teeth into the wasted flesh of his mate. This cannibalistic conclusion to a tale of sexual transgression is not unique to Maturin, but it is handled as a deft reminder of the relativity of desire. Love becomes literally an appetite, and desire becomes indistinguishable from murderous aggression. By walling these young lovers in the subterranean passage and listening to their moans, the parricide acts out the cultural mechanism that the gothic harbors at its core.

These few examples can begin to suggest how thoroughly invested in same-sex and transgressive incestuous desire the gothic seems always already to be. "The excess and ambivalence associated with Gothic figures were seen as distinct signs of transgression," Botting says. "Aesthetically excessive, Gothic productions were considered unnatural in the undermining of physical laws with marvelous beings and fantastic events."[34] It was thought unnatural, too, in the ways personal desires were organized and in the expression of excessive lusts and lurid passions. For Cindy Hendershot, "The Gothic fragments stable identity and stable social order." And, "Gothic bodies disrupt stable notions of what it means to be human."[35] It also disrupts stable notions of *how* to be human. In gothic novels, love between sisters, between mothers and daughters, fathers and sons, again and again challenges the status quo with the taboo around which the patriarchal system is organized. Other forms of extreme and excessive desire, violent sexuality, victimization, and erotic submission are at work in many of these novels. I call these works queer because there is no way that they merely contribute to the sexual status quo, and in some cases they militate strenuously against it.

Of course, in the larger picture, gothic fiction did nothing to stop the imposition of sexological thinking at the end of the nineteenth century. But the relation between sexology and the gothic can be reimagined and the discussion of sexual violence that has resulted from the rigidities of twentieth-century sexological thinking can be challenged, especially insofar as it has categorized and dismissed the importance of gothic fiction. Instead of relying on these rather crude twentieth-century rubrics for classifying sexual activity, I prefer to read these novels as an articulation of principles of pleasure that resist the sexological binaries that Sade and Sacher-Masoch have been made to represent. English gothic fiction in general, and *The Castle of Otranto, The Mysteries of Udolpho, The Italian, The Monk, Melmoth the Wanderer,* and a range of other novels in particular, offer different ways to speculate about sexuality. If Sade and Masoch have been canonized in attempts to establish a heteronormative system of the sexual imaginary, and if their erotic fantasies have been marshaled to regulate sexological thinking, then the system of sadomasochism should be exposed as a binary as false as any that culture cherishes.

What a simple, universalized theory of the "connection between cruelty and the sexual instinct" neglects are not only its sources and its specific dynamics but also its connection to the family and its deep involvement in various forms of same-sex fantasy that gothic fiction begins to bring more clearly into focus. Gothic novels articulate more complex "sexualities." Theories of sexuality that depend on the gothic—whether Walpole-Lewisism, or Lewis-Maturinism, or Radcliffe-Lewism—would be more varied, more sexually complex, less heteronormative, and more polymorphously perverse than any thus far considered.

In other words, sexuality needs to be rehistoricized in a way that will undo some of the obfuscation that twentieth-century understandings of sexuality have imposed. In an important essay, David Halperin demonstrates, by using examples from pre- and early modern culture, situations in which both sexual morphology and sexual subjectivity are richly articulated in literary and quasi-literary texts. He revises the notion of how to talk about the relation between behaviors and individuals, and he does so by building on Foucault's insights.[36] This is the challenge facing those who hope to "queer" literature of the past. It is not an attempt to read ourselves into the past but rather an attempt to understand how a different culture understood the kinds of extreme expressions of sexual style in the gothic that no twentieth-century interpretive binary can ever hope to explain.

To build on these observations would be valuable to queer studies to be sure, but it is also a significant addition to understanding the history of sexuality. In order to understand the peculiar sexual limitations of the present, it is necessary to fathom the extreme sexual behaviors and fantasies of the past. In that sense, this approach can contribute to liberatory thinking and transcend the essentialist-constructionist controversy for a queer connection that puts us in closer touch with the ways in which sexual practices were organized in the past. Queer gothic can do so in a way that will make it impossible to forget.

2

Gothic Fiction and the Erotics of Loss

Poor Conrad

Poor Conrad, set up to be the hero of Horace Walpole's *The Castle of Otranto* (1764), instead enters the novel as a mangled corpse, "dashed to pieces, and almost buried under [the] enormous helmet" that is the first sign of his father Manfred's future demise. His death motivates much of the gruesome action of the novel, but his broken form, this "disfigured corpse," rarely gets more than a perfunctory sigh of displeasure. It is time to look more closely at his "bleeding mangled remains" and to the place they hold in the deeper gothic plot that the novel subtly suggests.[1]

Manfred's hopes are crushed with the death of this "homely youth, sickly, and of no promising disposition, . . . [who] was the darling of his father" (15). The assiduities of such affection, however displayed, render Conrad singularly unprepossessing—Manfred's love is hardly the nurturing kind—but Manfred still attempts to use the boy as a sexual prop to keep his crumbling dynasty from falling about his head. Walpole says that Manfred's "fondness for young Conrad" (17) and his "impatience for [the] ceremonial" between Conrad and Isabella, his intended, are in part the result of his fear of an "ancient prophecy" (15). In this sense, the pathetic boy represents Manfred's failure to establish a legitimate line. But he is also a sexual surrogate for Manfred, and Manfred's fondness and impatience for the nuptials suggest that he has invested the wedding with a personal erotic significance. This is confirmed as soon as Conrad's body has been carried away. Instead of mentioning his wife or daughter, Manfred urges his servants to "take care of the lady Isabella"

(19). If his little darling cannot perform the ritual that privilege and power require, Manfred decides, he will have to marry the girl himself.

Isabella "felt no concern for the death of young Conrad" (20) but learns to her dismay that Manfred's concern will lead to her own victimization. By pressing his suit for her hand, Manfred causes her to flee, and the flight of Isabella within the gloomy confines of the castle's subterranean regions is one of the set pieces of the novel. This is not coincidentally the first gothic moment of erotic fear: "The lower part of the castle was hollowed into several intricate cloisters; and it was not easy for one under so much anxiety to find the door that opened into the cavern. An awful silence reigned throughout those subterraneous regions, except now and then some blasts of wind that shook the doors she had passed, and which grating on the rusty hinges were re-echoed through that long labyrinth of darkness" (27).

Walpole may not have known that he was offering terms for what would come to be known as "female gothic," but he did understand that female vulnerability had great fictional potential. Here Walpole does what becomes the hallmark of gothic fiction: In a single image he combines the sexual anxiety of a victimized female, the incestuous desire of a libidinous male, the use of the actual physical features of the castle to represent political and sexual entrapment, and an atmosphere deftly rendered to produce terror and gloom. The scene, retold hundreds of times in gothic fiction, is absolutely basic to the form. Because he understands that gothic fiction can represent abject terror and frenzied aggression in ways other fiction only approximates, Walpole's depiction of this moment, and others like it, takes on talismanic importance in the history of gothic fiction.

In a simple and practical way, the loss of Conrad as his own sexual agent leads Manfred on a sexual rampage that results in his brutal rejection of his wife Hippolita, the near-rape of his son's fiancée Isabella, and the grisly murder of his daughter Matilda, his one other hope for legitimacy. A gothic novel is about fear, specifically erotic fear, and the ways in which desire renders the family a hotbed, as Foucault might say, of sexualized brutality and nightmarish erotic tensions. But this sexual excess, this dysfunctionality, is traceable to that original moment of loss. If Conrad had lived—that is, if that vaguely homoerotic pact between powerful father and pitiful son had been allowed to survive—the structure of family, of community, and of culture would have been different. Of course, the loss of Conrad is already a given when the novel opens; his death enables the fiction. The paternal rampage is directly the result of the loss and disappointment that Conrad represents. But this fiction of paternal license is not just any fiction; it is the "dominant fiction," not just of gothic literature but also of Western culture in a larger sense.[2] Manfred's anger, his sexual voraciousness, and his deep regret are the qualities that begin to define subjectivity in Western culture, as Freud would point out. The practical loss of an heir, in other words, hints at a deeper loss as well. No one in the novel puts that deeper loss into words, but everyone feels its force, and a pall of melancholy hangs over the work even at its close, where Theodore, a young peasant, chooses Isabella because with her he can "forever indulge the melancholy that had taken possession of his soul" (110). Walpole creates a melancholic mood in this first gothic novel as a way of exploring his peculiar version of erotic desire: a desire founded on loss.

In his essay "Forgetting Foucault," David Halperin disagrees with what has come to be understood as Foucault's argument that "in the premodern and early modern periods . . . sexual behavior did not represent a sign or marker of a person's sexual identity; it did not indicate or express some more generalized or holistic feature of the person, such as that person's subjectivity, disposition, or character." Halperin goes on to "argue strenuously against this view," because he feels that Foucault has been misunderstood, that Foucault was speaking about "discursive and institutional practices, not about what people really did in bed or what they thought about it." For Halperin, "Foucault is analyzing the different modalities of power at work in premodern and modern codifications of sexual prohibition, which is to say in two historical instances of sexual discourse attached to institutional practices." Halperin goes on to argue, to prove in effect using a classical and an early modern example, that "first, sexual acts could be interpreted as representative expressions of an individual's sexual morphology. Second, sexual acts could be interpreted as representative expressions of an individual's secret subjectivity." Halperin is not claiming that either of these understandings is equivalent to the modern notion of sexual identity or, less, homosexuality. Instead, he states that "we need to find ways of asking how different historical cultures fashioned different sorts of links between sexual acts, on the one hand, and sexual tastes, styles, dispositions, characters, gender presentation, and forms of subjectivity, on the other."[3]

This argument raises a number of questions about how to treat sexual encounters and personal habits in the past. Halperin is not throwing open the doors to essentialist arguments but rather urging us to find ways of interpreting the sexual past so as to approach it in all its difference and to make sense of it in those terms. He is not saying that we should impose a gay reading or even interpret passages as gay because of what seems a recognizable configuration. Rather, he insists, we need to look for ways that history and culture can inform a reading, can establish a relation with the past, and in so doing tell us something about how sexuality functioned in different times and places.

Subjectivity is, of course, as loaded a term as sexuality, and we need to understand Halperin's examples—the Greek *knaidos,* on the one hand and an early modern pederast on the other—as both historically contingent and illustrative not of subjectivity per se but of a collection of traits and desires that begin to have cultural meaning. Before discussing the sexual identity of a *subject,* however, it is necessary to think more actively about the nature of early modern, even later early modern, *subjectivity.* The term, defined in the *Oxford English Dictionary* as "the quality or condition of viewing things exclusively through one's own mind or individuality; the condition of being dominated or absorbed in one's personal feelings, thoughts, etc.," entered common usage in English in the early nineteenth century, just at the moment when gothic fiction was all the rage. The pathetic remains of Walpole's puny weakling can begin to explain something about gothic subjectivity and about queer subjectivity as well.

Judith Butler explores the homoerotics of subjectivity in her book *The Psychic Life of Power,* and gothic fiction can help explain the historical subject in terms equally complex. As Butler observes, "If there is no formation of the subject without a passionate attachment to those by whom she or he is subordinated, then subordination proves central to the becoming of a subject. As the condition of becoming a subject, subordination implies being in a mandatory submission. Moreover, the desire to survive, 'to be,' is pervasively exploitable by desire."[4] If this is true, then how vividly gothic fiction dramatizes the condition of becoming a subject. Conrad's brutal dismemberment suggests the ways in which this process can go tragically wrong. Conrad's desire "to be," that is, can never be articulated in this world of patriarchal power. The loss that Conrad's mangled corpse represents is central to the formation of subjectivity in gothic fiction. His death at the opening releases Manfred's lurid energies and aggressive action, to be sure, but it also places that action in a realm that is "pervasively exploitable by desire."

Manfred's paternal rampage reminds us how brutalizing that private experience can be. For example, his daughter Matilda is brutally stabbed by Manfred himself in the novel's second vivid scene of transgressive sexual aggression:

> [Manfred] hastened secretly to the great church. Gliding softly between the aisles, and guided by an imperfect gleam of moonshine that shone faintly

through the illuminated windows, he stole towards the tomb of Alfonso, to
which he was directed by indistinct whispers of the persons he sought. The
first sounds he could distinguish were—Does it, alas, depend on me? Manfred will never permit the union.—No, this shall prevent it! cried the tyrant,
drawing his dagger, and plunging it over her shoulder into the bosom of the
person that spoke—Ah me, I am slain! cried Matilda sinking: Good heaven,
receive my soul!—Savage, inhuman monster! what hast thou done? cried
Theodore, rushing on him, and wrenching his dagger from him.—Stop, stop
thy impious hand, cried Matilda; it is my father!—Manfred, waking as from
a trance, beat his breast, twisted his hands in his locks, and endeavoured to
recover his dagger from Theodore to dispatch himself. (108)

The elaborate sexual fantasy involved in gliding through the darkness of
the chapel at the tomb of his deposed predecessor and discovering there his
daughter in conversation with a young man, the thrill of his erotically coded
blow, and the abject self-hatred of the climactic moment—all these effects
help to create a gothic primal scene. Reversing the trajectories of Freud's
Oedipal arrangement, Manfred has murdered his son so that he can marry his
daughter, but he is doomed to destroy her in the violence of his lust. Matilda
dies accepting her own submission, fulfilling the melancholic promise of
Conrad's death and asserting the will of the father. "To desire the conditions
of one's own submission is . . . required to persist as oneself," Butler says.[5]
Here is an example of what that can mean for a young woman who dares to
defy paternal power. Walpole's villain is the guilty patriarch whose incestuous
sexual violence becomes a nightmare of broken bodies and violated graves.
His attempts to force himself on the younger generation—Conrad, Isabella,
Matilda, and Theodore—are the direct cause of his dispossession. The normativity of paternal power is itself the perversion, and Walpole reminds us
that the son and daughter must be sacrificed to the increasingly impotent
and destructive sexual demands of the aging father.

Leo Bersani argues that "sexuality would not be originally an exchange of
intensities between individuals, but rather a condition of broken negotiations
with the world, a condition in which others merely set off the self-shattering
mechanisms of masochistic *jouissance*."[6] But the self-shattering mechanisms
of gothic fiction imply more than masochism in their challenge to normative
sexual dynamics. At the climax of *The Castle of Otranto* Matilda has put her
faith in the power of the family only to find her myth destroyed in a brutal
confrontation with her father. Her "broken negotiations with the world"
are dramatized vividly and with a singularity of focus that defies attempts

to see her as a simple (gothic) victim. She has dared to assume that from her female position she could reimagine the family from a maternal rather than a paternal perspective. Her bond with her mother, Hippolita, is what enrages her father, and it is a world of female intelligence and generosity that his brutalizing lust destroys. Bersani argues that "[m]asochism would be the psychical strategy which partially defeats a biologically dysfunctional process of maturation."[7]

Such a process is difficult to describe in psychological terms, but one like Matilda's, both incestuous and abusive, already complicates subjectivity with an abjection that the novel codes as female. Her particular victimization seems to function as a psychical strategy as well as symbolic one. Manfred's violence ultimately has meaning only in relation to Matilda's renegotiation of normative desire. The love she expresses, the vain hope that the aggressive dynamics of family life can be transformed by her death, makes Manfred's violence even more monstrous. At the same time, the gesture of rape is transformed in Matilda's suffering; she takes pleasure in the pain that in its odd way signals her father's love. But this is not a simple masochistic response to Manfred's sadism. Matilda's pathetic victimization represents a kind of abjection that queers the fantasy by substituting a bloody corpse for the object of sexual desire. As Theodore and Manfred fight over the bloody dagger, Matilda lies there in defiance of their homosocial love-fest. Her death adds to the mood of regret in this novel, and regret is again articulated at the novel's close. A queer reading might suggest that the regret is already implicit in the violence itself and that abjection is what the novel articulates as a gothic identity. Manfred finally wanders in the dissatisfaction of frustrated desire, disappointed friendship, and tepid, normalizing consummation.

In Matthew Lewis's *The Monk* (1796), loss is central to the erotic dynamics of this work as vividly as it is in *The Castle of Otranto*.[8] Throughout the novel, the desiring Ambrosio cowers in fear of the implication of his desires, killing his mother and raping his sister, all in an attempt to overcome the debilitating desire he has felt for the boy-girl novice Rosario/Matilda. In the most important subplot of the book, the figure of "The Bleeding Nun" torments young Raymond with a love that is both violent and incestuous. In this case the tender love between Raymond and Theodore is sacrificed to a victimizing and vindictive desire that nearly destroys Raymond. Ambrosio and the Bleeding Nun are both destroyed so that one kind of sexual union—that between a man and a woman—can flourish, but these unions are "the prey of grief and the sport of disappointment."[9] Because same-sex love is impossible, everyone becomes a victim.

As if to emphasize the degree to which Ambrosio is the "victim" of his desires, Lewis gives Rosario/Matilda a role in teasing out the uncontrollable and brutally violent desire that destroys those whom Ambrosio might have loved, his mother and his sister. The excessive emotion of what turns out to be the only "bed scene" in the novel, a scene between a sexually confused young man and his mother, seems in retrospect the emotional center of the work. Although it might seem that maternal desire motivates Ambrosio, the matricide depicted is a displacement of the same-sex desire that Lewis has already dramatized. The violent misogyny of the scene—he stifles her until she becomes a "Corse, cold, senseless, and disgusting" (304)—I would ascribe to the self-hatred of which Ambrosio seems the most exquisite victim. Of course, Ambrosio's excessive behavior could be described as a kind of heterosexual panic, an expression of destructive desire for the mother as a way of proving sexual normality.

The fact that "homoerotic" desire is central to Ambrosio's subjectivity would in itself explain why this novel does not fit the usual Freudian paradigms of sexual perversion. Ambrosio's desire is corrupt not because of its incestuous objects but because, for Lewis, all desire brings with it its own damning cost. Ambrosio is a victim as much as Matilda or Antonia. He is the victim of a culture that forbids his desire and renders him remote from his deepest urges; the victim of a fear of sexuality that makes it possible for him to express himself only in violent terms; and the victim of fear that makes it impossible for him to fulfill the gentle love he felt for Rosario and sends him first toward simple sexual excess, then toward necromancy, and later, inevitably, toward incestuous violence. Lewis reconfigures family relations in these terms as a way of making his hero the victim of his own desire. Ambrosio's evil genius of carnal knowledge, moreover, is the same person as the sweet young boy he befriended in the monastery gardens. Ambrosio's desire for the young novice has become a brutal self-victimization at the same time it is lurid and destructive. This sexual subjectivity would defy the explanatory models of later sexological theory in its complexities of shifting gender, eroticizing frustration, and already bitter regret.

In Judith Butler's terms, this dynamic of self-hatred and uncontrollable sexual violence is inherent to psychic structures themselves. In discussing the Freudian account of the psyche, she claims that

> melancholia describes a process by which an originally external object is lost, or an ideal is lost, and the refusal to break the attachment to such an object or ideal leads to the withdrawal of the object into the ego, the replacement of

the object by the ego, and the setting up of an inner world in which a critical agency is split off from the ego and proceeds to take the ego as its object. . . . Thus, the ego absorbs both love and rage against the object. . . . The effect of melancholia, then, appears to be the loss of the social world, the substitution of psychic parts and antagonisms for external relations among social actors.[10]

This is a mild way of putting the ecstatic dysfunctionality of Ambrosio, but it does make sense in the terms of his particular transgressions. Whatever motivates him, he seems to have moved into a psychic world that is completely detached from his fraternal relations and social responsibilities. He takes his ego as an object, as Butler describes, and in doing so makes those closest to him nothing more than the victims of the loss he has sustained.

Another way of looking at this extreme dysfunctionality is that proffered by Leo Bersani in his essay on "Foucault, Freud, Fantasy, and Power." Bersani turns to Freud's "Wolf Man" for a discussion of "frictional confrontations: the real or constructed primal scene of explaining or correcting the terror of the dream; the presumed fear of castration leading to the repression of desire for the father; the father's vulnerability as the child's resistance to his fantasized violence; . . . Freud's interpretive violence against the evidence he himself records," and so on.[11]

The violence in *The Monk* is as perplexing as any Freudian case study, and Ambrosio's "lustful delirium" bespeaks a fear of sexuality as terrorized and terrorizing as any primal memory. Lewis creates a family romance that both effeminizes his hero and makes him its victim. It is hard to resist calling this dynamic heteronormativity itself. The mother and sister he slays are the figures with whom he finally identifies: "blind, maimed, helpless, and despairing," Ambrosio learns the wages of his incestuous lust. If Bersani can read a scene of gay lovemaking into Freud's scene of castration, then how much easier to look for transgressive desire in the complicated permutations of Lewis's hero. The terrorized father and terrorizing child exist in relation to an entire family of erotic possibilities. At the center of their relation are the loss that generates this self-hatred and the resulting carnage that renders the violence in this novel so singularly telling.

A similar same-sex eroticism is central to the other mother plot, that of the conflict between the Prioress of St. Clare and the transgressive novice, Agnes de Medina. As Mother St. Ursula recounts the events leading to the incarceration of Agnes in the vaults of the convent, she makes it clear that the emotional lives of the nuns are deeply communal and that the "lovely," "gentle" Agnes was the "Darling of all that was estimable in the Convent"

(351). The prioress herself bestowed a "tribute of approbation" on Agnes and seemed to single her out for special attention.

This maternal approbation is precisely what is offended when Agnes turns out to have transgressed the laws of chastity. The prioress's love turns to "inveterate hate," and Agnes is shut up in a "narrow gloomy dungeon" beneath the sepulcher of St. Claire. When her brother Lorenzo finds her, this is what he sees: "He turned towards them, and by the Lamp's glimmering beams beheld in a corner of this loathsome abode, a Creature stretched out upon a bed of straw, so wretched, so emaciated, so pale, that He doubted to think her Woman. She was half-naked: Her long dishevelled hair fell in disorder over her face, and almost entirely concealed it. One wasted Arm hung listlessly upon a tattered rug, which covered her convulsed and shivering limbs: The Other was wrapped round a small bundle, and held it closely to her bosom" (369).

The "small bundle" is, of course, her dead child, who was unable to survive the ordeal of incarceration in spite of all its mother's love. The infant corpse makes the pathos of the scene almost grotesque, and the victimization of Agnes expresses more about the vindictive fury of the prioress than even her later destruction by the angry mob is able to do. Rather than see the scene as merely sensationalistic, however, it is possible to view this morbid outcome as a deeply paranoid reading of the sexual license of the convent itself. The family that emerges in this tale of erotic cruelty is the barren family of same-sex desire. Two mothers and a corpse may everywhere be implied in the Freudian model, but this particular configuration is never articulated. Because the prioress's love for Agnes threatens her own exercise of power, Lewis seems to claim, she must kill the child. At the same time, the pathetic and brutalized Agnes broods over her dead child in fear that her mother's love was not pure enough to save them both from the vindictive jealousy of her own mother's homoerotic delusion. The prioress goes to elaborate and violent extremes to protect her same-sex fantasy from the prying eyes of masculine desire only to find herself brutally exposed and finally destroyed by the violence of a mob. Agnes survives to rescue Raymond from his terrifying encounter with the Bleeding Nun and join him in a muted and disappointing conclusion.[12]

Lewis depicts figures, then, who cower in fear of the implication of their own desires; who brood in regret that a mother's love was not pure enough to save them both from the vindictive jealousy of another mother's homoerotic delusion; or who attempt to protect a female same-sex fantasy from the prying eyes of masculine desire, only to be brutally exposed and finally destroyed by the violence of a mob. There is no position of safety in this case, no "subjectivity" not shaped by violence and defined by loss. As Walpole does in his account of a broken family and the deeply felt regret that desire engenders, Lewis insists on the violence of subject-making. Rather than see these as the bizarre versions of subjectivity offered in gothic fiction, Lewis captures a feature of subjective experience that defines it in terms of these devastating absences. Should it surprise us that it took another gothic writer, Sigmund Freud, to codify such perceptions for the twentieth century? When it comes to exploring the depths of human experience, fiction precedes scientific investigation more often than not.

Mothers and Other Lovers

As Ann Radcliffe tells story after story of female victimization, she also constructs an alternative reading of the family. The disowned and dishonored heroine often searches for a lost mother in the confines of a castle or a convent, and at the same time she flees the aggressive attentions of an overly erotic father or father surrogate. In order to help her in her pursuit and to aid her in her flight, the heroine elicits the almost fraternal friendship of an emasculated young man, weak, wounded, and powerless, who becomes a surrogate brother as well as a lover and delivers the heroine from the villainous father into the arms of the erotically consoling mother. The Radcliffean heroine reanimates the family with sexual tension in ways that Freud never imagined. She creates a sisterly mother/brother to bond with her in attempts to defeat the father and marry the mother, and she learns a kind of power of her own in her solitary wanderings in the pernicious darkness of castles, convents, and various incommodious abodes. In Radcliffe's novels, heteronormativity is challenged and masochism seems a less useful way to describe the muted success that a Radcliffe heroine enjoys: outside culture Radcliffe's heroines and their bleeding lovers can establish a female-oriented sexual bond based on the kinds of protective emotionality that sadomasochistic culture would reject.[13] Bersani argues that "sentiments and conduct we might wish to associate with love can emerge as a resistance, in the Foucauldian sense, to the violence and avidity for power inherent in all intimate negotiations between human beings."[14] Radcliffe's novels play out this resistance in surprising ways, as I hope a discussion of *The Italian* will show.[15]

Ellena di Rosalba, in Radcliffe's *The Italian* (1797), moves from one ruthless enclosure to another until she is trapped in a seaside house in which her captors are planning her murder. For Ellena, this is not an unusual situation. As Claudia Johnson says, in *The Italian*, "the virtuous . . . often find themselves enclosed, impeded, imprisoned in dungeons, torture chambers, or dank subterraneous passages."[16] The murder seems to have no directly erotic valence until (appropriately) the moment at which the assassin, the monk Schedoni, pushes aside the gown from her sleeping form in preparation for stabbing her:

> Her dress perplexed him; it would interrupt the blow, and he stooped to examine whether he could turn her robe aside, without waking her. As the light passed over her face, he perceived that the smile had vanished—the visions of her sleep were changed, for tears stole from beneath her eye-lids, and her features suffered a slight convulsion. . . . His agitation and repugnance to strike encreased with every moment of delay, and, as often as he prepared to plunge the poniard in her bosom, a shuddering horror restrained him. Astonished at his own feeling, and indignant at what he termed a dastardly weakness, he found it necessary to argue with himself. . . . This consideration re-animated him; vengeance nerved his arm, and drawing aside the lawn from her bosom, he once more raised it to strike; when, after gazing for an instant, some new cause of horror seemed to seize all his frame, and he stood for some moments aghast and motionless like a statue. His respiration was short and laborious, chilly drops stood on his forehead, and all his faculties of mind seemed suspended. When he recovered, he stooped to examine again the miniature, which had occasioned this revolution, and which had lain concealed beneath the lawn that he withdrew.[17]

Ellena cries even while she is sleeping, and the dark, threatening presence of the monk only renders her plight more abject. This is not the same kind of erotic terror that Walpole rendered. Instead, the terror is that of a pathetic victim, lying under the knife with nothing more than a shudder. Ellena is saved, however, by the miniature she wears. It is a picture of her "father" that Schedoni recognizes as a portrait of himself. This surprising revelation, which turns out to be untrue, brings this couple into a familiar configuration. If this is the most intense private moment in the novel, it is also the most painfully familiar. The "father" threatens brutal violation that gothic readers already suspect. This midnight encounter of incestuous violation always already suggests the paternal, in Radcliffe and in many of her contemporaries. Paternal violence shapes the heroine just as the terms of her very existence seem to depend on his whim, or rather his pleasure. Even though Ellena accepts Schedoni as her father, she feels that something is amiss and never settles into a comfortable relation with him. But then why should she? As it turns out, he is in fact her father's murderer.

Incest is not always victimizing in this paternal way. While incarcerated in the unfriendly San Stephano convent, this same heroine finds herself befriended by the kindly Olivia, a nun who seems willing to risk her own safety in order to help the abject Ellena:

> Among the voices of the choir, was one whose expression immediately fixed her attention; it seemed to speak a loftier sentiment of devotion than the others, and to be modulated by the melancholy of an heart, that had long since taken leave of this world. Whether it swelled with the high peal of the organ, or mingled in low and trembling accents with the sinking chorus, Ellena felt that she understood all the feelings of the breast from which it flowed; and she looked to the gallery where the nuns were assembled, to discover a countenance, that might seem to accord with the sensibility expressed in the voice. As no strangers were admitted to the chapel, some of the sisters had thrown back their veils, and she saw little that interested her in their various faces; but the figure and attitude of a nun, kneeling in a remote part of the gallery, beneath a lamp, which threw its rays aslant her head, perfectly agreed with the idea she had formed of the singer, and the sound seemed to approach immediately from that direction. Her face was concealed by a black veil, whose transparency, however, permitted the fairness of her complexion to appear; but the air of her head, and the singularity of her attitude, for she was the only person who remained kneeling, sufficiently indicated the superior degree of fervency and penitence, which the voice had expressed. (86)

Ellena is attracted to a disembodied voice, albeit a very beautiful one, and a feeling of other-worldly melancholy. She identifies with this sound, and she also feels the desire to put a face to all this wealth of sensibility. This first view of Olivia in the lamplight as these sounds rush over her, this secret attempt to penetrate the veil, and the abject figure of her stance all suggest an erotic intensity that the brutality of this prisonlike convent only intensifies.[18] The love that grows between Ellena and Olivia could be described as an erotics of loss. Unbeknown to both, Olivia is the mother that Ellena lost to "death" in childhood, and Ellena is the child that Olivia lost when she fled her murderous brother-in-law's incestuous violence and jealousy. These depths of feeling color the emotional bond with the melancholy that Ellena heard in the voice, and the sublimity that surrounds their hushed and veiled forms is the abyss of loss rather than an unnamed fear or crimson terror.

"Unencumbered with disagreeable parents wishing to thwart her," Robert Miles argues in a discussion of the politics of the novel, "Ellena's conflict becomes internalized. She is opposed, not by a 'father' out there, but by scruples, in here. Her struggle is principally between desire and pride."[19] It is not pride, however, that causes her to fret over the fate of her lover. Rather, it is a form of desire constituted in loss. "Father" and mother both function in the constitution of subjectivity, and the results of this dynamic are subtle and far-reaching.

Critics have worried over the ineffectuality of Radcliffe's heroes, and Vivaldi is no different from the other wounded and absent males that this author celebrates. If Adeline in Radcliffe's earlier *The Romance of the Forest* (1791) heightens suspense and her own dread by imagining Theodore in chains, Theodore bleeding, and Theodore suffering untold torments, Ellena does all these and also imagines her dear Vivaldi dead:

> "His confinement must be severe indeed," said the afflicted Ellena, "since he cannot relieve my anxiety by a single line of intelligence. Or, perhaps, harassed by unceasing opposition, he has submitted to the command of his family, and has consented to forget me. Ah! Why did I leave the opportunity for that command to his family; why did I not enforce it myself!"
>
> Yet, while she uttered this self-reproach, the tears she shed contradicted the pride which had suggested it; and a conviction lurking in her heart that Vivaldi could not so resign her, soon dissipated those tears. But other conjectures recalled them; it was possible that he was ill—that he was dead! (368)

Ellena seems determined to imagine the worst—or is it the best? Given her continual victimization in his company, and indirectly because of him and his family, and given the comfort and safety she feels in the Convent of the Pieta, perhaps the safest Vivaldi would be Vivaldi the corpse.

Vivaldi, for his part, also seems to fantasize about Ellena's dead form more actively than her living one. When he hears that someone has died at the Villa Altieri, for instance, he reacts as follows:

> An indifferent person would probably have understood the words of the monk to allude to Signora Bianchi, whose infirm state of health rendered her death, though sudden, not improbable; but to the affrighted fancy of Vivaldi, the dying Ellena only appeared. His fears, however probabilities might sanction, or the event justify them, were natural to ardent affection; but they were accompanied by a presentiment as extraordinary as it was horrible;—it occurred to him more than once, that Ellena was murdered. He saw her wounded, and bleeding to death; saw her ashy countenance, and her wasting eyes, from which the spirit of life was fast departing, turned piteously on himself, as if imploring him to save her from the fate that was dragging her to the grave. (41)

Desire seems to depend on the fear of victimization, and death provides the erotic charge in this passage of interiority. The exquisite detail with which the scene is painted can only suggest that the fantasy is deeply rooted in the subjectivity of this unheroic gothic hero. This is not a vague fear of what might happen but a specific desire for what will.

Butler explains how and why all desire finds its sources in the erotics of loss. She quotes from Freud's discussion of his earlier essay "Mourning and Melancholia" in *The Ego and the Id,* where he remarks that "when it happens that a person has to give up a sexual object, there quite often ensues an alteration of his ego which can only be described as a setting up of the object inside the ego, as it occurs in melancholia." Butler's helpful gloss on Freud's remarks suggests that "melancholic identification permits the loss of the object in the external world precisely because it provides a way to *preserve* the object as part of the ego and, hence, to avert the loss as a complete loss. . . . Giving up the object becomes possible only on the condition of a melancholic internalization or, what might for our purposes turn out to be even more important, a melancholic *incorporation.*" For Butler, this *incorporation* is the way in which identification becomes a "magical, a psychic form of preserving the object."[20] This form of psychic experience could also be labeled "uncanny"; psychic life preserves this loss in a form that means it will be found—if ever it is found—with a specifically gothic mode of recognition.

Radcliffe typically leaves none of this to the imagination. Ellena is schooled in loss, and her melancholy temperament has much to do with the early "death" of her mother. She finds herself lost and alone throughout the novel, a loneliness broken only when she walks among the avenues of the Our Lady of Pity convent:

> on turning into the walk, [she] perceived several persons advancing in the shady distance. Among the voices, as they drew nearer, she distinguished one whose interesting tone engaged all her attention, and began also to awaken memory. She listened, wondered, doubted, hoped, and feared! It spoke again! Ellena thought she could not be deceived in those tender accents. . . . The voice spoke again; it pronounced her name; pronounced it with the tremblings of tenderness and impatience, and Ellena scarcely dared to trust her senses, when she beheld Olivia, the nun of St. Stephano, in the cloisters of the Della Pieta! (369–70)

"She listened, wondered, doubted, hoped, and feared!": This ecstatic expression of emotionality insists on more than romantic friendship between the younger and the older woman. This is the anxiety of erotic attraction

and it is precisely the anxiety that Olivia's "tremblings of tenderness" suitably repay. Ellena now learns that this dear, dear companion is in fact her
mother and that the loss she has felt can now be reworked into the heart of
their tearful bond. The loss is incorporated into the love that they share. But
how fascinating it is that Radcliffe sets these scenes of intense and uncannily
familiar female-female desire in the Convent of the Pietà. Pity, of course, is
the mood of this reconciliation, a melancholic recognition of the tears that
bind them. Suggestive, too, are the range of visual images that the Pietà calls
to mind. Our lady of pity is the grieving mother, grieving, that is, for the
broken, castrated son she holds in her arms.

Radcliffe's heroine must reexperience that primal "homosexual" attachment in order to give any significance at all to her love for Vivaldi. Vivaldi
understands this, for the first feelings he has toward Olivia are those of jealousy: "The fears of Ellena now gave way to affectionate sorrow, as, weeping
on the bosom of the nun, she said, 'farewell! O farewel, my dear, my tender
friend! I must never, never see you more, but I shall always love you; and
you have promised, that I shall hear from you; remember the convent della
Pieta!' . . . 'Ah Ellena!' said Vivaldi, as he gently disengaged her from the nun,
'do I then hold only the second place in your heart?'" (135).

Ellena does not exactly answer Vivaldi—she offers him a "smile more
eloquent than words" (135)—because she cannot offer him the response
for which he hopes. Her "affectionate sorrow" for Olivia cannot be so easily dissipated. This attempt at a (hetero)normative resolution is repeatedly
foiled, and Vivaldi's attempts to rescue Ellena and marry her are singularly
unsuccessful. He ends up in the prisons of the Inquisition, and she proceeds
to her long and threatening encounter with Schedoni. Radcliffe brings them
together at the close of the novel (of course), but a mood of "affectionate
sorrow" colors even the close, despite Vivaldi's servant Paolo's insistent "O!
giorno felice!" (415) with which she celebrates the inevitable wedding.

It is an oddly chastened Vivaldi—grilled by the Inquisition, witness to
his mother's perfidy, and confronted with the horrors of Ellena's putative
paternity—who offers Ellena his hand at the novel's close. Olivia smiles
on the pact, of course, but Radcliffe does more than insist on a maternal
nod of approval. She seems to insist that only to the degree that Vivaldi is
like Olivia will Ellena be willing to marry him. She colors this relationship
with the same "affectionate sorrow," that is, because she understands all
relationships in terms of loss. The ideal relationship is the one that Ellena
lost in childhood and rediscovered at the climax of the novel. The originary
same-sex love that had been foreclosed and repressed emerges to bless this

union of victims. The melancholy mood at the close of this novel is erotically charged—at her wedding Ellena cannot walk down the isle of Santa Maria della Pietà without calling to mind the "anguish" of earlier moments when she imagined that Vivaldi might have died (415)—and only the un-dead are offered as an alternative to patriarchal aggression. If Vivaldi finds himself in this maternal, female space at the novel's close, well, someone should tell him that this is the only place where love can flourish after all.

Charlotte Dacre's *Zofloya* (1806) retells the story of Radcliffe's *The Italian* from a darker and more brutal perspective more reminiscent of Lewis's *The Monk* as critics have suggested.[21] Originary loss is not reconstituted but exacerbated by violence and incest. Victoria di Loredani, the Venetian heroine of Dacre's novel, grows up in a seemingly happy family that is destroyed when her mother Laurina succumbs to the importuning devotion of a scheming lover. Her fall from grace and the resulting corruption of both Victoria and her brother Leonardo is the narrative lesson that is repeated at every turn. The paternal judgment becomes a narrative trope on the wages of maternal sin:

> "Laurina, unfortunate and once-loved wife! thou wilt make thyself answerable, by thy conduct, not only for the life and future actions of thy daughter, but for the *fiat* which will go forth respecting her, when she renders up her great account!—Ponder, then, well upon the mighty charge, that, by appearing before me at this awful moment, thou bringest upon thyself—yes, on *thy example*—Oh! thou who couldest desert thine innocent and lovely offspring—on *thy example* will the life and conduct of thy daughter *now* be formed!" (20)

This judgment is repeated so often that some readers have taken it to be ironic. But far from ironic, the judgment dramatically forecloses the love between Victoria and her mother, the female-female bond that might have supported her in the horrors that were to be her lot in life. Instead, her mother becomes her chief antagonist and the model for her own hideous fall. Radcliffe's uncannily hopeful recognition is turned inside out. Victoria recognizes her mother and despises her for all this loss has cost her.

Desire in the novel is again structured around this originary loss. Earlier, when her mother attempts to curb her interest in Berenza, the voluptuary whom she seduces and later marries, Victoria wants him all the more. Indeed, she uses her mother's example to explain her desire:

> She saw exemplified, in the conduct of her mother, the flagrant violation of a most sacred oath—she saw every principle of delicacy and of virtue apparently contemned—and, although the improper bias of her mind led her infi-

nitely to prefer the gay though horrible degradation in which she lived, to the retirement and seclusion so strongly insisted on by the dying Marchese, yet had she reflection and discrimination enough, fully to perceive and condemn the flagitious disregard those dying commands had received. But Victoria was a girl of no common feelings—her ideas wildly wandered, and to every circumstance and situation she gave rather the vivid colouring of her own heated imagination, than that of truth. . . . [W]hen Berenza singled her out, when he addressed her in the language of love, she then discovered that her sentiments were those of envy, and of an ardent consuming desire to be situated *like* that unhappy mother—like her, to receive the attentions, listen to the tenderness, and sink beneath the ardent glances of a lover. (28)

Butler's Freudian paradigm is brought out in such vivid relief as to almost seem a caricature. But it is not a caricature precisely because the desire to be like her mother forecloses the originary desire for the mother, with a result that is virulently destructive and finally self-defeating. I have written elsewhere about the importance of miscegenation to the climactic scenes of the novel.[22] There I say that the attraction between the dark moor Zofloya and the reckless heroine gives the novel coherence and that Dacre depicts female desire as a kind of victimization. By giving in to illicit desire, either incestuous or, more unusually, the result of miscegenation, Dacre encourages a "worm" that feeds on her being. Victoria's desire for the moor is symptomatic of the loss she suffers in the opening of the novel. She finds in his dark majesty the contours of the subjectivity her mother always already denied her. But of course it is a subjectivity defined in loss. And it leads her to an even more grasping, devouring desire, the reverse of the consolation that the Radcliffean mother could offer.

Victoria's obsession with the relationship between Henriquez and Lilla, which forms the bulk of the second half of the novel and introduces her to the character Zofloya, who aids and abets her desires, is articulated as a desire for Henriquez and a hatred of Lilla. In the way that the drama is played out, however, desire for Lilla is emphasized, not only as Victoria obsesses about her "fairy" beauty and plots her destruction, even as she is meant to be a protectress for her husband's brother's lover, but also in the violent confrontation between them that ends Lilla's life. There is no more powerful scene in the novel:

Nerved anew by this feeble attempt to escape her vengeance, Victoria pursued her flying victim. At the uttermost edge of the mountain she gained upon her, when Lilla perceiving that hope of escape was vain, caught frantic, for safety, at the scathed branches of a blasted oak, that, bowed by repeated storms, hung almost perpendicularly over the yawning depth beneath.—Round these, she twisted her slender arms, while, waving to and fro with her gentle weight over the immeasurable abyss, they seemed to promise but precarious support. (225)

Lilla is objectified as a victim, a pale reflection of Victoria who becomes the perfect answer to Victoria's surging rage. Her "slender arms" and wounded hand make her attractive as well as pathetic in terms the novel has established. She is an object of fascination to Victoria, obsessive erotic fascination. Lilla represents the devoted femininity that Victoria has sacrificed to her desire to be *like* her mother. Like her indeed. This is as intense a scene as the novel offers, and all the frustration of that originary foreclosure resides in its brutal, physical intensity. Victoria wanders in frustrating and horrifying normative desire, that is, because she has lost the mother whom she loved. Her hatred of her mother, of herself, and her deep and maddening loss heighten the cruel brutality of this climactic scene:

> Victoria advanced with furious looks—she shook the branches of the tree, that Lilla might fall headlong. Enhorrored at this terrible menace, the miserable girl quitted suddenly her hold, and on the brink of the mountain sought despairingly to grapple with the superior force of her adversary!—Her powers were soon exhausted, when clasping together her hands, and looking piteously upon that which had received the wound [Victoria has stabbed her], from whence the blood now streamed up to her elbow; she exclaimed, "Barbarous Victoria!—look down upon me, behold what thou hast done, and let the blood thou hast shed appease thee. Ah! Little did I think, when a deserted orphan, invited by thee to remain beneath thy roof, that such would be my miserable fate! Remember *that*, Victoria—have pity on me—and I will pray of heaven to forgive thee the past!" (225)

The encounter between pitiable innocence and vindictive fury is more pointed than similar scenes in Lewis and immeasurably crueler. In Lewis's *The Monk*, Ambrosio's final rape and murder of Antonia, as willful and violent as it is, does not share the premeditated murderous glee with which Victoria proceeds to destroy her opponent. Lilla's Radcliffe-like innocence only makes her a more entertaining victim:

> The only answer of Victoria was a wild laugh, and again she raised the poignard to strike.
> "Is it even so, then?" cried the despairing Lilla.—"Take then my life Victoria—take it at once,—but kill me I implore, with that same dagger with which you murdered Henriquez, because he loved me more than he did you!"

Fired to madness by this accusation, and the concluding remark, Victoria, no longer mistress of her actions, nor desiring to be so, seized by her streaming tresses the fragile Lilla, and held her back.—With her poignard she stabbed her in the bosom, in the shoulder, and other parts:—the expiring Lilla sank upon her knees.——Victoria pursued her blows—she covered her fair body with innumerable wounds, then dashed her headlong over the edge of the steep.—Her fairy form bounded as it fell against the projecting crags of the mountain, diminishing to the sight of her cruel enemy, who followed it far as her eye could reach. (226)

The terms of this description emphasize the extenuated pleadings and sufferings of Lilla. Almost lurid in its descriptions of this attenuated heroine, Dacre forces her reader to witness the cold-blooded fury of Victoria at close range. Unlike Berenza, who has been poisoned, and Henriquez, who falls on his own sword, Lilla alone receives the full force of Victoria's sadistic anger. The image of Lilla hanging from a tree over the abyss while Victoria shakes the branches would be comic if it were not so deeply implicated in Victoria's transgressive desire. This is not a neat execution of her amatory nemesis; it is rather an elaborate dance of death that continues to eroticize the poor Lilla even as it deprives her of life.

The blood, the pleading, and the violent stabbing all connect this encounter with other erotic encounters in the novel. Victoria, in bed with Berenza, is herself stabbed when her brother attempts to murder her paramour; the incestuous encounter reminds Victoria of the depth of her family connections at the same time that it fuses the bond between her and Berenza. Blood and violence are all part of Victoria's vocabulary of love from the very first, and even after she has fled this scene Victoria sees "those fair tresses dyed in crimson gore" and "that bleeding bosom" (226). The resonance cannot be accidental; the bloody female is herself the source of erotic desire in this scene. Although the bleeding Lilla invokes the name of Henriquez to stoke Victoria's rage, the presence that is felt throughout this scene of female-female victimization is the figure of Victoria's mother Laurina, herself a victim and a victimizer whom Victoria has internalized as loss and realized as hatred.

When Victoria meets that mother again in the robbers' cave where her brother Leonardo and Megalena have ended, she rejects her. In doing so she turns to the moor, who has befriended her with an affection that is as erotically charged as her relations with her mother are brutally cold. "[S]he loved, yet trembled at the inscrutable Zofloya" (245), and in the arms of this "presumed lover" (244) she tells him, "Wert thou always with me Zofloya, . . .

black melancholy and gloomy visions would never agitate my soul" (249). But her mother continues to be a source only of pain. When Leonardo asks if she can find it in herself to forgive her mother, Victoria's response recapitulates the maternal theme in particularly brutal terms:

> "Hah!—that is the very point," exclaimed Victoria, with a wild frightful laugh,——"that which I have been, my mother made me!——Mother," she pursued addressing the anguished Laurina—"why did'st thou *desert* thy children, to follow the seducer, who hath justly rewarded thee?—'Tis thou who hast caused *my* ruin; on thy head, therefore, will my sins be numbered.—Can I—oh can I reflect upon my deeds of horror, without arraigning thee as the primary cause?—thou taughtest me to give the reins to lawless passion,—for that I dishonoured my husband;—caused the death of his brother, and murdered a defenceless orphan!—For these crimes—all, all, I say, rising out of *thy example,* I am now a despised exile in the midst of robbers—of robbers, of whom the noble son who supports thee in his arms is *Chief!*—for this"—
>
> "Infamous, abandoned girl!" exclaimed Leonardo, "palsied be thy tongue!—can'st thou, wretch! without one compunctious pang, strew with sharp thorns the dying pillow of thy mother?—kneel, monster of barbarity! Kneel and solicit heaven and her for pardon."
>
> The fierce countenance of Victoria relaxed into a smile of contempt, and she remained immovable. (258)

This filial ingratitude is more than a convenient plot device. Victoria blames her mother in this particularly brutal way in part because of an insistent nature-versus-nurture argument that Dacre has tirelessly articulated. But beneath the thematic clarity of this encounter, another level of personal intensity is at work as well. Dacre sees this relation between mother and daughter as so totally formative that it could be seen as the basis of subjectivity.

When Victoria says "that which I have been, my mother made me," she gets at the very heart of gothic interest in the self. This moment brings us even closer to an understanding of the psyche in which maternal power is both all encompassing and peremptorily foreclosed. Victoria rejects her mother because of the pain she has caused. Rather than embrace the pain, however, as Ellena di Rosabla does in *The Italian,* she rages against it. Butler says that "survival, not precisely the opposite of melancholia, but what melancholia puts in suspension—requires redirecting rage against the lost other, defiling the sanctity of the dead for the purposes of life, raging against the dead in order not to join them." Victoria's rage at the mother she had lost is directed at other females in the novel and at other males as well. But she defiles the sanctity of mother-daughter love in this death scene precisely because of the intensity of that love. "Survival," after all, "is a matter of avowing the trace of loss that inaugurates one's own emergence."[23] Dacre realizes the violence and brutality of subjectivity, and Victoria plays out this violence, with the help of the radical alterity that Zofloya represents, to victimize everyone to whom she is close. It is a stunning, breathtaking display of personal aggression and rage. But of course Victoria is the victim, the one finally cast into the abyss. It is her own loss that she suffers in the end.

Subjectivity and Subjection

Kim Ian Michasiw claims that Dacre's *Zofloya* taught Shelley and Byron how to challenge the "myths of romantic selfhood." Michasiw discusses "the landscape of overindulged passion, overpowering yet inconstant sexual desire, elaborately and exquisitely planned and executed torments and murders" that Shelley borrows for his early *Zastrozzi* (1810) and *St. Irvyne; or, The Rosicrucian* (1811). Michasiw also suggests that Dacre's insistence on the "forced recognition that one's self is not one's own is a key moment in Shelley's works."[24] Even more suggestive, however, is a shared notion about the nature of subjectivity. Shelley's works borrow from Dacre's a desperate understanding of privacy and a bleak vision of the contours of subjectivity. They are so deeply steeped in pain and loss that they never quite gather the self-possession that even a gothic novel demands. They wallow in a kind of homoerotic bleakness that establishes the parameters of identity.

Zastrozzi, for instance, begins in a cave where the heroic Verezzi is chained to the wall in damp and gloomy confinement: "Oh! what ravages did the unified efforts of disease and suffering make on the manly and handsome figure of Verezzi!"[25] "Disease and suffering" could be the epigraph of gothic fiction. Here, though, it is a handsome man, not a defenseless girl, who is brutally victimized. Radcliffe has already prepared us for the unheroic heroism of the battered, brutalized, and bleeding—the castrated—male. In *Zastrozzi,* however, the male figure takes on a more immediate physical presence that suggests masculinity eroticized in an almost eerie approximation of death: "His bones almost started through his skin; his eyes were sunken and hollow; and his hair, matted with the damps, hung in strings upon his faded cheek" (8). Shelley uses this figure of broken masculinity as the basis of his gothic fantasy, and in doing so he suggests the ways in which loss can determine the workings of the uncanny.

The elegiac tradition, in the work of Gray and others, had already articulated the erotics of loss in the figure of a broken, wounded male. I have argued
elsewhere that the bloody, broken male is figured as loss in elegiac writing
and that at the heart of the elegiac tradition lies the blood-soaked figure of
castration. In his own elegiac poem *Adonais,* Shelley laments with the help
of the goddess of love:

> Stay yet awhile! speak to me once again;
> Kiss me, so long but as a kiss may live;
> And in my heartless breast and burning brain
> That word, that kiss, shall all thoughts else survive,
> With food of saddest memory kept alive,
> Now thou art dead, as if it were a part
> Of thee, my Adonais! I would give
> All that I am to be as thou now art!
> But I am chained to Time, and cannot thence depart! (ll. 226–34)[26]

Mourning in this case gives meaning to life, and desire is equated with
loss. The kiss for which the poet calls is the kiss that normative culture insists
upon. Subjectivity forecloses the same-sex love that Shelley evokes in this
poem and in his gothic novels as well. The poet laments a lover who is lost
to him, in other words, and Urania helps him give that love not a spiritual
but a burningly physical dimension. As the poet reaches out to his dead
friend he gives his "spiritualized love" a specific erotic structure. The lines
"In my thoughtless breast and burning brain / That word, that kiss, shall all
thoughts else survive" are reminiscent of Gray's Latin elegy in which the
poet urges his departed friend to "look down from your lofty seat on the
storm of human passion, the fears, the fierce promptings of desire, the joys
and sorrows and the tumult of rage so huge in my heart, the furious surges
of the breast . . . while my only wish is to mourn at your tomb and address
these empty words to your silent ashes."[27]

In *Zastrozzi,* the tale of vindictive desire and frustratingly unrealizable
love that follows is constructed around this figure of emasculation. The vivid
description of the hero's incarceration in the cave—"Languishing in painful
captivity, Verezzi passed days and nights seemingly countless, in the same
monotonous uniformity of horror and despair" (7)—suggests a subjectivity that has lost itself in utter abjection. And in the tale that follows Verezzi
seems unable to comprehend his status as "victim" (63) or the degree to
which his own desires are always already determined. He succumbs to the
enticing blandishments of the wicked Matilda, sacrificing the memory of his

beloved Julia, whom he thinks has died. For Shelley, though, the trajectory of this affection, or its object, is less important than Verezzi's own sexual passivity and the ways in which he becomes the object of affection himself. Like Dacre's Henriquez, that is, his importance lies in his own desirability. If not specifically homoerotic, this is a differently eroticized masculinity. Weakened, fainting, and in every way debilitated, his giving in to Matilda's demands is a kind of victimization. The passive male victim organizes a sexual dynamic that in subtle ways defies the normative.

Ultimately, Verezzi dies by his own hand. When Julia reappears he is horrified by his inability to give up Matilda, and he stabs himself with the "fatal poignard." "No peace but in the grave for me!" he exclaims as he collapses on the sofa (88). Debilitating and destructive as it is, desire turns back on itself. This auto-erotic gesture suggests that this has been a fantasy of male passivity that finally withdraws into itself. This passive, weakened male can never realize desire in any other form but that of loss. The grave, after all, is where he began.

In *St. Irvyne*, too, Wolfstein, the hero, has fallen in with a band of robbers and murdered their chief because of his threat to rape Magalena, a captive who becomes his companion and lover. At the same time, he finds himself more and more completely under the control of Ginotti, a brooding and mysterious figure who has been witness to the murder and demands that Wolfstein listen to his tale. It is the heart of Shelley's gothic-Romantic fantasy. Loss becomes a function of the romantic imagination:

> It was midnight. . . . The sky was veiled by a thick covering of clouds; and, to my heated imagination, the winds . . . whistled tidings of death and annihilation. I gazed on the torrent, foaming beneath my feet. . . . 'Twas then that I contemplated self-destruction; I had almost plunged into the tide of death, had rushed upon the unknown regions of eternity, when the soft sound of a bell from a neighbouring convent, was wafted in the stillness of the night. It struck a chord in unison with my soul; it vibrated on the secret springs of rapture. I thought no more of suicide, but reseating myself at the root of the ash-tree, burst into a flood of tears; never had I wept before; the sensation was new to me; it was inexplicably pleasing. I reflected by what rules of science I could account for it: *there* philosophy failed me. I acknowledged its inefficacy; and almost at *that* instant, allowed the existence of a superior and beneficent *Spirit*, in which image is made the soul of man. (182–201)

This act of subjection, this desire for a higher power, leads Ginotti into a defiant and unsatisfying conclusion. After this recognition of power, he is carried off in a visionary soul-selling that leaves him desperate and alone. Butler argues (in a discussion of Foucault's *Discipline and Punish*) that "the individual is formed or, rather, formulated through his discursively constituted 'identity' as prisoner. Subjection is, literally, the *making* of a subject, the principle of regulation according to which a subject is formulated or produced."[28] In his gothic fictions, Shelley understands implicitly the terms of that description. In fact, these works participate in the process that Foucault and Butler describe. Subjectivity is a form of subjection, and the powers in control, an unnamed jailer or an all-powerful Spirit, are the measure finally of abjection, the markers of loss. The gothic passivity that has elsewhere seemed only vaguely uncanny is exposed with all the glare of a visionary moment. This is a glimpse of the "real": "Ginotti's frame mouldered to a gigantic skeleton, yet two pale and ghastly flames glared in his eyeless sockets" (219). This is the horror that the gothic understands. It is the horror of subjectivity itself.

These works all suggest that subjectivity emerges from an originary loss that forecloses same-sex bonds in favor of brutal and brutalizing gendered alternatives. Walpole, Lewis, Radcliffe, Dacre, and Shelley all insist on a debilitating early love that renders the hero or heroine unfit for anything but sexual violence. I have ironically suggested that gothic fiction could offer an alternative structure of sexual violence, and in these works it is possible to see how such a structure could be formed. Freudian psychology is hardly more vivid or persuasive than these bizarre accounts. Popular and almost mythic in their cultural significance, moreover, these works can claim to pave the way for the psychological theorizing that emerged in the later nineteenth century. Gothic fiction informs that history as surely as that history informs gothic fiction.

Later chapters in this study build on these observations and further the claim that gothic fiction and Freudian psychology are symbiotic. For now, the first half of this claim begins to come clear. The next several chapters build on these ideas and help suggest one of the more important cultural implications of gothic fiction. Gothic fiction was the testing ground for theories of individual psychology before that psychology was fully articulated. That gothic fiction is always already queer explains a lot about psychology itself.

3

"Dung, Guts and Blood": Sodomy, Abjection, and the Gothic

The following account was reported in a London newspaper in September 1810: "On Thursday, *James Cooke, P. Hett, James Amos, alias Sally Fox, William Thompson, Richard Francis* and *James Pone,* the execrable miscreants, convicted of forming a club at the White Swan, in Vere-Street, to commit a vile offence, were placed in the pillory, pursuant to their sentence, between Panton Street and Norris-Street, in the Haymarket. The disgust felt by all ranks of Society at the detestable conduct of these wretches occasioned many thousands to become spectators of their punishment."[1]

The men were the victims of a long-term investigation that included both infiltration of the club and an elaborate system of entrapment that led them to incriminate themselves. This account turns on the notion of "disgust." Some are so used to hearing the term used in connection with sodomitical transgression that they have perhaps forgotten what it means. The *Oxford English Dictionary* lists as the first meaning "strong distaste or disrelish for food in general, or for any particular kind of food; sickening disinclination to partake of food, drink, medicine, etc.; nausea, loathing." This basic physical response to sexual difference is specifically bodily in its terms. "Distaste," "sickening," "nausea"—the words all suggest a kind of disease or dis-ease with the notion of sexual transgression because of the ways in which it threatens to invade the cultural body. This rebarbative physical response is never far from meanings that seem to apply more obviously to this cultural situation: "Strong repugnance, aversion, disappointed ambition, etc.; profound instinctive dislike or dissatisfaction."[2]

Because the men in question were no more or less foul-smelling than the spectators, the latter took it upon themselves to provide the even more foul-smelling matter by means of which the "execrable miscreants" could be identified:

> Shortly after twelve, the *ammunition wagons* from the neighbouring markets appeared in motion. These consisted of a number of carts which were driven by butcher's boys, who had previously taken care to fill them with the offal, dung &c appertaining to their several slaughter-houses. A number of hucksters were also put in requisition, who carried on their heads baskets of apples, potatoes, turnips, cabbage stalks, and other vegetables, together with the remains of divers dogs and cats. The whole of these were sold to the public at high price, who spared no expense to provide themselves with the necessary articles of assault.

The food, albeit rotten, produced for the ritual of disfiguration that followed reinforces the "disgust" motif that was introduced earlier. It was not enough to say that these sodomites were offensive but rather they needed to be made literally disgusting. The materials poured forth from the bowels of London, the materials with which the sodomites would be identified, and are reminiscent of the garbage that ran through those streets in the final triplet of Swift's "Description of a City Shower":

> Sweepings from butchers' stalls, dung, guts, and blood,
> Drowned puppies, stinking sprats, all drenched in mud,
> Dead cats, and turnip-tops come tumbling down the flood.[3]

Swift's poem of festive, celebratory disgust contrasts nicely with the festival of execration almost a century later, when the fetid materials that suggest the industry of an active city were marshaled for the purposes of a painful and grotesque labeling. The "dung, guts, and blood" showered on the offenders were meant to give these creatures an identity that was culturally controlled. By identifying them, that is, the crowd also rendered them hideously and horrifyingly recognizable for what they represented:

> The first salute received by the offenders was a volley of mud, and a serenade of hisses, hooting, and execration, which compelled them to fall flat on their faces in the caravan. The mob, and particularly the women, had piled up balls of mud to afford the objects of their indignation a warm reception. . . . The shower of mud continued during their passage to the Haymarket. Before they reached half way to the scene of their exposure, there were not discernible as human beings. . . . [Later, in the pillory] upwards of 50 women were permitted to stand in the ring, who assailed them incessantly with mud, dead cats,

rotten eggs, potatoes, and buckets filled with blood, offal, and dung, which were brought by a number of butchers' men from St. James's Market.

The markets of London furnished the materials with which the men were marked. Like the refuse of the butchers' stalls, they became by definition disgusting, loathsome, and nauseating. And the disgust gave rise to an energetic attack that was both vigorous and excessive. The process of identification took place as public spectacle, and like all identification it had a largely public function. These men were identified as monstrous, and the threat they posed was considered so serious that they had to be covered with filth as a sign of their crimes. Their befouling caused them almost to cease to be human. They were transformed into monsters to the degree that they threatened heteronormative culture with the dark, unknown otherness of sexual transgression. Like hideous monsters, these creatures were constructed as figures of deformity in order to display outwardly the inner depravity their sexual interests were imagined to reflect.

It might be argued that prisoners in the later eighteenth and early nineteenth centuries were always described in these terms. Studies such as Peter Linebaugh's *The London Hanged,* however, make it clear that the specific terms in which the newspaper report reveled were not common. The festivities and denunciations around hanging and pillorying are not as pointed as they are here, nor do they regularly insist on the inhumanity of the subjects involved.[4]

The terms of monstrosity are clear. The disgusting filth poured from the bowels of the eighteenth-century city, as it were, produced an identity that in its abjection ceased to be human. This subjectivity has been most usefully theorized by Julia Kristeva. In her study of abjection, *Powers of Horror,* she associates "dung, guts, and blood" and other forms of bodily effluvia with the kinds of processes described. For Kristeva, the matter that the body detaches, produces, and corrupts is a sign of abject identification. "Excrement and its equivalents," she says, "(decay, infection, disease, corpse, etc.) stand for the danger to identity that comes from without: the ego threatened by the non-ego, society threatened by its outside, life by death." She contrasts these things with "menstrual blood," which "stands for the danger issuing from within the identity (social or structural)."[5] The elaborate ritual in the pillory suggests a collapse of this distinction. The sodomite is a threat that comes from both without and within. He is the excremental non-ego and bloody identity, blended in this image of monstrosity. That is what makes his presence so uncannily tormenting.

These matters culminate, for Kristeva, in her consideration of the figure of the corpse. She argues that "it is the corpse ... that takes on the abjection of waste.... A decaying body, lifeless, completely turned into dejection, blurred between the inanimate and the inorganic, a transitional swarming, inseparable lining of a human nature whose life is undistinguishable from the symbolic—the corpse represents fundamental pollution."[6] In a chapter on Thomas Gray I have shown the ways in which that poet courts desire in the form of his own death in the *Elegy*.[7] The process is made devastatingly public in the ritual I have described. It is almost as if the sodomite serves as the figure of abjection for the culture at large and is being asked to bear the weight of culture's dis-ease with itself and its processes.

This dynamic, by which a figure is isolated and made to bear the anxieties of culture at large, has become a familiar one in Western experience. For instance, in a discussion of the role of anti-Semitism in Fascist thinking, specifically in Hitler's arguments in *Mein Kampf,* Slavoj Žižek argues that in order to "explain to the Germans the misfortunes of the epoch, economic crisis, social disintegration, moral 'decadence,' and so on" Hitler "constructs a new terrifying subject, a unique cause of Evil who 'pulls the strings' behind the scenes and is the sole precipitator of the series of evils: the Jew."[8]

Without in anyway trying to diminish the horrors of twentieth-century anti-Semitism, I suggest that this technique is a familiar one in Western culture: gypsies, blacks, Asians, and other ethnic and cultural groups have been handled similarly in different cultural and historical situations. So has the figure of the sodomite before, during, and after the period that Žižek is describing. The venom poured on the transgressive figures in the preceding quotations is that reserved for the cultural enemy, the figure that threatens the entire edifice of cultural respectability. And the sodomite does just that. Žižek adds, "The 'criticism of ideology' [that the Jew represents] consists in unmasking traditional allegory as an 'optical illusion' concealing the mechanism of modern allegory: the figure of the Jew as an allegory of Evil conceals the fact that it represents within the space of ideological narration the pure immanence of the textual operation that 'quilts' it."[9]

The sodomite functions similarly in late-eighteenth- and early-nineteenth-century culture, performing a critical action by his unserious display. Žižek explains how this can be so. The figure he describes is so valuable as a tool of cultural inversion because of a surplus of meaning that can only be understood in terms of enjoyment: "the surplus on which this mechanism relies is that fact that we impute to the 'Jew' an impossible, unfathomable enjoyment, allegedly stolen from us."[10] If that is true of the overdetermined figure of the

Jew in twentieth-century, anti-Semitic European culture, then it is also true of the overdetermined figure of the sodomite in eighteenth- and nineteenth-century British culture.[11]

The spectacle of identification that takes place in the pillory scene is excessive to the degree that it attempts to enact the kinds of enjoyment the sodomite has tried to keep secret. The scene is in one sense an attempt to reclaim this excess of sodomitical enjoyment and make it at the same time an identificatory process for the sodomites. We will make you the figures of our enjoyment, the process seems to suggest, and allow you to function in only the terms that we provide. The process of identification is so important because without it the sodomite cannot be recognized. The anger and exuberance of the attack on these men depended to a certain extent on the fact that they had been hidden, lurking as it were in the midst of an unsuspecting urban population. Sodomites must be dealt with so severely, the public seems to say, because otherwise we might not know who they are. We might mistake them for our friends.

As Jonathan Goldberg, citing Alan Bray, points out in his brilliant discussion of male-male relations in Marlowe's *Edward II* (1594): "Friendship and sodomy are always in danger of (mis)recognition," and what allowed "the proper intimacy between men to be called sodomy rather than friendship was ... precisely the transgression of social hierarchies that friendship maintained."[12] This political use of the concept of sodomy is crucial to an understanding of the way that the term functioned throughout the eighteenth century. The flexibility of the term, and the ways in which friendship and sodomy are in danger of "(mis)recognition," help explain much that is confusing about antisodomitical writing in the eighteenth century. This flexibility also begins to explain why the threat of the sodomite, his invisibility, the (mis)recognition of sodomite and friend, means that the terms of this ritualistic identification have broad cultural significance. No matter how vividly or how vilely some sodomites are identified, this suggests, others are lurking in the guise of friends, merchants, or even members of the clergy to threaten and undermine the bonds by which hegemonic culture is structured.

In *The Phoenix of Sodom; or, The Vere Street Coterie* (1813) this fear is articulated directly. The seeming invisibility of these figures, the notion that they might be masquerading as respectable members of society, makes them doubly vicious:

> How came a man of fortune and fashion to such a house?—I, therefore, shall repeat the question—What possible business could a man of rank, or

respectable merchant, or clergyman, or any other man in the character of a
gentleman, have, or what reasonable excuse can he make, for such frequent
attendance at a low, dirty public house, in the filthy avenues of Clare Market—the common and exclusive resort of the persons I have described. . . .
Even men in sacerdotal garb have descended from the pulpit to the gully-hole
of breathing infamy in Vere Street. (21–22, 24)

The author, who dilates on the possible horrors, seems almost carried away
with the vision he articulates. It is promiscuity of rank that worries him more
than perpetration of crime. The scandal, the horror, not only concerns this
crossing of class and social boundaries but also resides in the malleability of
terms like *man of rank, merchant,* or *clergyman.* The author cannot believe that
men whom he and society identify in one way can be available to other forms
of identification. "The gully-hole of breathing infamy" is a reference to anal
sex as surely as it is a reference to the club itself. Moreover, the author cannot
resist imagining this transgressive practice as so widespread as to be almost
universal: "Men of rank, and respectable situations in life, might be seen wal-
lowing either in or on the beds with wretches of the lowest description: but
the perpetration of the abominable act, however offensive, was infinitely more
tolerable than the shocking conversation that accompanied the perpetration"
(11). This quotation is surprising. The first horror, that of class transgression,
is familiar. From antisodomitical writing in the period as well as from trials
later in the century it becomes clear that a breakdown of hierarchy threatens
the social order itself. But why should the "conversation that accompanied"
it be so much more offensive than "the perpetration of the abominable act"?
Perhaps it is threatening to the degree that it moves beyond the merely physical into the realm of a possible emotional involvement. Love between men of
different stations would be much more threatening than simple sexual congress, and that is what at the most basic level Vere Street threatens. Liaisons
such as these threaten to bring culture to its knees.

The author of *The Phoenix of Sodom* is obsessed with questions of class
to be sure. Still, the story he tells concerns not a member of the clergy but
a much less distinguished figure. The author's most basic interests start to
emerge in the following telling lament:

I cannot pass this description of *ladies,* without making mention of another,
equally entitled to an external tribute due to delicacy; for it seems that one, of
no inconsiderable consequence to the dignity of the Coterie, is, by profession,
a Chimney Sweeper and Nightman, an employment not ill appropriate to
the delicate passions of which constitute his amusement. This lump of diab-

olism resides West of Hyde-park corner; and some time ago married a little
Catamite, called Miss Read, according to the rites of the Vere-street church;
and, of course, did that which all good husbands will do, took his precious
spouse to live in the house with him, the better to secure himself from the
effects of cuckoldom: but so it happened, that this *sweet-scented enamorata*
has a wife, unfortunately for the poor woman recognized by the Canons of
the Church of England; and, therefore, to pave the way for this little dung-hill,
Venus, he was introduced as a young man who wished to board and lodge
in a decent family. (28–29)

The offense here against the wife—the horror of a husband's male friend
turning out to be a lover—is measured in strictly financial terms. The author
seems unduly concerned with the details of how this man is being kept.
Although the tenant pays three guineas per week, "this knight of the gully-
hole regularly gave *Miss Read* the money every week, in order that he might
be considered an honorable and punctual pay master" (29). In other words
the illicit relation results in financial consequences for the married couple,
and the wife loses to the degree that the tenant gains. The extent of the
author's outrage might be considered understandable, however, if what really
is being threatened here is the system of heteronormativity. The author of
The Phoenix of Sodom laments "that a fine, elegant, perhaps beautiful woman,
should be doomed to have her bed encumbered with a wretch, who loathes
her person, squanders her fortune, and treats her with criminal contempt, to
indulge his damnable propensities, with (if I may be allowed the metaphor)
the *scavengers of Sodom!*" (30–31).

If the specter of the hidden sodomite looms so large over late-eighteenth-
and early-nineteenth-century culture, then that might be in part because the
stakes of sexual identification are so much higher at the cultural moment
when sexuality and sexual identity, as well as subjectivity and gender, are
being codified. After all, the processes that culminate in great sexological
pronouncements of the nineteenth century have their origins here. Discussions of sexual subjectivity from Symonds and Kraff-Ebing to Freud use the
conventions of gothic fiction to express the details of their understanding of
psychological states and internal processes. The dark corridors of interiority
with which we are now so familiar, the psychological struggles that typify our
understanding of subjectivity, and the violences of aggression and depression
are all couched in terminology familiar in gothic fiction. The connections
between the history of sexuality (and the growth of sexology) and the gothic
are not merely coincidental. They haunt each other with similarities that are
more intimately involved than has usually been claimed.

In Mary Shelley's *Frankenstein* (1818) the relation between subjectivity and sexuality, the sexuality of loss especially, gives the work its haunted quality. Victor Frankenstein's ecstatic childhood experience is interrupted by the introduction of Elizabeth Lavenza as his sister, playmate, and future partner. She pays for this intrusion, of course, with her life. The novel tells the tale of what become Victor's "unspeakable" longings. "It was the secrets of heaven and earth that I desired to learn," he says. In relation to other characters in the novel he is a son, brother, friend, and lover, but all the time he harbors a "fervent longing to penetrate the secrets of nature." As he says enviably of the microscope, he wants to "penetrate into the recesses of nature and show how she works in her hiding places."[13] This desire becomes an obsession, and when he does succeed in his quest he brings forth a monstrous creature that destroys all of those close to him. Like the sodomites in *The Phoenix of Sodom,* that is, Victor Frankenstein harbors a secret identity that threatens to destroy the culture of which he is a part.

Victor Frankenstein creates a second self out of the assorted body parts he finds in his secretive, nocturnal trips to graveyards and charnel houses. "Darkness had no effect upon my fancy; and a churchyard was to me merely the receptacle of bodies deprived of life, which, from being the seat of beauty and strength, had become food for the worm" (51). This macabre rewriting of Gray's *Elegy* hovers on the brink of an abyss. The vast sublime that stretches before the reader, however, is the sublime loathsomeness of abjection. Physical waste material becomes the basis of Frankenstein's secret life: "Now I was led to examine the cause and progress of this decay, and forced to spend days and nights in vaults and charnel houses" (51–52). Or again, "I pursued nature to her hiding places. Who shall conceive the horrors of my secret toil, as I dabbled among the unhallowed damps of the grave, or tortured the living animal to animate the lifeless clay" (54). The "secret" that Frankenstein discovers is the secret of life, or the secret life, that haunts heteronormative culture with its misshapen horror.[14]

Victor's creation of the monster is in some ways an expression of his loss, for the manner in which he roots through charnel houses and digs up graves suggests an obsession with the abject that melancholic subjectivity presupposes.[15] "I saw how the fine form of man was degraded and wasted; I beheld the corruption of death succeed to the blooming cheek of life; I saw how the worm inherited the wonders of the eye and brain. I paused, examining and analysing all the minutiæ of causation, as exemplified in the change from life to death, and death to life, until from the midst of this darkness a sudden light broke in upon me—" (52).

Victor's scientific obsession is a death-in-life that figures loss as the constitutive element of subjectivity. His creative vision, in other words, is steeped in death, and the life he produces is marked by the originary loss. It is no accident that Frankenstein's creature seems "monstrous"; Victor realizes that the terms of life are monstrous in their deep involvement with death.

The poor creature that Victor creates also realizes subjectivity through loss, not only because he is abandoned by his creator at the moment of birth but also because he finds that he is unacceptable, even to himself. The homoerotic force of originary desire is made perfectly clear. In the novel's primal moment the creature reaches out to Victor in a gesture that so defies our understanding of subjective attachments that we have been unable to see it for what it is: "I beheld the wretch—the miserable monster whom I had created. He held up the curtain of the bed; and his eyes, if eyes they may be called, were fixed on me. His jaws opened, and he muttered some inarticulate sounds, while a grin wrinkled his cheeks. He might have spoken, but I did not hear; one hand was stretched out, seemingly to detain me, but I escaped, and rushed down the stairs" (58).

This passage centers itself, as all gothic fiction does, on the confrontation with the horror that is oneself, the horror that one's relation to the world is painfully inappropriate and distorting to the privacy of self and that the life one wants so desperately is only death barely escaped. Moonlight creates a world between light and darkness and suffuses the scene with an unsettling glare. Just as the animated corpse seems a figure of death-in-life, so the moonlight is a light that suggests darkness. Later it becomes metaphorically associated with the creature.[16] Here it "force[s] its way through the window shutters" (52) as a way of suggesting that Frankenstein cannot shut out the light of knowledge he has discovered. Nor can he hide from the pursuit of his creation, who peeps into the bed in which Victor has sought refuge. A waking dream? The detail of observation—the eyes, the grin, and the hand—all suggest the grotesque reality of the vision. The personal pronoun *I* is the real center of attention, and the creature exists as an object to be observed, to be feared, and to be rejected.

This one act of love between Victor and his creation could have saved him and his loved ones from the monstrous fates that await them. "He might have spoken, but I did not hear": Victor chooses not to hear, not to accept, and not even to acknowledge this creature as his own. Instead, he chooses death, just as in his research he chose the dark path of death and corruption. Later, when creating a mate for this creature he destroys rather than completes his creation. Victor calls the creature a monster—"the miserable monster whom I had created"—as a way of separating it from himself. But Victor also always understands that the monster is a part of him, that part he would reject in his attempt to survive. This rejection breeds a violence that is cultural as well as personal.

The psychological is the social, as Victor so painfully discovers in the ensuing pages of the novel. His own life and the tragic lives of those around him are determined by his foreclosure of the secret (homoerotic) desire that the creature represents, and his culture—a system the novel encodes as patriarchal—is determined by a similar foreclosure and the violence that inevitably results from it. "Law," as Justine finds out in the course of her trial for the murder of young William, incorporates this violence as well. She is guilty, she admits, simply because the "Syndics" have accused her. The secret relationship between Victor and his creature—the real cause of William's death—is never suspected.

Frankenstein's creature—sensitive, intelligent, loving, and an alter ego, as it were, of whom he could take pride—comes to seem gargantuan, misshapen, scarcely human, and grotesque. In almost direct proportion to the ways in which he is treated he is violent, excessive, and threatening, not just to Victor's circle of intimates but to culture itself. Like the account of the pillorying of the sodomites, moreover, this tale turns on secrets that defy "nature" and in doing so transgress societal norms in ways that cannot be tolerated. Victor understands this, and as a result he attempts to reject, or repress, the signs of excess that he has harbored secretly. The creature is monstrous specifically because love is denied him, and he destroys Victor's intimates not just as an expression of Victor's aggressive desires, as some critics have argued, but also as a playing out of the consequences of sexual secrecy and the denial of love. Victor has dedicated himself to the act of creation out of an intense—indeed, excessive—pleasure.

Once this male-male bond is foreclosed in the novel the creature slips into a melancholic state that grows into hatred and violence. This foreclosure is paradigmatic, and it functions as the loss by which the self is forged. That it has to do with technology as well as subjectivity, or rather the technology of subjectivity, is why it remains so vitally alive. The relation between the psychological and the social come together in the figure of Frankenstein's creature. "If the melancholic turn is the mechanism by which the distinction between internal and external worlds is instituted," Butler says, "then melancholia initiates a variable boundary between the psychic and the social, a boundary . . . that distributes and regulates the psychic sphere in relation to prevailing norms of social regulation."[17] Frankenstein's creature turns the psychic life outward so as to make this boundary permeable and to render the social a function of the subjectivity that I have been describing.[18] Loss and the foreclosure of the homoerotic bond is the basis of modern culture.

If the creature's subjectivity is at the center of the tale, then it is also an account of the terrors of identification, of reaching into the dark and frightening depths of soul to produce a figure to be labeled and marked as monstrous. The novel plays out the terms of Victor Frankenstein's rejection of this creature and the violence implicit in its terms. The creature becomes the measure of Victor's abjection, as I have elsewhere argued, and torments him, his creator, by destroying all those he holds dear.

This process starts at the moment of the creature's inception, when Victor dreams that he holds the corpse of his mother in his arms: "I slept, indeed, but I was disturbed by the wildest dreams. I thought I saw Elizabeth, in the bloom of health, walking in the streets of Ingolstadt. Delighted and surprised, I embraced her; but as I imprinted the first kiss on her lips, they became livid with hue of death; her features appeared to change and I thought that I held the corpse of my dead mother in my arms; a shroud enveloped her form, and I saw the graveworms crawling in the folds of the flannel" (58).

Victor understands the secret he has created as a threat to the happiness of his prospective marriage and to the concept of family itself. Critics have suggested that Victor's crime is the appropriation of the maternal power to give birth and that this maternal nightmare can be connected to that theme.[19] At the same time it is important that at this crucial moment of self-confrontation Victor destroys in his imagination the women who are close to him. They are sacrificed to a male same-sex fantasy because it is impossible to imagine male-male desire outside of the confines of heteronormativity. If Victor has reached into the depths of nature to pull out a grotesque secret about himself, then he has defied the dictates of family and home. In the terms of the novel he cannot do so without becoming a threat to society and, inevitably, a pariah, in fact, a monster. Like the sodomite, that is, Frankenstein's monster must bear the brunt of cultural responsibility for everything that Victor cannot face about himself.

The murder of little William, with which the creature's reign of terror is inaugurated, is a culturally fitting sign of the dangers of Victor's excessive involvement with his desires. The sweet if not quite so innocent little boy—he torments the creature with his status and the position of his family—is sacrificed in a cruel scene meant to show the full horror of Victor's position. Henry Clerval's death is more telling, however, because of the intimacy the two men have shared and the possibility that Clerval seems to offer for an alternative to Elizabeth's assiduous attentions. Throughout the novel Clerval functions as a second self, a poetic, emotional counterpoint to the intellectualized Frankenstein. He is the one sent to discover what is wrong with Victor and who stands by him, even in his greatest obsessive behavior. Victor deeply feels the loss of this friend:

> I entered the room where the corpse lay, and was led up to the coffin. How can I describe my sensations on beholding it? I feel yet parched with horror, nor can I reflect on that terrible moment without shuddering and agony. The examination, the presence of the magistrate and witnesses, passed like a dream from my memory, when I saw the lifeless form of Henry Clerval stretched before me. I gasped for breath, and throwing myself on the body, I exclaimed, "Have my murderous machinations deprived you also, my dearest Henry, of life? Two I have already destroyed; other victims await their destiny: but you, Clerval, my friend, my benefactor——"
> The human frame could no longer support the agonies that I endured, and I was carried out of the room in strong convulsions. (176)

At this point, when the authorities identify Victor as a murderer, he claims the identity for himself. The "lifeless form of Henry Clerval" mocks him with its spectacle of emasculated masculinity. Victor passes into convulsions precisely because of the threat that this compromised masculinity poses. He knows how and why his friend has been sacrificed, and he now must confront the question of identity, directly and without compromise.

In doing so, of course, he sacrifices the other person closest to him. Elizabeth's death is the most grotesque and painful of them all: "Why am I here to relate the destruction of the best hope, and the purest creature of earth? She was there, lifeless and inanimate, thrown across the bed, her head hanging down, and her pale and distorted features half covered by her hair. Every where I turn I see the same figure—her bloodless arms and relaxed form flung by the murderer on its bridal bier. Could I behold this, and live? Alas!" (195).

It is a critical commonplace to suggest that Victor is responsible for these deaths.[20] The rhetoric of alter ego must not exonerate him from the deepseated anger and hatred these acts imply, but the confrontation is really a self-confrontation, an unwillingness to accept the deepest truths about himself. He is willing to sacrifice the love of his friend, and he refuses to acknowledge his lack of love for Elizabeth. These secrets turn him into the monstrous creature he has created. The creature metes out vengeance that is a measure of the horror of identification.

The process that had led the creature to this extreme behavior, then, involves his rejection by society as well as his creation by Victor. He is made monstrous to the degree that he is unknown and unnamable.[21] If he represents a dread and unspeakable desire on the part of Victor, a desire that places him outside the family and at odds with even himself, then he also represents culture's refusal to do anything with this intense excess but identify it, reject it, and attempt to destroy it. Victor has no choice but to attempt to destroy it as well. At the same time, of course, he destroys himself. In doing so he has created the myth that belongs to modern culture, and he has given his name to that myth. Frankenstein and his creature have become one in the popular imagination because culture makes certain that Frankenstein's desire is turned back on himself. "In *Frankenstein*," Bette London argues, "where the female subject drops out of sight, the discomfort accrues to the masculine collective: the male artist, spectator, and spectacle. And as the notorious slipperiness of Frankenstein's signature suggests, the composition of masculinity, at least in the novel, cannot be fixed."[22] The discomfort that London describes is closer at times to madness.

Madness is always a possibility, just as it is when questions of sexuality are addressed. When he tells of sodomitical sexual activity, the only conclusion that the shocked author of *The Phoenix of Sodom* can draw is that of madness:

> That the reader may form some idea of the uncontrollable rage of this dreadful passion . . . that a person in a respectable house in the city, frequently came to [t]his sink of filth and iniquity, and stayed several days and nights together; during which time he generally amused himself with eight, ten, and sometimes a dozen different boys and men! . . . It is said that this animal is now in a mad-house; which, in my apprehension, is the natural consequence of transactions which can only be produced by a temporary insanity. (17)

Sexual desire is figured as a kind of madness, just as the paranoid relations between men become a kind of madness in the novels I am discussing. In the novels, though, the degree to which the mad, the threatening other, becomes part of one's own abjection is precisely where sexuality emerges. The "animal" that stalks the pages of this novel, however, cannot be so easily confined.

A kind of insanity is the subject, too, of the gothic masterpiece of the 1820s. James Hogg's *The Private Memoirs and Confessions of a Justified Sinner* (1824) dramatizes the nefarious doubling between Robert Wringham and the satanic Gil Martin. In the first of the novel's two parts, "The Editor's Narrative," the bookish and lonely Robert Wringham forms an emotional attachment to his lively and athletic older stepbrother, George. Gradually Robert, variously described as "devilish-looking," "moody and hellish looking," with "a deep and malignant eye," becomes a kind of "shadow" to George, who tries in vain to avoid the inevitable physical confrontation that leaves Robert a bloodied victim, symbolically castrated and feminized. George begins to see Robert as a "limb of Satan" and starts to feel that he is haunted by "some evil genius in the shape of his brother."[23]

George sees his brother as a monstrous alter ego. After they have argued and fought at a tennis game, Robert emerges "bloody and disgusting" (25), and George and his friends see him as an "unaccountable monster" who "actually tried to get in alongst with them" (25) and ruin their camaraderie with his lurid, disfigured form. George continues to be harassed, stalked, and even haunted by his brother: "the attendance of that brother was now become like the attendance of a demon on some devoted being that had sold himself to destruction" (37). The tension between the two brothers—bitter rivalry, jealousy (on Wringham's part), and sheer hatred—threatens to erupt into violence on a number of occasions. It is not long before George is murdered by the brother who despises him.

This tale of displaced desire and misdirected libido raises a number of questions about brotherhood, identity, and the nature of male-male desire. The blood that flows throughout the opening section—Wringham emerges from every encounter but the last as a bloodied victim—suggests the abjection that is always already implanted in this account. Robert is the bleeding, castrated male because he has no access to the power and position that George represents. He hovers about, antagonizes, and finally murders George because of the desire to identify with all he represents. Instead, he is identified as "a horrible monster" (41) who dares transgress the bound of social respectability. In his abjection he becomes the poor, disgusting thing that those who oppose him continue to claim. Robert steps behind George in the dark shadows of the Edinburgh night and stabs him with a rapier from behind—"the fellow in black rushed from his cover with his drawn rapier, and gave the brave young Dalcastle two deadly wounds in the back, as quick as arm could thrust, both of which . . . pierced through his body" (78). He completes the process that he began on the tennis court, the process that identifies him as desperate, abject, and a mere parody of masculinity. That the murder can be read also as a kind of male rape does nothing to contradict this view, for this is the rape of a powerless, monstrous, and, finally, castrated male.

In the second part of the novel, "Private Memoirs and Confessions of a Sinner, written by himself," Robert tells of being haunted by a double. In a narrative that suggests a paranoid relation to the world he admits seeing the "beauty of women . . . as the greatest snare to which mankind are subjected" (113). Isolated in his particularly virulent misogyny, he becomes "open" to the seduction of the mysterious Gil Martin, who teaches Calvinist "justification" as a creed that legitimates acting out suppressed desires, which leads Robert into a series of self-justifying acts of violence against other men. Not surprisingly, the only relations charged with emotion are those between men. Hogg is exposing the inner workings of a culture that objectifies women and places male relations under strict scrutiny. "I had heart-burnings, longings, and yearnings, that would not be satisfied" (182), Robert Wringham tells readers. His desire literally consumes him, and his alter ego becomes a function of ego itself.

In discussing this novel, Eve Kosofsky Sedgwick says, "As [Robert] pushes blindly, with the absurdly and pathetically few resources he has, toward the male homosocial mastery that alone and delusively seem to promise him a social standing, the psychologized homophobic struggle inside him seems to hollow out an internal space that too exactly matches the world around him" (114).[24] The double works as an effective fictional representation of this replicated vision. Gil Martin has intimate knowledge of his subject because internal paranoia and cultural conditioning are one and the same. The paranoia Robert Wringham expresses, in other words, is the paranoia that culture breeds in any, in all, tempted to transgress the narrow limits of the normal. Robert Wringham recognizes that the guilt he feels, as well as the special justification he claims, are prices that culture exacts for offering him even his tentative place at its margin. In this late-gothic novel, then, subjectivity is the source of the haunting. Transgression and perversity have been planted within the individual psyche in order to do the work of culture more effectively. Gothic fiction has dramatized this transition and has decried its effects in various ways, but nowhere more effectively than here.

Dennis A. Foster maintains that the narrative form of confession reproduces "patterns of desire, guilt and obligation." Confession offers itself as form for the second part of *Memoirs and Confessions* for religious as well as personal reasons. In describing the ways in which confession functions within family and religion Foster notes, "Confession is not an incidental narrative form within these institutions: it is the mode by which people enter into discourse with their culture. . . . It represents an attempt to understand the terms and the limits by which the people are defined, both as they listen to the confessions of others and as they recount their own transgressions."[25]

Robert Wringham tells his story because he cannot understand the limits of the human, cannot accept them. Desire exists here as something already frustrated and disappointing. His desire turns to guilt precisely because he cannot accept the implications of desire. For Foster, "Desire makes sense only if one can imagine that some other exists who already has the desirable thing, and who might therefore provide the desiring subject with what he needs."[26] In Wringham's case that "some other" does exist, but he is unable to imagine that he can be provided with what he really wants. That is the measure of his loss, and it is also a measure of his monstrous villainy.

Both novels and the Vere Street scandal suggest the complication of identification and sexual transgression in the early nineteenth century. The urge to identify the sodomite is born out of fear, and identification seems a phobic enterprise. To identify oneself in these works, or to accept the identifications made publicly, is to admit the kind of monstrosity, or monstrous villainy, that the Vere Street trial reports make a public spectacle. That is what identification meant throughout the nineteenth century, and it is why the topic is so vexed and politicized for twentieth-first-century gays and lesbians. Coming out may seem an answer to this history until it becomes obvious that coming out is exactly what a phobic culture desires. That point will become more obvious in the later chapters of this study; here I claim, on the basis of these examples, that identification is a ruthless process of labeling and can turn subjects against themselves.

PART 2

Gothic Culture

4

The Horrors of Catholicism: Religion and Sexuality in Gothic Fiction

Catholicism emerges from the historical setting to play an active role in most gothic novels. In Horace Walpole's *The Castle of Otranto* (1764) a Catholic chapel provides one of the key sites of the action, and the unassuming Father Jerome, the local cleric, holds a significant position in the denouement of the action. More to the point, however, is the mood of religious sentiment that suffuses the whole. When Manfred decides to divorce his wife Hippolita in favor of his dead son's fiancée Isabella, the transgression is personal and sexual—the incestuous implications of such a bond are by no means ignored—and also a violation of the religious law that sanctifies marriage. Manfred asks the priest to persuade his wife "to consent to the dissolution of our marriage and retire into a monastery."[1]

Hippolita's continual prayers emphasize this connection and involve her daughter Matilda in her world of private devotion. When Matilda is murdered by her father, moreover, she has been meeting Theodore, a young peasant, in the chapel of Otranto, and her stabbing has all the markings of martyrdom as well as of Manfred's incestuous sexual aggression. To a certain extent these two things are the same. Matilda's blind belief in her father, her devotion to his power and wisdom, and her refusal to accept him as inherently evil all lead to her demise; as she dies she blesses him and prays for his forgiveness. I have argued earlier in this volume (25) that Manfred has reversed the trajectories of Freud's Oedipal arrangement, murdering his son in order to marry his daughter. He destroys his (other) daughter in the violence of his lust.

Manfred's incestuous sexual violence becomes a nightmare of broken bodies and violated graves. Manfred is dispossessed because he attempts to dispossess the younger generation. The powerful and self-absorbed father victimizes his own children in this novel, and he sacrifices them to the exigencies of paternal power. The family is the true victim of Manfred's lusts, and in this novel it can never really recover. At the same time, as Father Jerome reminds the hero, Manfred offends more than the family: "Profane prince! . . . is it at the altar that you choosest to insult the servants of the altar?—But, Manfred, thy impious schemes are known. Heaven . . . know[s] them" (93).

By placing this violence in the chapel of Otranto and suffusing the scene with the air of a religious sacrifice, Walpole makes a subtle connection between the heteronormativity of sexual violence and the patriarchal law of the father upon which Catholicism insists. "The following work was found in the library of an ancient catholic family," Walpole writes in the preface to the first edition of the novel, and "the principal incidents are such as were believed in the darkest ages of Christianity."[2] The gothic terms of the work—sexual hysterics and violently destructive abuse—have greater meaning because of the religious terms in which they are couched. Sexuality, that is, depends on a religious context to exert its full cultural significance. Sexuality and religion are not opposite poles from which to understand the action of the novel; they are inextricably bound in the cultural imagination. Walpole understands that clearly enough to couch his sexual excesses in religious terms.

Later gothic fiction makes this connection explicit by returning again and again to convent and monastery as a way to explore same-sex and otherwise transgressive desire. It is no accident that these repeated dramatizations of love between men and love between women take place in the later eighteenth and early nineteenth centuries. These dramatizations are not ancillary to the history of sexuality or a byproduct of a development in sexology. Because they anticipate sexological analysis at precisely the moment when these questions had begun to be explored, they could serve as chapters in the history of sexuality. It is a commonplace to suggest that "homosexuality" emerged in the 1870s, when it was named and codified, at least tentatively.[3] But an earlier and very necessary process of popularization exists: Catholic gothic fiction and the history of sexuality, for this moment at least, overlap in countless ways.[4]

When in *The Monk* (1796) Matthew G. Lewis uses the details of conventual life to suggest lurid forms of sexual excess such as necromancy, incest, matricide, and same-sex love, he does not need to explain his choice of a Catholic setting, a Mediterranean country (Spain, not Italy in this case), or religious life.[5] All these things, to the English imagination at least, made such easy, rational sense that Lewis could assume a general understanding of (and even assent to) his extravagant posturing. Although reviewers criticized Lewis's excess, they never suggested that his portrayal of Catholic monastic life was inappropriate.[6] If the novel can be considered sensational that is not because anyone objected to the portrayal of the characters themselves—oversexed and violent priests and victimizing and vindictive nuns. Devil worship, self-abuse, and other lurid sexual possibilities were common popular perceptions of conventual life in Mediterranean countries.

The Gordon Riots in 1780 revealed the depth and breadth of anti-Catholic feeling in England in the later eighteenth century.[7] The Catholic Relief Act passed by Parliament in 1778 was meant to alleviate the plight of Catholics in the smallest ways, but it was widely viewed as a threat to English independence. As Colin Haydon argues, "The Act seemed objectionable on a number of counts. It seemed to violate the Protestant constitution as established in 1689. . . . It formally suspended the old restrictions on Popish priests and it was felt that this new license might allow them to win converts. Above all, it aided a group which had long been represented by those in authority as dangerous and seditious."[8] The depth of this feeling is expressed in such popular publications as the *Appeal from the Protestant Association to the People of Great Britain* (1779): "To design the Advancement of POPERY, is to design the Ruin of the State, and the Destruction of the Church; it is to sacrifice the Nation to a double Slavery, to prepare Chains both for their Bodies and their Minds": this was the kind of language that used in popular pamphlets to inspire resistance to the Relief Law.[9] With cries of "No Popery" rioters raided the homes of prominent Catholics and Catholic sympathizers in London and other important centers. "At the chapel in Duke Street, a dead dog with a crucifix between its paws was hung up against a wall of the building," and at other places chapels were smashed and altars were paraded through the streets.[10] Some of the violence of the Gordon Riots, in other words, makes the excesses of gothic fiction seem almost tame.

Of course by the time most gothic novels were written there were other reasons to fear Catholicism, or at least to fear the political forces that emerged from Catholic countries. The anti-Jacobin feeling of the 1790s, combined with a horror at the perceived barbarities of the French Revolution, exacerbated the mood that Haydon described and meant that villainous continentals were all the rage. The logic of anti-Catholicism is not exactly congruent with the political conservatism of the anti-Jacobin movement, but neither public sentiment at large nor the bulk of popular gothic novels can be accused of being systematically political, thematically consistent, or even regularly coherent. The fear expressed in anti-Catholic writing of the 1790s was as deeply rooted as it was in the 1780s, as the rhetoric of both Jacobin and anti-Jacobin writing suggests.[11] The barbarities reported from France, the excesses of the response to historical injustice, and the horror at public execution were balanced by the seeming overthrow of the religion that had haunted English imaginations throughout the century.[12]

At the same time, not coincidentally, attitudes about sexuality were similarly shaped by attitudes toward Catholics and Catholic countries. Throughout the eighteenth century it was a commonplace that sodomy was imported from Italy and France, if not from more exotic locales, and often monasteries and convents were seen as locales where same-sex desire could flourish. In one of the standard texts of the eighteenth century a familiar quotation makes these relations explicit. The writer is complaining about the "fashion" of men kissing one another in public:

> This *Fashion* was brought over from *Italy,* (the *Mother* and *Nurse* of *Sodomy*); where the *Master* is oftener *Intriguing* with his *Page,* than a *fair Lady.* And not only in that *Country,* but in *France,* which copies from them, the *Contagion* is diversify'd, and the Ladies (in the *Nunneries*) are criminally *amorous* of each other, in a *Method* too gross for Expression. I must be so partial to my own *Country-Women,* to affirm, or, at least, hope they claim no Share of this *Charge;* but must confess, when I see two Ladies *Kissing* and *Slopping* each other, in a *lascivious Manner,* and *frequently* repeating it, I am shock'd to the last Degree.[13]

This passage is not unique in the eighteenth century, nor is it out of keeping with the other passages I have considered: Sodomy is a contagion that has spread from the Continent, a disease that threatens the island nation like rabies or the plague. In almost the same breath but parenthetically, it emerges from a convent. The Catholic connection is subtle but insistent. Italy and Italians, the religion, politics, and culture all combine to represent sexual transgression. In "The Import of Sodomy," John C. Beynon cites several cases in which sodomy and Italy are connected in suggestive ways. Bernard Mandeville, in his *A Modest Defense of the Public Stews* (1724), for instance, names Pope Sixtus VI as the source of sodomy. Because he attempted to suppress female courtesans, the argument runs, men turned to one another for sexual solace. It is intriguing to think that a pope could be cited as the source of sodomy, but that idea is in keeping with the religio-political climate that I have described.[14]

In his discussion of attitudes earlier in the century Cameron McFarlane says that "just as the representation of the sodomite is refracted through the social structures of the gender and class hierarchies, it also intersects with a discourse of xenophobia directed particularly toward the Catholic countries of France and Italy." McFarlane makes it clear how politically (in the larger sense) useful the association "Italian/Catholic/sodomite" became throughout the country and how it functioned in political satire as well as in broadsides such as *Satan's Harvest Home.*[15] Charles Churchill codifies these attitudes for the later century in his poem "The Times":

> With our island vices not content,
> We rob our neighbours on the continent;
> Dance Europe round, and visit every court,
> To ape their follies and their crimes import.
> To diff'rent lands for diff'rent sins we roam,
> And richly freighted, bring our cargo home,
> Nobly adventurous to make vice appear
> In her full state, and perfect only here. . . .
> ITALIA, nurse of ev'ry softer art,
> Who, feigning to refine, unmans the heart.[16]

In one short passage Churchill attacks the notion of the Grand Tour, the vice of Catholic countries, and the danger of foreign trade. He emphasizes the criminal and sinful aspects of sexual transgression and suggests that Italy is a particular danger for young English travelers. Later in the poem he makes the terms of his fear of the Continent more specific: "Women are kept for nothing but the breed; / For pleasure, we must have a GANYMEDE, / A fine, fresh, HYLAS, a delicious boy, / To serve our purposes of beastly joy" (331–34). In talking about how to educate a son, he advises:

> Give him no tutor—throw him to a punk,
> Rather than trust his morals to a monk;
> Monks we all know—we, who have lived,
> From fair report, and travelers, who roam,
> More feelingly. (639–50)

Churchill is circumspect in his expressions, but the implications are clear. Monks transgress in ways that are threatening to English manhood. English travelers are physically threatened by priestly predators, the poem suggests, and by establishing a contrast between living and traveling Churchill hints that even to leave England is to risk one's life and reputation. At the same time, of course, as E. J. Clery reminds, "Throughout the eighteenth century, Italy formed the highlight of any European tour."[17] Endless eighteenth-century accounts—memoirs, letters, maps, paintings, and music—celebrate Italy as the fountain of art and culture for several generations.

In addition to the possible experience of a deep cultural awakening, many adolescent British travelers used the tour as an opportunity for sexual experimentation as well as other kinds of physical and emotional excess. Because classical culture offered so many models of same-sex love to the educated traveler it is no wonder that certain activities and locations became associated in the British mind. If the prime exemplar of the intellectualization of the process happens to be German ("art historian, archaeologist, and chief librarian of the Vatican, the German scholar Johann Joachim Winckelmann infused his influential vision of Greek antiquity with all the telltale signs of homoerotic desire," as one scholar puts it), that does not mean that English travelers throughout the century were not alive to the same enticing possibilities.[18]

As satiric comments by Smollett and others make clear, the Grand Tour was also infamous as a source of sexual adventure, and various accounts of continental travel emphasize the sexual excess that was implicit in the Italian adventure.[19] The catalog for a 1996 exhibit on the Grand Tour, for instance, states that Italy held the lure of various kinds of travelers: "outcasts of a more permanent kind, Jacobites, bankrupts, or homosexuals, seeking relief and some form of security."[20] This image of homosexuals on the run is surely a nineteenth- rather than an eighteenth-century image, but the suggestion that homosexuality—or, more properly, sodomy—loomed above the image of Italy in the eighteenth century is surely correct.

Of course, as the litany of "Jacobites, bankrupts, or homosexuals," suggests, it is not easy to separate the sexual and the political—or rather the religio-political. In discussing early modern England, Alan Bray points out that sodomy was a political rather than a sexual signifier. In "Homosexuality and the Signs of Male Friendship in Elizabethan England" Bray describes the ways in which sodomy could be used as an accusation, especially in cases of religio-political subversion and vice-versa. Renaissance sodomy, he says, "was not only a sexual crime. It was also a political and a religious crime and it was this that explains most clearly why it was regarded with such dread." He goes on to explain how "the ubiquitous association of sodomy with treason and heresy was put together and why one encounters it so commonly in the polemics of Reformation Europe."[21]

Approaching the topic from a different direction, Mark D. Jordan shows how sexual activity between men was proscribed by the early Christian church. His work demonstrates how the labels *sodomy* and *sodomite* were adopted to regulate various behaviors—sexual, political, religious, and social—and indicates that their usefulness for early "fathers" of the church stemmed from their flexibility. This flexibility suggests that sodomy has never been just one thing in the Western cultural imagination any more than its use has promoted one sexual practice to the exclusion of all others. Jordan also argues that "as elsewhere in Europe, English sodomy legislation seems to have been enforced infrequently. Where sodomy cases appear in the surviving historical sources, they typically involve some other factor—political scheming, racial or religious or class prejudice, personal enmity."[22]

Before the eighteenth century in England questions of sexual relations between men were extraordinarily complex. The label *sodomite* was flung at politicians and papists as well as at people from Italy, France, and Spain—from just about anywhere but England. By implication, the term was meant to regulate Englishness as much as to describe any particular form of sexual behavior. That remained true throughout the eighteenth century, to be sure, and the difference before and after 1700 is not as vivid as some historians have suggested.[23] Such associations did not end with the Age of Enlightenment; in some cases they even intensified. That is what some rhetoric of the Gordon Riots suggests, and it is what the more extreme language of the 1790s articulates.

Given this context it is not surprising that Matthew G. Lewis can titillate with the possibility of same-sex desire in *The Monk* merely by invoking Catholicism, a monastery, and an emotional bond between a handsome priest and a blushing novice. In another study I have explored the homoerotics of the scenes in the novel in which the novice gradually confesses his love for the older priest.[24] In *The Monk,* Lewis seems to delight in outrageous details and scandalous transactions. Sexual transgression is the norm, as characters find that their lusts force them to violate religious vows, invoke Satanic powers, and destroy the bonds of family and friendship. The seemingly virtuous monk Ambrosio gives into so many different "lusts" that it is difficult to separate avarice, jealousy, and pride from his campaign of sexual victimization. His growing bond with the young novice, Rosario, becomes a lurid sexual adventure when that novice turns out to be a woman, Matilda, who has been a model for the portrait of the Madonna to which Ambrosio is devoted.

That his excess of prideful devotion has led him to these lurid scenes of sexual perversity is a given in the novel. The connection between Catholicism and bodily lust is made explicit in various ways. Confessional confidence leads to sexual abuse; lust is exercised by means of devil worship; and the monastery and convent are scenes of violence, victimization, and death. Such familiar scenes help make clear the ways in which the easy relation between Catholicism and sexual perversity has a political as well as a social valence. After all, almost all the violence in the novel is answered in direct political terms with mob violence and the destruction of the convent and monastery as well as the brutal physical destruction of the prioress and several of the more violent nuns. Sexual excess and political subversion seem to go hand in hand with religious fervor. The connection is not accidental. Religious fervor is sexual in its expression, and if sexuality is always already political so is religion. The politics of religion and sexuality in the experience of gothic fiction, at least, have much in common.

Ronald Paulson has explained how the French Revolution influenced gothic writers and gave their work a currency that it might not otherwise enjoy. He also explores the ways in which the fear and fascination inspired by events in France could affect a novel like *The Monk:*

> Lewis exploits the dramatic resonances of the Revolution and its anti-clericalism, but simultaneously portrays the rioting mob as blood-thirsty, completely out of control, animal-like in its ferocity. The convent of St. Clare represents corruption, superstition, and repression, but its overthrowers, no more admirable than the tyrants, are capable of the same atrocities or worse. In the same way, many observers (conservative and otherwise) by 1793 saw the brutally oppressed masses of France usurping the tyrannical roles of their erstwhile oppressors.[25]

I have elsewhere argued that Lewis was afraid of the torrent of passion that could be released when repression was overthrown.[26] That happens in the individual case of Ambrosio and in the general case of the mob that destroys the Prioress of St. Clare. But it is important to remember that Lewis seems to take an explicit interest in the violence and even celebrate it. Otherwise the details of destruction would not be so vivid or the dramatization of excess so extensive. Lewis invests such scenes with an almost erotic excitement precisely because he connects them with the thrill of sexual transgression and the fear of uncontrollable sexual excess. Ironically, this technique does not decrease the relation between religion and sexuality but rather increases it.

At this moment the yet-uncodified history of sexuality emerges at sites like these. The automatic association of Catholicism with political/sexual transgression makes it available for the exploration of sexual difference. Ambrosio and Rosario are pushing the envelope of sexual definition, as it were, precisely because they are always already transgressive to the English imagination as monks, as Catholics, and as Mediterranean. Lewis uses this transgressive potential to confront readers with the possibility of same-sex desire. The monastery is a precursor of the sexual laboratory, and in a sense it functions as the controlled environment in which the habits of an unfamiliar species can be studied. The horror that such an examination generates is a built-in protection for the observer. Lewis may not have the dispassionate zeal of an investigator like the twentieth century's Alfred C. Kinsey, but he does perform a similar function for the later eighteenth century. Male-male relations are being examined, even if they are held up as a sign of horror and disgust. Like William Beckford's exotic use of the East as an examination of pederasty, that is, Lewis uses his "exotic" locale to make the connections he is seeking both revelatory and automatic.[27] He uses a Catholic setting and context in order to make these readings available to his age. They form a part of the sexuality; the particular configuration of two men of different ages in a monastery occupies a different place in the eighteenth-century cultural imagination from any other configuration of two men. More is allowed, more is even assumed, than otherwise would be even possible.

Ann Radcliffe's less excessive gothic is no less involved in establishing a context for same-sex desire. As an answer to the rigors of patriarchal law, Radcliffe offers the kindly maternal convent in which relations among women are celebrated and in which particular female-female bonds are valued and even honored. In describing the situation in *The Romance of the Forest* (1791), for instance, Robert Miles argues, "Radcliffe's heroine on a threshold looks both ways, inward toward 'maternal' sensibility with its delusive image of subjective wholeness (delusive, because the heroine is still caught within a patriarchal structure, the family 'house' or abbey), and outwards towards a patriarchal order of repression and deferral."[28]

In *The Italian* (1797) Radcliffe creates a context in which this maternal fantasy is no longer delusive. Ellena, Radcliffe's heroine, wanders through the novel in a state that could be described as melancholy. She experiences loss as fundamental and determining. As the novel develops it seems that Ellena must reexperience a primal "homosexual" attachment in order to give any significance at all to her love for the hero, Vivaldi. The attachment inevitably offers itself in a convent, Santa Maria della Pietà, where Ellena finds herself drawn to a single nun—"Among the voices of the choir, was one whose expression immediately fixed her attention; it seemed to speak a loftier sentiment of devotion than the others, and to be modulated by the melancholy of an heart, that had long since taken leave of this world" (86).

This first attraction develops into a kindly friendship that quickly becomes the center of Ellena's convent existence. Later, when the nun is revealed to be Ellena's mother, the scene in which they express love for one another is too powerful to admit anyone else into their circle. Vivaldi understands his exclusion, for the first feelings he has toward Olivia are those of jealousy. "'Ah Ellena!' said Vivaldi, as he gently disengaged her from the nun, 'do I then hold only the second place in your heart?'" (135, see also chapter 2 of this volume).

E. J. Clery makes it clear that for writers like Radcliffe "the basis of the nightmare vision of Italy [is] the Roman Catholic Church. Whereas the classical heritage united Western Europe in the eighteenth century, religious difference led to alienation and antagonism, and Italy was in this respect regarded by Protestant nations as the epicentre of spiritual corruption." Clery feels, however, that "Radcliffe and other gothic writers in fact participated in a gradual liberalizing of religious ideas." The aestheticizing forces of gothic fiction, Clery argues, meant that the convent was a fulcrum for change in this context. In Radcliffe, she claims, the convent is idealized "as a refuge for women, a place where they could escape crisis in the patriarchal family and secure some autonomy." Of course in *The Italian* the convent can also be a place of constriction and malevolence. What makes the difference, a distinction that Clery does not make but which seems essential, is the question of desire. Clery says that Radcliffe inspires "a curious empathy with the Catholic Other."[29] She does so precisely by means of this deep, erotic maternal motif, which is the legacy of Radcliffe as much as any interest in aggressive fathers. In each of the novels a grim paternal figure threatens the heroine emotionally and physically. But in each the subjective experience of maternal love, exoticized as ghostly or eroticized as religious, spiritual, and conventual, offers a consoling alternative to the experience of solitude that a lonely female faces.[30]

Other gothic writers, especially those actively pro-Catholic in their narrative agenda, do not cancel these resonances; they simply make them less immediately obvious. Regina Maria Roche's *The Children of the Abbey* (1797), restrained in its use of wicked monks and nuns, nevertheless tells a tale that deeply intertwines religion and sexuality. The heirs of Dunheath Abbey, Amanda Fitzalan, the heroine of the tale, and her brother Oscar, are nefariously disinherited and forced to struggle separately for survival. Her widowed father sends Amanda to live with friends, but she quickly becomes the victim of jealous competitors. She is beautiful and unassuming, but a rumor spreads that she is somehow dishonorable. Out of the welter of suspicion and disappointment Amanda finds solace in the form of a Catholic nun. The nun does not accuse, threaten, or victimize in any way, but even in this novel the consoling force of the convent is often suggestive. As Roche describes Sister Mary when Amanda first encounters her, "She was fifty . . . her skin was fair, and perfectly free from wrinkle, the bloom and down upon her cheeks as bright and soft as on a peach. . . . She wore the religious habit of the house which was a loose flannel dress, bound round the waist by a girdle, from which hung her beads and a cross, a veil of the same stuff descended to the ground, and a mob cap and forehead cloth quite concealed her hair."[31] The fetishization of the nun's downy skin, as well as the implied fascination with her aging virginity and simple, coarse habit, give an erotic quality to scenes that transpire in the convent, scenes that in other ways represent a consoling escape from the exigencies of heteronormative desire.

Later, when Amanda's father dies, she collapses and remains "a considerable time in a state of insensibility" (3.1.1). She is overcome by his death, and in addition to knowing that she is friendless and unsupported she is also trapped by circumstances. Sister Mary is determined to break into Amanda's solitude and help her confront her future. As Amanda recovered she "found herself in a bed laid upon the floor in the corner of the outside room. . . . She saw someone sitting by the bed, and perceived sister Mary" (3.1.1). The nun responds to her grief and makes it possible for Amanda to loosen the grip on her heart: "'This is indeed a charitable visit,' cried [Amanda], extending her hand, and speaking in a low broken voice. The good-natured nun jumped from her seat on hearing her speak and embraced her most tenderly. Her caresses affected Amanda inexpressibly; she dropped her head upon her breast, and wept with a vehemence which relieved the oppression of her breast" (3.1.2–3).

Sister Mary does not turn out to be Amanda's lost mother, but she offers the consolations of one. Her ability to caress and press the girl to her brings a response that is more powerfully physical than practically anything else that has happened to Amanda. As if to emphasize the intimacy of this scene Amanda expresses concern about being undressed, and she "requested sister Mary to assist her in putting on her clothes" (3.1.3). Amanda finds that she can hardly be separated from the nun: "Amanda went to bed every morning, and was nursed with the most tender attention by sister Mary, who also insisted on being her companion at night" (3.1.5). Later, when the friendless Amanda moves into the convent, "a little room, inside the prioress's chamber, was prepared for Amanda, into which she was now conveyed, and the good-natured sister Mary brought her own bed, and laid it beside hers" (3.1.21).

Of course, I am not arguing that the two women were having secret sexual encounters in this room, but I do think that the convent allows Roche to establish an intimacy between them that would otherwise be suspect.

The climactic scene of maternal confrontation in the novel also takes place in a chapel. Amanda, wandering around Dunreath Abbey, "sighed whenever she passed the Chapel which contained the picture of her mother" (3.12.231). Gothic elements and religio-erotic ones work together here to create the kind of primal scene that makes gothic so elemental and so irresistible. ("The silent hour of twilight was now advanced, but the moon-beams that darted through the broken roof prevented the Chapel from being involved in total darkness. Already had the owls begun their strains of melancholy on its mouldering pillars, while the ravens croaked amongst the luxuriant trees that rustled around it" [3.12.238–39]).

Like many gothic heroines before her, Amanda wanders through the darkness in hopes of encountering some hint about her mother and, through her, her own past. The expression "reverential awe" uses religious terminology to explain family relations. This results in an intensification of domestic relations. Other gothic heroines have also felt the loss she feels at this moment of confrontation. Radcliffe's heroine Ellena, for example, must reexperience a primal female-female attachment in order to give any significance to her love for Vivaldi. Something like that is going on here as well. Amanda experiences loss—deeply imbedded and original—just as Ellena does. Her "agony of grief," this passage suggests, concerns her past and present as well. Her subjectivity is encoded in this midnight confrontation, and the ghostly maternal figure makes its clear that Amanda's subjectivity is grounded in loss.

This powerful scene can hardly prepare her for the confrontation that awaits her when she returns the next night and pursues her object in her mother's own chamber. The excitement is palpable as Amanda moves forward with a temerity that marks her as a gothic ingénue. At the same time, the scene has all the quality of a dream: darkness, sudden moonlight, a room of indeterminate size, and finally the consoling portrait once again. But she finds that all is not what it seems:

> Amanda . . . at last came to the door, it was closed, not fastened; she pushed it gently open, and could just discern a spacious room; this she supposed had been her mother's dressing-room; the moon-beams . . . suddenly darted through the casements. . . . She advanced into the room; at the upper end of it something white attracted her notice: She concluded it to be the portrait of Lady Malvina's mother. . . . She went up to examine it; but her horror may

be better conceived than described, when she found herself not by a picture, but the real form of a woman, with a death-like countenance! She screamed wildly at the terrifying spectre, for such she believed it to be, and quick as lightening flew from the room. Again the moon was obscured by a cloud, and she involved in utter darkness. She ran with such violence, that, as she reached the door at the end of the gallery, she fell against it. Extremely hurt, she had not the power to move for a few minutes; but while she involuntarily paused, she heard footsteps. Wild with terror, she instantly recovered her faculties and attempted opening it . . . at that moment she felt an icy hand upon her's! (3.13.243–44)

This scene of horrified confrontation is a classic gothic encounter. The ghostly presence—maternal and enabling even if not her actual mother—shimmers with erotic feeling. After all, the girl prowling through the castle in the middle of the night has suffered emotional stress and personal disappointment of various kinds. But still she thinks that the dark, gothic chamber will offer some kind of satisfaction, some thrill of discovery. That the thrill becomes physical—that the cold, white figure follows her, chases her, and places its hand on hers—gives the scene a peculiar power that earns it a place among the other gothic novels I am discussing. Amanda is drawn to the chapel as a way of discovering something about her lost mother. Instead, she confronts a ghostly, unknown presence that clasps her with an icy grip. An almost direct reversal of the kindly embraces that Amada experiences with Sister Mary, this icy hand reminds her that the religious sublime can be anything but consoling. Here she must confront her deepest fears.

The quasi-religious confrontation leads, after a number of imaginative complications, to the novel's resolution. This woman, her own mother's stepmother and enemy, has been the cause of Amada's disinheritance, and she now pours out her guilt and apology to the appalled heroine. Like the Radcliffe resolution, that is, Roche insists on a confrontation with this maternal other before the past can be reclaimed. The terms of subjectivity are based on a lost female-female bond. That it is recovered through the offices of a nun after prowling through a chapel in a mood of religious intensity makes perfect sense.

William Henry Ireland returns to the extremes of Lewis. In Ireland's *The Abbess* (1799), for instance, the church relics of the Convent of Santa Maria Novella in Florence already display an excess that borders on the disgusting: "The most conspicuous figure was that of the Virgin, in massive silver, supporting on her left arm the Infant Redeemer, and, in her right hand, holding a small sphere of gold, said to contain three drops of her precious milk. Her head was encircled with a rich diadem of immense value, and her neck decorated with a string of diamonds, from which hung pendant a cross of gold, valuable only as containing a piece of the true Cross."[32] The riches of the Catholic Church, the bad taste in which they are displayed, and superstition are all encoded in this "conspicuous" statue of the Virgin.

It is inconceivable that a convent with such a presiding genius could offer the kinds of consolations that Radcliffe's Convent of the Pieta (in *The Italian*) almost automatically implies. The abbess has more in common with Lewis's scheming prioress than with Radcliffe's maternal figures. The features of her personality are apparent in her first description, in which "the Madre Vittoria Bracciano . . . wore indeed a religious habit, but was ill-calculated to adorn it, every worldly feeling predominating in her heart. Benignity, meekness, patience, and charity, such heaven-kissing attributes, were not the inmates of her breast. No—pride, cruelty, malice, and revenge; such were the passions that feigned triumphant over her mind. Her desires were too licentious and with difficulty bridled, even by the situation she held" (1.1.6–7).

This classic antireligious tirade is conventional enough in its terms. The beautiful exterior hides a mean, even vicious, interior; the position of religious superior depends on the stature of the family; and spiritual commitment is not included in the description of the abbess's qualities. Licentiousness is the key here, of course, because the abbess's willingness to give in to her desires is what motivates much of the malevolent action of the text. The "religious habit" is part of an elaborate disguise. Rather than prohibiting transgressive behavior, the habit allows her license to indulge carnal appetites in ways that a nonreligious woman never could.

The abbess is not alone in her nefarious practices within the walls of the convent. When the young and handsome Conte Marcello Porta finds himself attracted to Maddalena Rosa, a young boarder, he is accosted by a monk, Padre Ubaldo, who promises to lead him to a private assignation with the girl. Ireland describes the midnight meeting of these two men and their progress through the gloomy vaults of the convent, and then, in an almost gratuitous aside, he includes a scene of religious excess: "They proceeded to the passage; at the entrance of which, within a niche, rested a stone figure of the Virgin. The Monk placed the lamp on the ground, and, having bared his left shoulder, knelt before the image and seemed to offer up a prayer; then, loosening the knotted rope that girded his loins, struck himself several times with violence—the Conte turned from the sight with disgust. The Monk arose, and, having replaced his vestment, proceeded up the passage" (1.1.23).

This odd scene of religious masochism serves no purpose but to under-line the villainy of the monk and remind readers that religious devotion and sexual excess are often one and the same. The abuse of devotion, this exagger-ated and almost histrionic posturing, disgusts Marcello because his devotion is pure and unsullied. It is unclear why the monk performs this self-abuse in front of Marcello—unless, of course, he hopes to involve Marcello in some sadomasochistic fantasy involving himself rather than the abbess. After all, in dark and secret convent passages like these, anything is possible. Same-sex transgressive behavior is as likely as—or more likely than—the male-female encounter that awaits Marcello. Besides, the novel makes it clear that desire is always compromised, always excessive, and devotion by its nature is exces-sive and disgusting.

Maddalena Rosa is the daughter of the Duca Bertocci, who put her in the convent when his wife died. Because she is the object of Marcello's desire she becomes the victim of the abbess's jealous rage, as her erotic dream conve-niently predicts:

> As she slept, a vision floated before her fancy. She thought, that she again saw the amiable stranger in the church. His air was dignified, and he seemed more interesting, if possible, than when she had first beheld him. Suddenly, the grate which separated them mouldered away. He flew towards her, and knelt at her feet. At that instant, Maddalena imagined some one held her arm; turning, she thought the ghastly and forbidding figure of Padre Ubaldo stood at her side. The youth then vanished, and in his place stood the Madre Vit-toria. Rage marked every feature: in her uplifted hand she grasped a naked poignard. (1.4.124–25)

The dream, a précis of the action to come, is set in a church where fires moulder in grates. The implicit suggestion of sexual attraction and its always already transgressive potential gives urgency to the dream. As Maddalena turns to the stranger who confronts her with his devotion to her person, the priest Ubaldo, "ghastly and forbidding," grabs her and compels her to respond not to a less transgressive choice but to an even more illicit and demeaning one. In other words, the erotic embrace with Marcello immedi-ately gives way to monkish compulsion and abbessian domination. The easy substitution of the abbess for the lover is suggestive. Given the erotic context, as she raises the "naked poignard" to threaten Maddalena's life she could also be seen to be threatening the young boarder with rape. Gothic narrative depends on such easy associations, and here the context of the church and the threat of religious figures make Maddalena a more exquisite victim than her social position would suggest. Ireland is using the freedom of dream narrative to suggest at once illicit desire, jealousy, and compulsion. His version of the convent, that is, spells out in detail an entire range of transgressive potential.

As the dream continues, Ireland articulates the other, more familiar aspect of convent life, which Radcliffe and Roche have both emphasized, the nurturing of friendship and possibility of intimacy between two girls. Here again that possibility is written out as loss. It seems that Maddalena is forced to endure these hardships alone:

> The form of her friend Marietta, pale and emaciated, then glided before her. Casting on her a look of ineffable pity, she disappeared; and suddenly the scene faded before her. She found herself in a spacious apartment, the walls of which were hung with black velvet, and in the middle stood a bier. Maddalena thought she surveyed the chamber, but no one was present; and she then proceeded to view the face of the deceased. She advanced to the spot where the coffin rested; but, as she bent over, and raised the pall, the earth opened and received it. A female figure glided along, who, smiling, seemed to approach her. It was again the nun Marietta. Maddalena thought she flew to meet her; but the figure changed to that of a handsome youth. She eyed him with attention, but could not recollect him. He clasped her to his breast in transport, and, at that moment, Maddalena awoke. (1.4.125–126)

Maddelana dreams that she loses her friend Marietta in death. It may be that she understands that this tender intimacy will be sacrificed to heteronormative narrative, because when she flies to meet her friend the handsome youth steps in her place. This begins to suggest an erotic intimacy between the two women, an intimacy the convent setting encourages. In an odd reversal of the situation in the first part of the dream where the abbess replaces the lover, here the lover replaces the friend. Pointedly, almost insistently, Maddalena remains the subject of loss, and she can hardly remember the handsome Marcello. When he grabs her, she awakes. He breaks the spell of the dream—the spell of sisterly erotic love in a convent setting, that is—and pulls her back into the reality around her.

The abbess displaces Marcello in Maddalena's arms because she has mistaken his interest in the girl for an attraction to herself. The scene in which Marcello makes love to the abbess, Victoria Bracciano, is rich in sexually suggestive description: "At that moment, her beautiful hand pressed that of the Conte. What a delicious thrill ran through his feverish veins! Conceive the most delicate, small, and transparent hand, that ever nature formed, through which the branching streaks of blue were plainly visible. . . . Imagine fingers pulpy, round, and tapered, each joint of which was an opening rose-bud; and, to complete the picture, add nails long and beautifully formed, at the extremity of which appeared a tinge of the carnation" (1.5.147).

The description continues in painstaking physical detail, and each fetishized body part adds to the erotic and transgressive qualities of the scene. That this is a nun who is being physically described and erotically coded, of course, only adds to the narrative thrill. The scene climaxes when she at last removes her veil and the conte realizes that he has been caressing the wrong woman. The abbess's outrage at his obvious confusion—"a malignant fire darted from those eyes, which beamed before the languid rays of love" (1.5.157)—is only mollified when the conte pretends to love her. Her false expressions of love in turn leads to her extravagant expressions of love that redound on him and the boarder when they are discovered in one another's arms ("You have wounded my pride. . . . Every scheme that Hell can suggest to an injured and despised woman, shall be put in practice to destroy you" [1.8.238–39]). The violent response leads to misery upon misery for the heroine, and the conte is consigned to endless searching and pleading for his now-sequestered love.

Later, when the abbess's wicked henchwoman Sister Beatrice tells the young Giancinta that in the convent they "live in sisterly friendship" (2.2.55), it is merely the prelude to deception, victimization, and violence. Ireland's anti-Catholic interests seem like misogyny, and in this case as in other male gothic it would be wrong to downplay situations that seem misogynous to modern readers. At the same time, though, a novel such as this can be especially revealing of ways in which religion and sexuality play themselves out in terms of one another. Women do find friendship in the convent, and they relate to one another with the intimacy of Radcliffe's characters at times. Both Marietta and Giancinta share deeply personal moments with Maddalena. When Marietta is on her deathbed, she gives Maddalena "a small crucifix of gold, which," she says, "I have ever worn within my bosom. It was the gift of my mother. . . . Keep it, Maddalena, in remembrance of me." Then she adds an intimate promise: "And at the silent hour of midnight, when thou art wont to chant thy hymn of praise, look upon it; for, if departed spirits ever visit those they loved on earth, I will, at that solemn hour, be with thee" (1.6.177).

The intimate promise, sealed soon after with a kiss on the lips, suggests that Marietta is willing to haunt Maddalena and that she feels her love is strong enough to cross from the world of the dead to the world of the living. To make this promise she uses a crucifix that she has worn on her breast. The tiny, precious, fetishized religious object gives their love a kind of holiness, and the sacrilegious promise takes on the quality of a religious vow. For these two inhabitants of the convent, this language may be all that is available to them. At the same time, they can use religion to justify even these muted expressions of same-sex love.

If the convent offers a perversion of maternal love and the victimization of innocence, the prisons of the Inquisition, into which Marcello and Maddalena are ushered at the moment when her father seems ready to relent, offer a higher register of lurid sexual excess. To the English imagination the Inquisition represented the perverse extreme to which religion and law could tend in a Catholic setting. The religio-political institutionalization of sadomasochistic pleasure within the prisons of the Inquisition was a regular feature in gothic fiction from *The Monk* to *Melmoth the Wanderer* (1820) and beyond. Ireland takes pleasure in dilating on the fevered imaginings of his incarcerated hero and heroine and makes sure that the terms of these fantasies are not ignored. The conte, for instance, wanders in his dreams through scenes of sadistic excess:

> Now, [Marcello's] fertile imagination paints the suffering Maddalena—the cords tearing her tender frame—her form pale, languid, and almost expiring—again the torture forces her back to hated life—her groans distract his soul—with anguish he awakes.
>
> Again he slumbers—the horrid scene continues—he strives in vain to render her assistance—now, he is habited as a criminal, in the Act of Faith, he approaches the faggot—Maddalena Rosa is already chained to the stake—now, the ardent flames consume her garments—her beauteous hair now blazes—her flesh is scorched—her limbs wreathe in anguish—she cries for mercy—he hears her shrieks—again he wakes—the piercing cry still vibrates in his ear. (3.1.6)

The erotic fantasy brings various gothic obsessions together. The Inquisition is a useful trope for religio-political violence, and when coupled with the excessively victimized female, as it is here, it begins to suggest the ways in which such dominant fictions work in private fantasy. Ireland used these materials to write such an overheated passage because they were connected in the English imagination to sexual license and sadomasochistic pleasure. This religious torture, the auto-da-fé, reverberates with a special quality of suffering. As the heroine is consumed in Marcello's imagination, readers are invited to fantasize about the sexually titillating details of the horrors of Catholicism. The erotics of religious torture emerged so readily from Marcello's imagination because they were already available in the lurid projections of British culture.

As the last volume of the novel develops both characters are tormented by the sadistic inquisitors in quasi-pornographic terms. Marcello is tortured because he will not break his vow and explain what he was doing in the convent after hours. "'Put him to the question, then,' exclaimed the Judge":

> The familiars, in an instant, tore off the Conte's habiliments, when a loose gown was thrown over his body. Cords encircled his wrists, which were then passed through pullies. Again, the question was put; but the Conte refused to answer. . . . The officials drew the ropes, and the Conte was suspended by his hands to the ceiling. He was for some moments kept in this painful situation. . . . During this interval, a ponderous mass of lead was attached to his ankles; . . . every limb was stretched in the most dreadful manner, and he experienced unutterable agonies. . . . During this torture, the question was repeatedly posed; but the Conte maintained a resolute silence. In an instant, the rope was slackened, and he came with violence to the pavement. The sudden jerk dislocated every joint: the torment was too acute, and an agonized groan escaped his lips. (4.1.20–22)

With this detailed description of physical torture, more elaborately detailed than similar scenes in *The Monk* or *Melmoth the Wanderer,* Ireland seems to take pleasure in the image of the stripped and suffering male. By taking such care with description he eroticizes the broken male body just as Radcliffe and Dacre do.[33] But if Radcliffe and Dacre are interested in redefining masculinity, Ireland takes a lurid interest in the suffering figure. He pushes the familiar image of the wounded (castrated) gothic hero to an extreme, stretching him on the rack and jerking him suddenly to earth. He torments him with physical torture and insists on outlining the details of that torture for the reader. Often such a fate is only imagined in gothic fiction. Groans and muffled beatings are common, but in this case the reader is forced to watch as the hero is tied and stretched—indeed, almost dismembered. Like his contemporary the Marquis de Sade, in other words, Ireland takes pleasure in presenting the suffering male form.[34] The ghoulish spectacle depends on the hallowed chambers of the Inquisition for its resonance, and its full effect as pornographic titillation depends on the quasi-religious valence of the scene. The notion of the Inquisition, in other words, enables Ireland to bring all these concerns together in a single image.

When Maddalena is brought forward for similar treatment, the effect is strikingly different. She is told that her "agonizing shrieks shall pierce Marcello's hardened bosom, and force the secret from his lips":

> The command was immediately issued—the familiars quitted the Conte, and seized the delicate form of the statue-struck Maddalena——already, they began to tear the garments from her tender limbs——already, the barbarians had rent the veil, that had concealed her *alabastrine* bosom, from which her palpitating heart was bursting.—The big tears trickled down her pallid cheeks, like flaky snow, which the Sun's heat dissolves upon the marble's cold and polished surface.——Now, her long auburn hair escaped the fillet, which had negligently bound it—one hand was raised, to cover her naked breast—the other, uplifted, seemed to supplicate Heaven's protection. (4.1.44–45)

Ireland uses this moment to present a stripped and supplicating female character, and once again the sadomasochistic intentions are palpable. The tenderness of Maddalena's limbs is emphasized because that is what will be violated in the torture to follow. The hand covering her naked breast also suggests vulnerability and tenderness. But the other images here—the *alabastrine* bosom and the cold and polished surface of marble, with which her cheeks are compared—suggest cold rigidity and polished smoothness. For all the pain and supplication apparent in the pose, there is also a rocklike hardness to her stance that even the threat of torture cannot pierce. When, in response to the suffering she faces, Marcello gives in to his tormentors and offers to break his vow in order to save her, she chides him almost brutally, considering his situation, and insists that he not tarnish his honor: "'Shame! Shame!' cried Maddalena: 'how I blush at your pusillanimity. Resume your wonted courage: be the man of honour; or live despised by her, whose life you thus basely seek to purchase'" (4.1.48).

If he is weak and broken by the torture he has experienced, then she is strong, strong enough to preserve them both and their honor as well. In a classic gothic reversal he must take strength from her, and she must inspire the courage that she can alone respect. Maddalena becomes a slightly sadistic figure, chiding her hero for his weakness and giving him an example of greater strength and greater ability to withstand suffering. Like the abbess, in other words, Maddalena knows what it means to be a woman in a culture that fixates on male power and sensibility.

Later, their pain is rewarded. The suffering hero and heroine are vindicated, and the true villains of the piece are exposed. Padre Ubaldo and his accomplice are condemned to death at the stake, and the abbess is condemned to a physically and emotionally degrading series of penances. She faces exposure and ridicule both in her convent and in the streets of Rome. In her private moments of reflection, the reader is told that "the pangs of death would have been bliss, compared to those torments which the Madre endured. Sometimes, she cursed herself for having yielded to the agonies of the moment, and divulged her crime. Now, she painted the degrading punition which she was doomed to suffer" (4.2.97). Her bold and transgressive defiance of laws both human and divine here redound on her head. This scene of reflection, this dramatization of inner torment, compares interestingly to the scenes of physical torture. The notion of an "avenging Deity" is calculated to implant fear in the soul of the abbess. Because they are always already victims in this gothic tale, Marcella and Maddalena suffer less at the hands of the inquisitors than does the proud and imperious abbess. Her physical, sexual indulgences come back to haunt her as she stands in shame before her fellow nuns. The body that was so vividly eroticized earlier now becomes a sign of misery and self-contempt.

The novel turns uneasily to domestic arrangements and a hastily achieved union that pale beside the scenes I have just discussed: "The Conte Marcello . . . proceeded to Bertocci palace; where he was received by the Duca with every mark of affection, while pleasure animated Maddalena's tender bosom, on again beholding, after so many painful vicissitudes, the man she loved" (4.2.202). This is not nearly as powerful as the frantic outbursts quoted earlier; it is so muted as to be as meaningless because it is in narrative terms. The domestic arrangements have less power than the excessive physical and emotional torment of the inquisition. The religious valence of the scenes of torment—several tormentors are duplicitous monks seeking vengeance—renders them more thrillingly transgressive than anything that happens at the Bertocci palace. The resolution is incapable of containing the power the scenes of religious excess have generated. In general, the Mediterranean, Catholic setting allows narrative license that makes transgression the rule rather than the exception. A close examination of these works exposes an association between Catholicism and transgressive sexuality so deeply felt as to be almost invisible.

In terms of what this association accomplished culturally, the possibilities of sexual experience could be coded into these exotic narratives, disguised by time and space into a culture that was understood to be transgressive by definition, rather than discussed openly and in possibly a dangerous way. The possibilities for expression were therefore endless. Catholicism is not a vague feature of the background in most gothic novels; it is, rather, an active element in the romance of personal relations. The horrors of Catholicism play a more active role in the history of sexuality than has previously been acknowledged.

5

Psychodrama: Hypertheatricality and Sexual Excess on the Gothic Stage

In *The History of Sexuality* Michel Foucault proposes "four great strategic unities, which, beginning in the eighteenth century, formed specific mechanisms of knowledge and power centering on sex." These are, first, a hysterization of women's bodies; second, a pedagogization of children's sex; third, a socialization of procreative behavior; and, fourth, a psychiatrization of perverse pleasure.[1] These processes, and the cultural discomfort they engender, have been vividly dramatized, not as an accident of theater history but because the history of sexuality and the history of gothic drama are causally related. The kinds of issues explored in the plays discussed in this chapter suggest that the processes Foucault describes were codified first in the popular imagination before sexologists and psychologists articulated them. The sexological history of the nineteenth century, that is, began on the gothic stage.

Mathew G. Lewis's *The Castle Spectre* (1797), Joanna Baillie's *De Montfort, a Tragedy* (1798), and Percy Bysshe Shelley's *The Cenci* (1819) are familiar titles to historians of the theater. All three had some life on the Romantic stage, and Shelley's play has been performed at regular intervals throughout the nineteenth and twentieth centuries.

Gothic drama, like so much else gothic, began with the imagination and peculiar fantasies of Horace Walpole, who completed *The Mysterious Mother*, his lurid and underrated tale of incest and murder, in 1768, just a few years after writing the intriguing novel *The Castle of Otranto* (1764). He never published the play but circulated it among friends, and it enjoyed considerable succès d'estime. Although the work never hit the stage, later in the century it was published with Walpole's *Works* (1798) and influenced playwrights as wide-ranging as Shelley, Byron, and Maturin.

Transgressive sexual desire determines the denouement of Walpole's tragedy. In this play the heroine, the Countess of Narbonne, hides an unspeakable crime by her haughty demeanor and challenges those who would urge her to reveal it. The play revolves around a "secret sin" that the countess seems to hide, and others in the play determine to "worm the secret out."[2] In the final act it is revealed that the crime the countess has been hiding is a bold and desperate act of incest. She, in grief at her husband's death, slipped into the bed in which her son's "damsel" was supposed to be expecting him. As the countess later puts it:

> Yes, thou polluted son!
> Grief, disappointment, opportunity,
> Rais'd such a tumult in my madding blood,
> I took the damsel's place: and while thy arms
> Twin'd, to thy thinking, round another's waist,
> Hear, hell, and tremble!—thou didst clasp thy mother! (60; 5.371–76)

Edmund, the son she addresses, has just married Adeliza, the daughter he engendered in this incestuous union. Edmund's love for Adeliza not only compounds the incestuous implications of the plot but also underlines the welter of erotic emotions that simmer within the confines of the family. The countess, who has spent the course of the play, the course of her life, really, plotting to keep these two characters apart is confronted with their secret marriage. The countess's "pollution" of her son, and the consequences for all the characters, is predictably devastating.

Walpole articulated regret that his play could never be performed. In writing to the Irish poet and playwright Robert Jephson, who asked for advice about play writing, he said, "Am I fit to give counsel, who have written a tragedy that can never appear on any stage?" When he did so he added that "there is one subject, a very favorite one with me, and yet which I alone was accidentally prevented from meddling with, Don Carlos." After dilating on the attractions of this plot—"yet how many capital ingredients in that story! Tenderness, cruelty, heroism, policy, pity, terror!"—however, Walpole admitted that "why I gave up that fruitful canvas, was merely because the passion is incestuous as is most unfortunately that of my *Mysterious Mother*."[3]

Don Carlos (1676) by Thomas Otway (1652–85) centers on a King Philip II of Spain, who fears that Elizabeth of Valois, his wife, is involved in an incestuous liaison with his son, Don Carlos. That the father is mistaken does not

prevent the play from dealing in excessive detail with the prospect of incest
and its disruption of peaceful domestic arrangements.[4]

> *King.* Oh Woman-kind! Thy Myst'ries! Who scan
> Too deep for easie weak believing man!
> Hold! Let me look! Indeed y'are wondrous fair,
> So on the out-side *Sodoms* Apples were.
> And yet within, when open'd to the view,
> Not half so danng'rous, or so foul, as you.[5]

What is at issue is woman's culpability; her duplicity, erroneously imagined, makes her foul and disgusting. The mention of Sodom's apples, which
suggest bitterness and gall, also hints suggestively at same-sex desire and
incest. Remember that after Lot and his daughters flee Sodom they lie with
him as a way of preserving his seed when they are all alone in the mountains.[6]
From this haunting resonance the play moves into a more explicitly gothic
realm. The king's uneasiness transforms the scene:

> *King.* 'Tis night: the season when the happy take
> Repose and only wretches are awake:
> Now discontented Ghosts begin their rounds,
> Haunt the ruin'd Buildings and unwholesome Grouds:
> Or at the curtains of the restless wait,
> To frighten 'em with some sad tale of fate.
> When I would rest, I can no rest obtain;
> And in sad Dreams torment me o're again.
> The fatal bus'ness is e're this begun:
> I'm shock't to think what I have done. (1:124; 5.1)

"The sad tale of fate" that Otway tells—one of incest, jealousy, and murder—holds for Walpole the charm of obsessive and debilitating incest. Surely
his fascination with this familial transgression is telling. Incestuous moments
from earlier plays and stories attract his attention, and he returns to the topic
again and again.

Jill Campbell relates the trope of incest to the love among men that is
evident in his correspondence. She argues that "the physical expressions of
passion that would make Walpole's declarations of love for his male corre-
spondents transgressive and unspeakable appear, just slightly displaced, in
the scenarios of emphatically embodied heterosexual incest which sometimes
conjoin those declarations."[7] This is a difficult argument that Campbell goes
on to complicate. It does, however, raise the question of the attractions of
incest for a writer always looking for ways to defy the dictates of sexual nor-

mativity. (Although Campbell's use of the word *heterosexual* unnecessarily confuses the issue here. Incest is a powerful enough trope to stand alone in most accounts of its force.) Incest fascinates Walpole, in other words, because with it he can defy the dictates of the "normal," which were in every way anathema to him.

I have elsewhere quoted Foucault's claim that "incest . . . occupies a central place; it is constantly being solicited and refused; it is an object of obsession and attraction, a dreadful secret and an indispensable pivot" in a society "where the family is the most active site of sexuality, and where it is doubt-less the exigencies of the latter which maintain and prolong its existence."[8] Like other gothic writers, Lewis in particular, Walpole understood that, and he probed incest with a marked insistence in all his works of drama and fiction. For Walpole, however, incest was more than a theme or a trope. He insisted on making it a spectacle, and even though *The Mysterious Mother* was never presented onstage Walpole imagined his depiction of the sexual-ized family as a theatrical event. "I am not yet intoxicated enough with it, to think it would do for the stage, though I wish to see it acted," he told his friend George Montagu.[9] Moreover, Walpole "contrived aristocratic 'closet' readings of the play within his immediate circle" and maintained a conflicted relation to the work throughout his life.[10]

The spectacle of the countess's horror in the last act of the play is excessive in ways that the trope might lead one to expect. When she learns that her son Edmund has married the daughter whom the countess bore as a result of an incestuous encounter with Edmund, her consternation is extreme:

> Confusion! Frenzy! Blast me, all ye furies!
> Edmund and Adeliza! When! Where! How!
> Edmund and Adeliza! Quick, unsay
> The monstrous tale—oh! Prodigy of ruin!
> Does my own son then boil with fiercer fires
> Than scorched his impious mother's madding veins!
> Did reason reassume its shattered throne,
> But as spectatress of this last of horrors?
> Oh! Let my dagger drink my heart's black blood,
> And then present my hell-born progeny
> With drops of kindred sin!—*that* were a torch
> Fit to light up such loves! And fit to quench them! (58; 5.1.291–302)

Walpole creates the spectacle of horror in this scene around the figure of a married couple. When in the next scene the happy couple come to the count-ess for her blessing there is nothing but horror and despair. In the figure of incest, that is, Walpole finds a way to dramatize the horror of the marriage bond. In this case the marriage is by definition a perversion of the bonds of normative culture that it is meant to secure. Walpole designed his play to make the explosion of disgust and revulsion coincide with the articulation of the marriage of the young pair. This is an antimarriage plot, one that designs a denouement that defies the dictates of patriarchal culture and places horror and loss when love and devotion would reside. This is no accident.

Elin Diamond's much-cited essay *"Gestus* and Signature in Aphra Behn's *The Rover"* begins to outline the ways in which the theater can function as I suggest. Diamond describes the libertine Willmore's gesture of detaching a small portrait from the courtesan Angellica's elaborate display of portraits of herself, in Behn's play, and she examines "this gesture as a 'Brechtian *Gestus*' or 'gest,' a moment in performance that makes visible the contradictory interactions of text, theater, apparatus, and contemporary social struggle." Diamond then explains how "the movement of painted flats, the discoveries of previously unseen interiors, introduced a new scopic epistemology" and demonstrates the ways in which details of theatrical production can be used to expose the fetishization of the prostitute/actress and the ideological contradictions implicit in her representation in the dreamlike candlelit interiors of the late-seventeenth-century theater.[11]

Walpole's demonization of normative relations in the climactic moment of *The Mysterious Mother* can never have the full effect of the Brechtian gest because the apparatus of the theater is missing in this most closeted of closet dramas. But the intensity of private readings, the spectacle of projection that takes place when these scenes are read, may have an analogous effect to the one that Diamond describes. The reactions to the play are extreme enough to suggest that he succeeded in challenging the status quo. Frances Burney prides herself on "the spleen [she] had conceived against [Walpole] upon reading his tragedy, which had been so great as to make me wish never more to behold his face."[12] Coleridge, too, thought the play "the most disgusting, detestable, vile contribution that ever came from the hand of man. No one with a spark of true manliness, of which Horace Walpole had none, could have written it."[13]

The excesses of the play seem to be read as Walpole's own excesses—or rather as his particular lack. The contradiction has as much cultural significance for the man-loving man as Behn's play does for the role of the actress/prostitute. Unmanliness is revealed by means of sexual excess, Coleridge seems to say, just as Edmund is unmanned by the news that his bride is in fact his daughter. Walpole's interest in this incest plot unmans him because it places him in lurid relation to the erotics of family life. Freud would have understood this relation and could probably have learned from it. Walpole is the pioneer of gothic drama because he is willing to look at these primal scenes of bourgeois ideology and expose them for what they are. If that also says something about his sexuality, a concept only beginning to be understood in the later eighteenth century, it is because he insisted on his position outside the normativity that he would attack.

William Mason sent Walpole "some prudent cautions about locking up your *Mother* (who in conformity to your character is your daughter too)."[14] Mason's casual comment suggests how readily his friends reread the play as a feature of his own identity. Of *The Mysterious Mother,* Horace Mann told Horace Walpole in 1779 that "the subject may be too horrid for the stage, but the judicious management of it by preparing the reader for the catastrophe, the sublime ideas and expressions so admirably adapted to the personages, make it a delicious entertainment *for the closet.*"[15] For Mann—and, it seems, for Walpole himself—this drama was too extreme, too excessive to be suitable for the London stage. He may also have understood that whatever value his work had as public entertainment it was also gauged to satisfy the needs of private fantasy. In this sense Mann's closet might share the resonance of the twentieth-century edifice in which the sexuality locked in fear and self-loathing expresses itself in violent excess.

Lewis's *The Castle Spectre,* Jeffrey Cox argues, "stands as the greatest theatrical success of the gothic drama, and it also serves as an exemplary model of gothic dramatic technique and tactics." For Cox, plays like *The Castle Spectre* "challenge the controlling preconceptions about nineteenth-century drama" and "provide an opportunity to explore the complex interactions between authors, texts, genre, the literary institution of the theater, and larger cultural or ideological constructs during the late eighteenth and early nineteenth centuries."[16] Cox explains that the cultural monopoly of the two licensed theaters at Drury Lane and Covent Garden, although there were various alternative theatrical spaces throughout the century, "was still the central fact for the institution of the theater at the moment of the gothic drama's arrival, but there were important challenges to patent houses as the century came to a close." He also suggests that the spectacles allowed in nonpatent theaters—naval spectaculars, equestrian shows, and pantomime—introduced new modes of music, gesture, scenery, spectacle that affected the ways in which plays were produced in official theaters as well. He points to "enormous advances in theatrical techniques, with . . . major innovations in lighting, scene-painting, traps, and special effects."[17]

Like the Restoration then, the late eighteenth century also witnessed a new scopic epistemology. Cox calls this new effect "sensationalism," and he connects it to the political and social tensions that emerged from an uneasiness around the topic of revolution in general and the French Revolution in particular. For him, "Gothic drama is the most subtle theatrical attempt of the 1790s to resolve the ideological, generic, and institutional problems facing playwrights of the day."[18] Although the literary politics of sensationalism has been largely misunderstood, the sexual tropes introduced in these plays are not any less sexual for their uses in political metaphor. Moreover, the sexual has a revolutionary force of its own. The politics of the plot and the contours of the action all have their source in sexual desire. The sensationalism of these plays, that is, and of *The Castle Spectre* in particular, begins to suggest a revolution in the coding and decoding of sexual identities just at the moment such identities are being produced for the purposes of homophobic cultural labeling.

The Castle Spectre concerns the fate of Osmond, the illegitimate earl, who, it is gradually revealed, has murdered his brother, Reginald, in order to take possession of his title and wife, Evelina. One of the play's dark secrets involves the fate of this wife, who with her husband has been missing since their disappearance some years before. Their daughter Angela, brought up by peasants, is now in Osmond's power. He has planned to destroy her, but because she bears an uncanny resemblance to her mother, whom Osmond loved, he decides to marry her instead. As he presses his suit and attempts to convince her to be his, her friend and suitor Earl Percy, whom she has met and loved under an assumed identity while at the peasants', infiltrates the castle in which she is incarcerated and attempts to liberate her from Osmond's clutches. In the end he succeeds, but only after she has discovered her lost father, heard the tale of her mother's death, and had a longing encounter with that devoted woman's eerie ghost.

Throughout these gothic intricacies the castle looms large. Scenes take place in "the Castle-Hall" (1.2, 2.2, 3.2) and "the Castle Hall: [when] The Lamps are lighted" (4.1); "the Armoury" (2.1); "Angela's Apartment" (4.2); "the Oratory" (4.2); "a Vaulted Chamber" (5.2); "a gloomy subterraneous Dungeon, wide and lofty" (5.3); and outside the castle walls, with "a View of the Conway Castle by Moon-light" (5.1). The gloomy, lamp-lit spaces—and even the lofty, well-lit ones—create a special mood. As Paul Ranger notes, "An atmosphere of moral gloom was prevalent in the gothic castle."[19]

The theatrical effects that began to transform the stage in the late eighteenth century are marshaled to evoke the dark and brooding landscape of psychological distress. Lewis's stage directions for the dungeon scene, for instance, read like a passage from a gothic novel:

> A gloomy subterraneous Dungeon, wide and lofty: The upper part of it has in several places fallen in, and left large chasms. On one side are various passages leading to other Caverns: On the other is an Iron Door with steps leading to it, and a Wicket in the middle. Reginald, pale and emaciated, in coarse garments, his hair hanging wildly about his face, and a chain about his body, lies sleeping upon a bed of straw. A lamp, a small basket, and a pitcher, are placed near him. After a few moments he awakes, and extends his arm. (212; 5.3)

Unlike a novel, however, this description is meant to describe an actual scene. Nothing is left to the imagination.[20] The scopic epistemology of gothic drama insists that the emaciated male form is fetishized as the lost origin of the dramatic action—the lost father in this case—and the source of psychological dread. The spectacle of pale, broken, and effectively castrated masculinity answers earlier anxieties in the play with a physical presence that mocks Osmond's preening, patriarchal threats with weakness, debility, and need. Lack, that is, establishes itself as the center around which this drama revolves.

This sign of broken masculinity is complemented in the play by the astonishing device of the ghostly appearance of Evelina, Angela's mother and also Reginald's dead wife, who appears at the end of act 4. From deep within Angela's apartment—the oratory is represented by the inner chamber at the back of the stage—the ghost walks across the stage with the self-possession of a gothic heroine. Angela hears plaintive music and watches in panic as the doors to the oratory unfold:

> The folding-doors unclose, and the Oratory is seen illuminated. In its center stands a tall female figure, her white and flowing garments spotted with blood; her veil is thrown back, and discovers a pale and melancholy countenance; her eyes are lifted upwards, her arms extended towards heaven, and a large wound appears upon her bosom. Angela sinks up her knees, with her eyes riveted upon the figure, which for some moments remains motionless. At length the Spectre advances slowly, to a soft and plaintive strain; she stops opposite Reginald's picture, and gazes upon it in silence. She then turns, approaches Angela, seems to invoke a blessing upon her, points to the picture and retires to the Oratory. The music ceases. Angela rises with a wild look, and follows the Vision extending her arms towards it.
>
> Angela. [Stop,] say, lovely spirit!—Oh! Stay yet one moment!

> The Spectre waves her hand, as bidding her farewell. Instantly the organ's
> swell is heard; a full chorus of female voices chaunt 'jubilate,' a blaze of light
> flashes through the Oratory, and the folding doors close with a large noise.
> (206; 4.2)

This wounded and bloody female figure, like the emaciated male form
described earlier, is a source of consolation and hope to the desolate Angela.
The figure of Evelina emerges from the depths of the scene in order to disrupt the victimizing patriarchal order with her corpselike challenge. Brutally
stabbed and with a look of melancholy longing, she brings an otherworldly
presence onstage.[21] Angela reaches out to the figure as the answer to her
prayers. It is the figure who will release her from her present torment; the
beckoning, disfigured form is celebrated as the answer to the perplexities of
Angela's incarceration. Like the emaciated Reginald, that is, the wounded
Evelina brings hope in the form of hypertheatricalized lack.

Slavoj Žižek offers terms by means of which this theatricalized relation of
death to life in *The Castle Spectre* can be understood. In discussing *Hamlet*,
he argues:

> [I]s not *Hamlet,* in the last analysis, a drama of *failed interpellation?* At the
> beginning we have interpellation in its pure form: the ghost of the father-king
> interpellates Hamlet-individual into the subject—that is, Hamlet recognizes
> himself as addressee of the imposed mandate or mission (to revenge his
> father's murder); but the father's ghost enigmatically supplements his com-
> mand with the request that Hamlet should not in any way harm his mother.
> And what prevents Hamlet from acting, from accomplishing the imposed
> revenge, is precisely the confrontation with the *"Che vuoi?"* of the desire of the
> Other: the key scene of the whole drama is the long dialogue between Hamlet
> and his mother, in which he is seized by doubt as to his mother's desire—What
> does she really want? What if she really *enjoys* her filthy, promiscuous relation-
> ship with his uncle? Hamlet is therefore hindered not by indecision as to his
> own desire; it is not that "he doesn't know what he really wants"—he knows
> that very clearly: he wants to revenge his father—what hinders him is doubt
> concerning the *desire of the other,* the confrontation of a certain *"Che vuoi?"*
> which announces the abyss of some terrifying, filthy enjoyment."[22]

This discussion of "failed interpellation" suggests that ghostly appear-
ances invoke a particular form of subjective response that can be understood
as a mission. At the moment in which the ghostly paternal order is issued,
however, its terms are complicated by permutations of desire that defy the
hero's attempt to do the right thing. Hamlet's doubt concerning "the desire

of the other," which in his case is represented by maternal sexual desire that he dreads might exclude him, makes it difficult for him to determine how to fulfill the demands of the ghostly directive. The resulting spectacle of tragic inaction in *Hamlet* leads to the debacle of death and degradation against which the paternal ghost warned.

What is resonant here is the implicit connection between the ghostly appearance and anxiety over a kind of "filthy" promiscuity that *Hamlet* and *The Castle Spectre* share. The "desire of the other" is the challenge in this case as well—Evelina plunges Angela into the bloody center of a family romance—and it is staged so as to make the crucial gestus of the dramatic presentation unmistakable. Interpellation involves a lurid invocation of the erotics of the family, and if Angela is a little more deliberate in her response to the ghostly invocation than was her Shakespearean predecessor, then that may in part be because the ghost of Evelina invokes maternal lack as a kind of blessing. Her bloody, wounded, and emaciated form offers Angela an escape from the victimizing paternal order that would destroy her. The defiant masochism she projects onto the gothic stage in quasi-religious terms offers Angela an escape from the torment facing her as it forces her back into the incestuous triangle from which she has emerged.

In her description of the gestus in *The Rover*, Diamond said that it revealed the implicit contradictions within contemporary ideology. If the shade of Evelina is kindly and beneficent, she also admonishes the heroine to avenge her own murder and rescue her languishing mate. Her bloody form breaks through the conventions of eighteenth-century ideology to suggest the violence to which the female is subjected at the same time it renders Evelina diaphanous and other-worldly. The contradiction concerns, of course, the situation of the heroine, who must struggle to keep herself out of the hands of the villain yet not sacrifice feminine passivity.[23] The appearance of the ghost in *The Castle Spectre*, bloody and beckoning, seems to eroticize heroic femininity just as we learn that Evelina died to protect her husband from Osmond's vindictive dagger. Loss is eroticized, as it were, precisely because the female in a virulently patriarchal culture is always already lost.

Lost, too, are the other figures who circulate at the edges of patriarchal culture. The otherwise superfluous references to the slave trade that animate the play at critical moments can be understood in these terms. Contemporary reactions to the play decried its allusions to the slave trade and to discussions of the degree to which blacks could be considered human.[24] Lewis stages his black characters so as to maximize the political valence that they bear, at the same time that he dismisses them as meant only for effect. "I thought it would give a pleasing variety to the characters and dresses, if I made my servants black; and could I have produced the same effect by making my heroine blue, then blue I would have made her."[25]

This infamous comment bears little relation to the situation in the play, in which black characters are allowed to articulate the tenets of the antislavery movement. "Twenty years have elapsed," Hassan tells Saib, "since these Christians tore me away [from my wife and native land]; they trampled upon my heart, mocked my despair, and, when in frantic terms I raved of Samba, [they] laughed and wondered how a negro's soul could feel" (1.2; 161). That momentary performance defies cultural assumptions and allows the audience to imagine a humanizing and sentimental response to slavery. It does not liberate slaves to dramatize their liberation; rather, it eroticizes their feelings of loss so as to heighten the transgressive dynamic by means of which the play challenges the status quo as it reinforces it.

Joseph Roach makes a similar point in *Cities of the Dead: Circum-Atlantic Performance*. In describing a performance of Shakespeare's *Macbeth* (1664) in which Native American chiefs ("kings") were placed onstage to satisfy demands of the crowd, Roach explores "some of the symbolic representations of that contest [between peoples and nations in contemporary North America] as staged through intercultural performances."[26] Plays such as John Dryden's *The Indian Emperor; or, The Conquest of Mexico by the Spaniards* (1665) and Thomas Southerne's adaptation of Aphra Behn's *Oroonoko; or, The Royal Slave* (1694) also demonstrate the dynamic of intercultural performance that interests Roach. "Aside from the oft-parodied exaggeration of confused motives in Dryden's heroic plays," he argues, "his dramaturgy or reprised characters deepens the scheme of surrogation on which he constructed this drama of superabundance, miscegenation, and sacrifice."[27] Roach demonstrates how these ideological concepts were articulated in the theater apparatus of the late seventeenth century, and, like Diamond, he insists that "English theater helped British subjects to imagine a community for themselves by making a secular spectacle out of the deeply mysterious play of ethnic identity and difference."[28] If Roach can make such a claim concerning the urgency of ethnicity and foreignness in the later seventeenth century an analogous claim about sexuality can be made in the later eighteenth century and in gothic drama in particular.

In *De Monfort: A Tragedy* Joanna Baillie pushes this challenge one important step further. The play centers on the deep and long-standing hatred the central character feels for his boyhood companion Rezenvelt. At first the plot makes it seem that there has been a dark crime on Rezenvelt's part, but it soon transpires that the only infraction has been the result of an awkward challenge that Lady Jane, De Monfort's sister, describes in this way: "You dar'd him to the field; both bravely fought; / He more adroit disarm'd you; courteously / Return'd the forfeit sword, which, so return'd, / You did refuse to use against him more; / And then, as report says, you parted friends."[29] But De Monfort explains that he has nurtured "hate! Black, lasting, deadly hate" for Rezenvelt and nothing more.

Paul Baines and Edward Burns describe De Monfort as "a contradictory being, lurching from self-control to wildness and back to restraint, unpredictably." As they also note, "Some critics have detected homoerotic overtones in De Monfort's passionate characterization of Rezenvelt; it is at least true that he seems to conjure or invent him as much as discover him."[30] Anyone could be forgiven for interpreting De Monfort's obsession with Rezenvelt as an erotic obsession. In fact, the play dramatizes the consequences of same-sex desire between these men and exposes its full (and fully contradictory) function in patriarchal culture. De Monfort's early speeches express life-long obsession with Rezenvelt:

> Oh that detested Rezenvelt!
> E'en in our early sports, like two young whelps
> Of hostile breed, instinctively reverse,
> Each 'gainst the other pritch'd his ready pledge,
> And frown'd defiance. As we onward pass'd
> From youth to man's estate, his narrow art,
> And envious gibing malice, poorly veil'd
> In the affected carelessness of mirth,
> Still more detestable and odious grew
> There is no living being on this earth
> Who can conceive the malice of his soul,
> With all his gay and damned merriment,
> To those by fortune or by merit plac'd
> Above his paltry self. (262; 2.2)

De Monfort has nurtured this grievance and exacerbated its effects in terms that are almost laughable. It begins to seem Rezenvelt's "mirth" as much as anything else that causes De Monfort this discomfort. The insubstantial basis on which this hatred is based is in part what makes it dramatically convincing, and it is also what makes it available to a reading like that described. Rezenvelt's merriment is "gay and damned" because it is not properly deferential. De Monfort claims:

He look'd upon the state of prosp'prous men,
As nightly birds, rous'd from their murky holes,
Do scowl and chatter at the light of day,
I could endure it; even as we bear
Th' impotent bit of some half-trodden worm,
I could endure it. But when honours came,
And wealth and new-got titles fed his pride;
Whilst flatt'ring knaves did trumpet forth his praise,
And grov'ling idiots grinn'd applauses on him;
Oh! Then I could no longer suffer it!
It drove me frantick.—What! What would I give!
What would I give to crush the bloated toad,
So rankly do I loathe him! (262; 2.2)

This eerie combination of contempt, jealousy, caricature, and disgust can hardly be explained by terms that are offered. Instead, it is inevitable that we see these two men in a complex relation that is more like a doomed love affair than simple antipathy. Eve Kosofsky Sedgwick has offered a way to theorize this intense male rivalry. "[I]n any male dominated society," she says, "there is a special relationship between male homosocial (*including* homosexual) desire and the structures for maintaining and transmitting patriarchal power." Male friendship and erotic male relations, that is, are not necessarily different, according to Sedgwick's scheme, in the ways they are expressed or culturally interpreted. "For historical reasons," she says, "this special relationship may take the form of ideological homophobia, ideological homosexuality, or some highly conflicted but intensively structured combination of the two."[31]

In order to understand how the relation between De Monfort and Rezenvelt functions, and before approaching the climactic scene between them, it is necessary to look more closely at the other intensely erotic relation in the play, that between De Monfort and Lady Jane. "While it is always assumed that [De Monfort] is the protagonist of the play that it is named for him," one critic says, "Jane is also a De Monfort and in many ways the dominating presence in the play."[32] The early intimacy between the siblings opens the play with a tender and touching alternative to the bitter rivalry that later emerges between the two men. Describing her brother, Lady Jane says:

But he who has, alas! forsaken me
Was the companion of my early days,
My cradle's mate, mine infant play-fellow.

Within our op'ning minds with riper years
The love of praise and gen'rous virtue sprung:
Thro' varies life our pride, our joys, were one;
At the same tale we wept: he is my brother. (256; 2.1)

In direct contrast to the De Monfort-Rezenvelt bond, the emphasis here is on virtue, shared experience, and unity. This fraternal intimacy is later intensified, in passages quoted earlier, when De Monfort opens his heart to Jane because she loves him. The image of them in each other's arms, in tears of recognition and deeply felt joy, ends the scene with this alternative emotional bond promising to save De Monfort from the destructive power of hatred.

Later in the play another female character, out of jealousy for Jane's impressive carriage and elegant wardrobe, starts the rumor that Jane has come to the German town where the play is set in order to meet with Rezenvelt, with whom she suggests Jane is romantically involved. It is hearing this rumor that brings about the play's catastrophe. The news acts as a catalyst, causing De Monfort to plan and execute the murder of Rezenvelt: "Was it for this / She urged her warm request on bended knee? Alas! I wept, and thought of sister's love, / No damned love like this. / Fell devil! 'tis hell itself has lent thee aid / To work such sorcery . . . If, by some spell or magick sympathy, / Piercing the lifeless figure on that wall / Could pierce his bosom too, would I not cast it? [Throwing a dagger against the wall]" (284, 286; 3.2).

The murder takes place, as the stage directions for act 4 suggest, in "Moonlight. A wild path in a wood, shaded with trees. Enter De Monfort, with a strong expression of disquiet, mixed with fear, upon his face, looking behind him, and bending his ear to the ground, as if he is listening to something" (288; 4.1).[33] De Monfort's psychological conflict is depicted in the darkness, the trees, and the moonlight. "How hollow groans the earth beneath my tread," he says as the scene opens (189; 4.1). Shortly, there is the sound of an owl crying in the night, and his distress is further explored: "Foul bird of night! What spirit guides thee here? / Art thou instinctive drawn to scenes of horror?" (189; 4.1). When Rezenvelt wanders into the same scene, as the audience now knows to meet his death, the owl screams again. "How such hooting is in harmony / With such a night as this! like it well. / Oft when a boy, at the still twilight hour, / I've leant my back against some knotted oak, / And loudly mimicked him, till to my call / he answer would return, and thro' the gloom / We friendly converse held" (290; 4.1).

It is a small point, perhaps, that what De Monfort hears with horror and foreboding, Rezenvelt understands as a game, a playful relation between himself and the uncanny. Of course, the analogy between these relations and the interpersonal relations that the play projects is suggestive. De Monfort reads horror into scenes that Rezenvelt sees as playful and intimate. Rezenvelt seeks intimacy where De Monfort experiences foulness and disgust. Baillie uses the midnight scene to suggest the ways in which an intimate friendship can be turned into hatred and horror.

Instead of staging the murder, however, Baillie moves the action to "The inside of a Convent Chapel, of old Gothick architecture, almost dark; two torches only are seen at a distance, burning over a new-made grave. The noise of loud wind, beating upon the windows and roof, is heard" (291; 4.2). After a procession of nuns and a "solemn prelude" on the organ, the murder is reported. "Oh! I did hear thro' the receding blast, / Such horrid cries! It made my blood run chill," one nun reports, "twice it call'd, so loudly call'd, / With horrid strength, beyond the pitch of nature. / And murder! Murder! Was the dreadful cry" (292; 4.2). In the next scene, set in "A Cloister in the Convent" (295; 4.2), the spectacle of the murder is startlingly introduced. To move from the gloomy horror of the wood to a torchlit and musical procession of nuns causes the murder to stand in stark contrast to this vision of homosocial order and devotion.

Nothing that is said by the nuns or monks can dispel the force of the action described in the stage directions. First, De Monfort is led in from the innermost recesses of the set: "A folding door at the bottom of the stage is opened, and enter Bernard, Thomas, and the other two Monks, carrying lanterns in their hands, and bringing in De Monfort. They are likewise followed by other Monks. As they lead forward De Monfort the light is turned away, so that he is seen obscurely; but when they come to be in front of the stage they all turn the light side of their lanterns on him at once, and his face is seen in all the strengthened horrour of despair, with his hands and cloaths bloody" (296; 4.3).

The spectral presence of De Monfort—Baillie is insistent about the exact lighting for the effect she seeks—places him in a realm that seems almost supernatural. The sudden but pointed light upon his face disembodies him and renders his despair more visually powerful than it would otherwise be. The blood in the scene completes the image and calls to mind the ghostly spirit that appears onstage in *The Castle Spectre*. The blood adds to the horror of the scene, to be sure, and it also suggests the kind of abjection that the murderer now assumes. His murder, as self-destructive as it is vindictive, is already measured as a kind of loss, one only his death can answer. Bloodied, emasculated, and rendered powerless, De Monfort's lack obtrudes where love for the friend might have transformed him. That it cannot do so is a measure of the tragedy.

After a brief interchange in which his despair and near-madness are expressed by seeming haunted by the memory of "murder" and by trauma-induced raving, the body is brought onstage: "Enter Men bearing the body of Rezenvelt, covered with a white cloth, and set it down in the middle of the room: they then uncover it. De Monfort stands fixed and motionless with hor-rour, only that a sudden shivering seems to pass over him when they uncover the corpse. The Abbess and Nuns shrink back and retire to some distance; all the rest fixing their eyes steadfastly upon De Monfort" (297; 4.3).

If De Monfort seemed ghostly, Rezenvelt appears here and at the end of the play as an outright ghoul. An illustration of this scene, reproduced as figure 1 in Ranger's study of the play, represents the body in its shrouded form. De Monfort shrinks back as if he has seen a supernatural figure. When the shroud is pulled back, his "sudden shivering" suggests the degree to which he is moved by what he sees. The scene, as the abbess and nuns back away, centers on the confrontation between the two men, one living and one dead. This is the configuration that culture has demanded for the expression of love between men. De Monfort stands transfixed because he understands what he has always already—in this culture anyway—lost. This is the haunting that has always been implicit in the relation between the two men. De Monfort is haunted by the man with whom he was locked in a devastating emotional bond.

After the bloody climax the plot turns, almost inevitably, to the relation between brother and sister. The final act involves several scenes between De Monfort and Jane. At first he shrinks from her when she visits him in his cell: "Away, away! / Shall a disgrac'd and publick criminal / Degrade thy name" (302; 5.2). She, however, commits herself to him forever:

> Dark lowers our fate,
> And terrible the storm that gathers over us;
> But nothing, till that latest agony
> Which severs thee from nature, shall unloose
> This fix'd and sacred hold. In thy dark prisonhouse;
> In the terrifick face of armed law;
> Yes, on the scaffold, if must needs be,
> I never will forsake thee. (303; 5.2)

This overstatement of a sister's commitment—touching as it is—suggests something more than sisterly affection. It is a selfless gesture and reminiscent of the terms such intimacy may have included. That becomes even more apparent when De Monfort responds to Jane's encouraging words. He rises, as it were, to her challenge in language that makes the hint of incest even stronger:

> But for thy sake I'll rouse my manhood up,
> And meet it bravely; no unseemly weakness,
> I feel my rising strength, shall blot my end,
> To cloth my cheek with shame. (303; 5.2)

That Lady Jane is able to "rouse" his "manhood" as no one else in the play; that she is the one to inspire him to cast off his "unseemly weakness"; and that she, finally, is the hero of this family romance, these all begin to suggest that homoerotics have been displaced in favor of incest, as Jill Campbell argues can happen in Walpole's works as well.[34] This elaborate triangle of incest, jealousy, hatred, and murder is reminiscent of Walpole's fascination with similar tropes. The sexual configuration of brother-sister-friend renders this dynamic unmistakable. Such scenes are calculated to bring the tension out of the closet of Walpole's private fantasy and onto the gothic stage. This particular version of the family romance exposes some of the more lurid demands of cultural organization and normative domestic relations.

The play ends after De Monfort's execution, with both his body and Rezenvelt's on display. Jane, who "advances to the table and looks attentively at the covered bodies," takes the occasion to comment on her loss and what it means to her:

> That I, within these sacred cloister walls
> May raise a humble, nameless tomb to him,
> Who, but for one dark passion, one dire deed,
> Had claim'd a record of as noble worth,
> As e're enrich'd the sculptur'd pedestal. (313; 5.4)

In other words she becomes a cloistered nun, that all-too-familiar location for transgressive females in gothic fiction. She immures herself because of the depth of her loss. The "one dark passion" to which she alludes is the hatred that De Monfort felt for his companion, but it could as easily be the underlying emotion that the depth of his feeling betrayed. It could even be the incestuous bond between himself and his sister. In any case, the "one dark passion" has destroyed him, as it would destroy others throughout the course of the century to follow. In this scene the two covered (ghostly) bodies spectacularly perform the spectral and equate same-sex desire with violence, hatred, death, and (last but not least) chaste, life-long devotion. The male figures are eroticized in death because it is only through loss that the terms of their erotic relation can be fully understood.

Shelley, who lives in twenty-first-century-imagination as an equally eroticized male corpse, addresses some of these same concerns. His infamous play *The Cenci* brings them to a fitting, if temporary, resolution. In a thoughtful and still very useful rumination on the early-nineteenth-century stage—its vast theaters, histrionic acting style, and dramatically debilitating system of star performers who made themselves the center of every production—Stuart Curran suggests that "in *The Cenci* Shelley is creating a vehicle for full-bodied, even wildly emotional acting."[35]

The response the printed play received, however, suggests that contemporaries could not recognize this reflection of their theatrical system. The reviewer in the *Literary Gazette,* for instance, wrote that "of all the abominations which intellectual perversion, and political atheism, have produced in our times, this tragedy appears to us to be the most abominable. We have much doubted whether we ought to notice it; but as watchmen place a light over the common sewer which has been opened in a way dangerous to passengers, so have we concluded it to be our duty to set up a beacon to this noisome and noxious publication." Moreover, the play was "a dish of carrion, . . . the production of a fiend, and calculated for the entertainment of devils in hell."[36] The language of disgust is telling in this instance, and the abomination results from a cultural threat rather than from any specific horror at the story being told.

In his preface, Shelley argues that *The Cenci* dramatizes a story of "moral deformity" that is "eminently fearful and monstrous. . . . The person who would treat such a subject must increase the ideal and diminish the actual horror of the events."[37] To accomplish that, Shelley pushes the scenes of grotesque transgression—incest and parricide in particular—offstage so it is reported rather than represented. That leaves him only the effects of transgression to represent onstage, and on those effects Shelley builds the hyper-theatrical power of his play.

Cenci is a delectable gothic villain. As Curran argues, "The paternal power in this play is almost mystical, a direct reflection of God's authority and the Pope's. A daughter's rebellion, like an angel's, opens an intolerable breach in the fixed hierarchy of nature, which tyranny or no, must be maintained."[38] Another way of describing this paternal power is that which Žižek has based on Lacan's psychoanalytic theory. In this case the "Name-of-the Father" has broader implications than even as wicked an individual as Cenci can embody.

In discussing "the enigma of the status of the father in psychoanalytic theory," Žižek describes

> the non-coincidence of symbolic and real father means precisely that some non-father (maternal uncle, the supposed common ancestor, totem, spirit— ultimately the *signifier* "father" itself) is "more father" than the (real) father. It is for this reason that Lacan designates the Name-of-the-Father, this ideal agency that regulates legal, symbolic exchange, as the "paternal *metaphor*": the symbolic father is a metaphor, a metaphoric substitute, a sublation [*Auf-hebung*] of the real father in its Name which is "more father than father himself," whereas the "non-sublated" part of the father appears as the obscene cruel and oddly impotent agency of the super-ego.[39]

By raping his daughter Cenci tries to encompass the "mystical" power of the paternal, but that illegitimate claim is precisely what causes the most intimate members of his family to murder him. "More father than father himself," Cenci expresses the erotic exploitation inherent in patriarchal power. The first sign that he is more complex than a severe or even a mean parent is the obvious and unnatural pleasure he takes at the deaths of his sons. As he announces to a party gathered at his home:

> My disobedient and rebellious sons
> Are Dead!—Why, dead!—What means this change of cheer?
> And they will need no food or raiment more:
> The tapers that did light them the dark way
> Are their last cost. The Pope, I think, will not
> Expect I should maintain them in their coffins.
> Rejoice with me—my heart is wondrous glad. (249–50; 1.3.43–50)

In a play that centers on parricide this speech, anticipating the crime as it does and invoking a further paternal power, the pope, perverts paternal relations and renders the family a locus of violence and horror rather than love and intimacy. Is sexology really necessary when Shelley sees through the permutation of paternal power in such a way? Cenci's staging of this antipaternal stance, this mockery of paternal love and celebration of paternal slaughter, amounts to his internal theater of poisoned family relations, dysfunctionality writ large.

Žižek suggests a way in which this complex paternity might be understood. Freud was already aware of the implications of obscene paternity, he says, when, "in *Totem and Taboo,* he wrote that, following the primordial parricide, the dead father 'returns stronger than when he was alive'—the crucial word here is 'returns,' which indicates how we should conceive another mysterious sounding proposition of Lacan—that father is a symptom: the symbolic father is a symptom insofar as it is the 'return of the repressed' primordial father, the obscene and traumatic Father-Enjoyment that terrorized the horde."[40]

The father in this play, brutal and victimizing as he is, feels himself like the "return of the repressed" that Žižek describes. The return of the repressed, that is, is anticipated in a play like *The Cenci* and reveals as much as any Freudian case study about family, desire, incest, and parricide and their relation to "civilization and its discontents." Shelley's attempt to create a theatrical space for these concerns, his hypertheatricalized drama of excess, dilates on the horrors of patriarchal culture by focusing on its origins in the family. This is a family romance that even Freud could envy.[41]

Cenci's larger crime, his rape of this daughter Beatrice, is threatened in terms that resonate throughout the play:

> She comes not; yet I left her even now
> Vanquished and faint. She knows the penalty
> Of her delay: yet what if threats are vain?
> Am I now not within Petrella's moat?
> Or fear I still the eyes and ears of Rome?
> Might I not drag her by the golden hair?
> Stamp on her? Keep her sleepless till her brain
> Be overworn? Tame her with chains and famine?
> Less would suffice. Yet so to leave undone
> What I most seek! No, 'tis her stubborn will
> Which by its own consent shall stoop as low
> As that which drags it down. (273; 4.1.1–12)

Cenci's fantasy of paternal power, as violent and even sadistic as it is, equates paternal incest with a brutalizing attempt to overpower the will of his daughter. Žižek says that "traditional authority is based on what we could call *mystique of the Institution.* Authority bases its power on symbolic ritual, on the form of the institution as such. The king, the judge, the president, and so on, can be personally dishonest, rotten, but when they adopt the insignia of Authority, they experience a kind of mystic transubstantiation."[42] For Cenci this ritual of abject submission redefines the family as a gothic institution that victimizes innocence and renders paternal power absolute. What is shocking about his excessive language of threat and victimization is his ability to take them seriously and assume that his position as husband

and father gives him the right to treat his daughter as a sexually brutalized victim in this way. Beatrice's mad scene after her father rapes her makes the terms of this relation even clearer:

> My God!
> The beautiful blue heaven is flecked with blood!
> The sunshine on the floor is black! The air
> Is changed to vapours such as the dead breathe
> In charnel pits! Pah! I am choked! There creeps
> A clinging, black, contaminating mist
> About me . . . 'tis substantial, heavy, thick,
> I cannot pluck it from me, for it glues
> My fingers and my limbs to one another,
> And eats into my sinews, and dissolves
> My flesh to a pollution, poisoning
> The subtle, pure, and inmost spirit of life!
> My God! I never knew what the mad felt
> Before; for I am mad beyond all doubt!
> [More wildly.] No, I am dead! These putrefying limbs
> Shut round and sepulchre the panting soul
> Which would burst forth into the wandering air! (262; 3.1.12–28)

In this context it takes Beatrice's madness to invoke a fully gothic setting. But in her raving, the heroine takes the action of the play into charnel pits, misty gothic passages, and the grave.[43] In doing so she turns herself into a revenant; dissolves her body in the poison of violation; and turns her living, vibrant self into a ghostly representation of herself. The uncanny result dramatizes female victimization in the patriarchal system more vividly that any other dramatic effect. In a sense she becomes her own ghostly specter, an Evelina come to deliver an Angela from the horrors of her situation into a redefined and reimagined realm.

Only Mary Wollstonecraft, in her quasi-gothic posthumous novel *The Wrongs of Woman* (1798), creates as vivid a context in which to reveal the position of the woman in a male-dominated world. Terry Castle has explained the disembodiment of character in gothic fiction as haunted, "[Freud's] central insight—that it is precisely the historic internalization of rationalist protocols that produces the uncanny—not only sheds light on the peculiar emotional ambivalence the Enlightenment evokes in us (it has both freed and cursed us), it also offers a powerful dialectical model for understanding many of the haunting paradoxes of eighteenth-century literature and culture."[44]

A play like Shelley's suggests that rather than using Freud to understand what is going on we could use the details of this kind of drama to expand psychologists' understanding of the dysfunctional family. Sexology emerges from a cultural context in which a play like this is possible, whether or not it was staged. Shelley reveals as much as any sexologist about abusive power within the family and the attempt to resist that power. What is uncanny is that Beatrice turns herself into a ghost precisely because her father has rendered her unable to reside comfortably in her own body.

Later, when Beatrice defies Cenci's demand that she appear before him, the terms of the relation become even clearer. He drops to his knees and enunciates:

> God!
> Hear me! If this most specious mass of flesh,
> Which thou hast made my daughter; this my blood,
> This particle of my divided being;
> Or rather, this my bane and my disease,
> Whose sight infects and poisons me; this devil
> Which sprung from me as from a hell, was meant
> To aught good use; if her bright loveliness
> Was kindled to illumine this dark world;
> If nursed by thy selectest dew of love
> Such virtues blossom in her as should make
> The peace of life, I pray thee for my sake,
> As thou the common God and Father art
> Of her, and me, and all, reverse that doom!
> Earth, in the name of God, let her food be
> Poison, until she be encrusted round
> With leprous stains! Heaven, rain upon her head
> The blistering drops of Maremma's dew,
> Till she be speckled like a toad; parch up
> Those love-enkindled lips, warp those fine limbs
> To loathed lameness! All-beholding sun,
> Strike in thine envy those life-darting eyes
> With thine own blinding beams! (276; 4.1.114–36)

Cenci's contempt for his daughter indicates that he assumes she is an extension of himself. His incestuous desire turns her into an infection that courses through his body. The wildly excessive expression of his subjectivity is precisely what deprives her of an independent and inviolate existence.

He claims that, like Satan, he has given birth to her, his sin, and he uses this ejaculation to condemn her and describe the scabrous, diseased female form as a projection of himself and his transgressive desire. Monstrous, she is visualized here as the female threat to patriarchy, the abject victim that all culture is constructed to expose.

After Cenci's murder, which happens offstage, and after Beatrice and her mother and brother have been apprehended, she articulates the horror of her situation as a ghostly encounter:

> If there should be
> No God, no Heaven, no Earth in the void world;
> The wide, grey, lampless, deep, unpeopled world!
> If all things then should be . . . my father's spirit
> His eye, his voice, his touch surrounding me;
> The atmosphere and breath of my dead life!
> If sometimes, as a shape more like himself,
> Even the form which tortured me on earth,
> Masked in grey hairs and wrinkles, he should come
> And wind me in his hellish arms, and fix
> His eyes on mine, and drag me down, down, down!
> For was he not alone omnipotent
> On Earth, and ever present? Even though dead,
> Does not his spirit live in all that breathe,
> And work for me and mine still the same ruin,
> Scorn, pain, despair? (298; 5.4.57–72)

In this speech she uses gothic detail to express her inability to escape from all-encompassing patriarchal power. She dramatizes the rape—creates his gray and wrinkled form that overpowers her—as a way of emphasizing the cultural configuration that enables this destructive relation. "Even though dead" he controls her fate—not as a ghost, although his presence is ghostly, but as the form of power itself. It is a vision of the patriarchy that assures her position as a victim.

Žižek maintains that "what . . . we have to bear in mind apropos of the primordial Father-Enjoyment is again the logic of 'deferred action'; the fact that the non-symbolized father changes into the horrifying spectre of the Father-Enjoyment only backwards, retroactively, after the symbolic network is already here."[45] Beatrice Cenci insists that her father be revealed as the primordial power, the "horrifying spectre" of paternity that haunts the gothic and reveals the spectacle of victimization that patriarchal culture embodies.

Gothic drama anticipates later developments in sexology and offers its own terms for explaining the rigors of cultural and the effects of normative sexual organization. It sees the family as the hotbed, as it were, of sexual conflict and explains the ways in which domestic space is always already eroticized. The details of these plays suggest that the myth of domestic regularity was never terribly secure. Unnatural desires structure the family and undermine the limits of the real. At the same time, of course, the exploration of transgressive desire reaffirms the power of the normative.

As titillating as sexual transgression of various kinds becomes in these plays, and as spectacularly as it is dramatized, as Foucault's analysis suggests, it constructs the mechanisms of knowledge and power that extend cultural control into the deepest recesses of desire. Sexual excess in these plays, in other words, only increases the effectiveness of the "strategic unities" that will root out desire and use it as an element of control. Only the culminating effects of identification, which remains suggested, have a more totalizing effect. These plays offer a level of preparatory work that anticipate Freud and offer an intriguing background to his paradigm-shifting insights. Indeed, had he known these plays, we might talk of a "Baillie syndrome" or the "Walpolian displacement." Instead we are left to make this claim for ourselves.

6

"The End of History": Identity and Dissolution in Apocalyptic Gothic

"The discourse on 'endism,'" Christopher Horricks argues in an essay on Baudrillard and the millennium, "consists of opposing views held by two groups. There are those who either mourn or deny the death of Enlightenment values, and so attempt to maintain their foundations against the perceived irresponsibility of the postmodernists. . . . Others are instead counter-Enlightenment, and support a radical rethinking of value and the claims of history. In short, there is a theoretical and philosophical struggle over the end of history, and therefore the meaning of the millennium."[1]

Arguments about the value and meaning of history are hardly new. Writers in the eighteenth century already questioned the "Enlightenment" view of history and looked for ways to reimagine its force and reconsider its ends. Jacobin thinkers in the 1790s especially thought it fit to challenge the accepted view of history and offer a radical alternative. For William Godwin, that alternative takes a fascinating form. In his unpublished essay "Of History and Romance" he addresses the question of history in similar terms:

> The writer of romance then is to be considered as the writer of real history; while he who was formerly called the historian, must be contented to step down into the place of his rival, with this disadvantage, that he is a romance writer, without the arduous, the enthusiastic, and the sublime license of imagination, that belong to that species of composition. True history consists in a delineation of consistent, human character, in a display of the manner in which such a character acts under successive circumstances, in showing how character increases and assimilates new substances to its own, and

how it decays, together with the catastrophe into which by its own gravity it naturally declines.[2]

Godwin is arguing about different versions of history, but he is doing so in a context in which a threat to established values is palpable. His desire to turn to human character is a measure of his willingness to engage in millennial thinking about history. Even more important for my purposes here is the outcome of this rethinking: Godwin equates history with the growth and decay of an individual being, and in doing so he implicitly argues for the contingency of events and the "catastrophic" conclusion to human endeavor. This is a radical perspective on history to be sure, and it is also a radically new conception of the meaning of human experience. Godwin might pay narrative lip service to the value of human life, but in a novel like *Caleb Williams* he dramatizes a portrait of human "decay" that is difficult to avoid and impossible to resist.

In this chapter I discuss three works that in very different ways challenged Enlightenment notions of history and deconstructed narrative so as to say something radical about the meaning and value of subjective experience. Identity itself becomes an issue here, as do the ways it can or cannot be historically realized. These works push at the limits of identification in order to discover what lies beyond. *Caleb Williams* (1794), *The Last Man* (1826), and *Dr. Jekyll and Mr. Hyde* (1886) are uncannily millennial because they refuse to accept the status quo and seem to desire instead the kind of cataclysmic dissolution that millennial thinking often implies. Emerging as they do from the final decade of the eighteenth century and from early and late in the nineteenth century, they tell an important story about the function of apocalyptic gothic fiction at a time when sexuality and sexual identity were beginning to have particular cultural valence. These works are not so much reflections of developments in the history of sexuality as episodes in an ongoing process of reassessment and revaluation that produces radical rethinking of the meaning of identity and its function in post-Enlightenment culture.

Male-male relations are so often the basis of a gothic plot that their significance may sometimes be missed. The figure of two men locked in a physical and psychological bond—whether friendship or rivalry—so intense that they are spiritually a single being is everywhere in gothic fiction. This often sensational configuration is emotional and erotic in ways that defy conventional descriptions of male friendship or rivalry. These works use male-male relations to explore questions about identity and dissolution, questions that the sexological purveyors of the history of sexuality had hardly begun to ask. They also use them to confront larger questions about "decay" and "catastrophe"—the end of human experience—that are familiar from the modern millennial moment.

In her influential study *Between Men*, Eve Kosofsky Sedgwick argues persuasively that a certain strain of gothic fiction finds an analogy in Freud's case history of Dr. Schreber, the state judge who published an account of his own bizarre psychological experiences later studied by Freud. For her it is clear that "paranoia is the psychosis that makes graphic the mechanisms of homophobia." Sedgwick describes a "large subgroup" of classic gothic novels "whose plots might be mapped almost point for point onto the case of Dr. Schreber: most saliently each is about one or more males who not only is persecuted by, but considers himself transparent to and often under the compulsion of, another male."[3] In Freud's case history, Schreber, with shame but without equivocation, tells of his sense that an ever-watchful God had chosen him for a special communication. In order to receive this communication, which would come in the form of divine rays, preferably through his anus, Schreber felt that God insisted on his dressing in woman's underwear in order to create the "voluptuousness" appropriate to the "wife" of God. Freud interprets Schreber's paranoia as an elaborate displacement in which Schreber avoids confronting his own homosexuality. The abjection implicit in Schreber's position—under God and afraid of him and also completely dependent on his love—equates desire with a kind of alienation from the self that produces a different personality, almost a different person, and behaviors that Schreber cannot fully understand.

Ignoring the homophobia that is rife in Freud's text, I find two things useful in this case history. First, Freud has made explicit the connection between paranoia and sexuality; and, second, he shows how, in the Schreber case, the source of patriarchal law becomes the agent of sexual transgression. Schreber "loves" the God who is watching and who will punish him. Law and desire, in other words, are inextricably bound in the workings of Schreber's private "nightmare." But Schreber's private nightmare is, in fact, the nightmare of culture itself. God, authority, and law become the brutal, victimizing aggressor in a sadomasochistic configuration of desire.

Schreber's obsession with God and God's desire to penetrate him, his fixation on a divine plan, suggests that Schreber is using God as a way of confronting himself. Žižek is helpful in explaining why this relation should be both erotic and victimizing. Schreber is struggling with questions of identity (I am ... , God is ...), and his inability to make distinctions leads to a peculiar form of psychosis. In *For They Know Not What They Do*, Žižek quotes Hegel's proposition, apropos of God, that "*identical* talk ... *contra-*

dicts itself. Identity, instead of being in its own self truth and absolute truth, is consequently the very opposite; instead of being the unmoved simple, it is the passage beyond itself into the dissolution of the self." He explains that identity is inert and incomplete: "this tedious point at which a set encounters itself among its elements, at which a genus encounters itself in the shape of its own species. . . . More precisely," he says, "instead of encountering itself, the initial moment comes across in *its own absence.*"[4]

This encounter with an identity constituted only in absence begins to explain why these narratives of same-sex desire can only be couched in terms of melancholic loss and debilitating self-contempt. Schreber's abjection before God is an attempt to fix (or transfix) himself with an identity. What his case study suggests, however, is that the self is dissolved in the attempt to fix identity. Identity becomes a kind of dissolution; it fails to serve any function but the measure of loss.

Caleb Williams, The Last Man, and *Dr. Jekyll and Mr. Hyde* illustrate three different versions of this dissolution. They place an abject male in the midst of confrontation with himself and from that confrontation draw conclusions that have broad cultural significance. The "identity thinking" in each case brings about a dissolution of the self that begins to assume millennial proportions. If identity is pursued to the point of absence, as it is in these three texts, then what does that imply for the history of sexuality, or even for history itself?

William Godwin's *Caleb Williams* tells of the personal obsession of a young man for the elusive secrets of an older, mysterious benefactor. James Thompson suggests that the novel is a story of "surveillance" in which both psychology and politics are at work and paranoia becomes a political as well as a psychological condition. "To put this as simply as possible," Thompson explains, "surveillance in *Caleb Williams* should be seen not merely in terms of the function of an authoritarian state, the professionalization of the police force, and the development of the penitentiary. . . . As an anarchist, Godwin was vitally interested in the mechanisms by which the state extended its influence of power into the lives of individual subjects."[5] That sounds uncannily like the relation Sedgwick described. Because the power of the state is felt in individual lives, that is, the novel has resonance in personal as well political terms.

One area in which these two functions overlap concerns the regulation of same-sex sexual activity that was already active in the 1790s, an era that had accustomed the public to the need for subterfuge and secrecy. Fear about events in France, knowledge that Jacobin writers like Godwin were potentially subversive, and general anxiety about social unrest led to a more paranoid social structure at the time Godwin was writing *Caleb Williams* and beyond. As Thompson notes, habeas corpus was suspended and government spying became routine in the 1790s.[6] Given the sexual surveillance that took place at this time the already-familiar language of indescribability and secrecy began to have a new legal status and in the public mind became tantamount to conviction. Already what Sedgwick calls *the* open secret was articulated in a number of different ways. In gothic fiction especially, this unspeakable secret of heteronormative culture existed as a violence, a horror, a monstrous other that could threaten the entire fabric of culture.[7]

The "surveillance" that haunts *Caleb Williams* as well as *Frankenstein* (1818), James Hogg's *Private Memoirs and Confessions of a Justified Sinner*, and other early-nineteenth-century works has a political function that is publicly celebrated. The Bow Street magistrates, forerunners of the secret police, began a system of surveillance and infiltration that more than once resulted in the public exposure and physical abuse of men involved in same-sex sexual activity, especially in clubs organized for men to meet and socialize. Like the gothic figure of the monster who is also part of the self, these men were rendered horrifying by their very natures. The trial and punishment that resulted made them posthuman victims of a culture that could not tolerate their refusal to play by the rules.[8]

Caleb Williams anticipates this drama of dissolution in a vivid portrayal of male-male desire. Caleb's obsession with his master, Falkland, and the history of Falkland's relation with his enemy, Tyrrel, are the dramatic center of the work. The socially fraught relations between these three men are sexualized in various ways. Caleb's interest in Falkland has sexual overtones from early in the novel, and he talks openly, even aggressively, about his "love" for his benefactor; Falkland, who in turn is described as small of stature, delicate, and intelligent, becomes locked in rivalries with both Caleb and his uncouth neighbor Tyrrel; Tyrrel mocks Falkland "as an animal that was beneath contempt" and clearly displays his jealousy of this ladies' man; and Falkland, in a fit of rage, stabs Tyrrel from behind.

Sexuality is understood in terms of power in each of these relations. Desire personalizes power inequalities in a way that makes the police state an inevitability, as Thompson argues. The minute that Caleb finds his master interesting enough to "know," Caleb's entire story falls into place. He seeks knowledge and then he is sought by it. When Falkland becomes the hunter, with law on his side, Caleb is doomed. Once drawn into the ideological structure of desire, that is, he is trapped in the structure of the law, from which there is no escape. Throughout the novel, the trope of secret knowledge, spying, which is political and social as well as private and personal, creates situations that demand violent resolution.[9] It is almost as if the spying is an act of sexual violence: "My act [of lifting the lid of Mr. Falkland's trunk] was in some sort an act of insanity; but how undescribable are the feelings with which I looked back upon it! It was an instantaneous impulse, a short-lived and passing alienation of mind; but what must Mr. Falkland think of that alienation? To any man a person who had once shown himself capable of so wild a flight of the mind must appear dangerous" (138–39).[10]

Caleb's "act of insanity" is made to feel like an act of personal, physical violation because the secret that Falkland hides can only be personal and physical. The novel pushes at these definitions, of course, and insists on a reassessment of what such violation means. What is personal and physical is also psychological in a way Godwin insistently explores. The self-alienation of which Caleb speaks is as powerful and debilitating as any act of violence perpetrated in the novel. The feelings he articulates in this passage return at the end of the work to suggest that he has sacrificed himself to a pursuit of secret sexual knowledge that eludes him.

Uneasy male-male confrontations structure all of *Caleb Williams*. Caleb spies on and confronts his nemesis, the "master" Falkland, and a similar haunting relation is established between Falkland and Tyrrel. The terms of this antipathetic relation are telling. The two are seen as a distopic pair. Tyrrel is "muscular and sturdy" like a statue that "might have been selected by a painter as a model for that hero of antiquity" (19). Falkland, in contrast, has "polished manners . . . particularly in harmony with feminine delicacy" (22). Tyrrel is portrayed as an "untamed, though not undiscerning brute" (21), and Falkland as eminently dignified ("though his stature was small, his person had an air of uncommon dignity" [12]). From the moment Falkland returns from Italy, he and Tyrrel are at odds. They spar in public and seem unable to remain calm in one another's company.

The uncannily named poet Clare sees a danger in this relation, and on his deathbed he tells Falkland so: "Beware of Mr. Tyrrel. Do not commit the mistake of despising him as an unequal opponent. Petty causes may produce great mischiefs. Mr. Tyrrel is boisterous, rugged, and unfeeling; and you are too passionate, too acutely sensible of injury. It would be truly to be lamented, if a man so inferior, so utterly unworthy to be compared with you, should be capable of changing your whole history into misery and guilt. I have a painful presentiment upon my heart, as if something dreadful would reach you from that quarter" (37).

Clare has a sense that the fates of these two "unequal" figures are mysteriously intertwined, and he rightly predicts a future of "misery and guilt." Just after the prediction Falkland, uninvited, visits Tyrrel at his home and tries to reason with him. He does not get very far in this project but does manage to articulate his deepest fear: "A strife between persons with our peculiarities and our weaknesses, includes consequences that I shudder to think of. I fear, sir, that it is pregnant with death at least to one of us, and with misfortune and remorse to the survivor" (31). The intimate, private moment is tense and emotionally charged. It is "erotic" in the sense that the adversaries circle and taunt each other even as they seem to be attempting rational conversation. It is no accident that they are having this conversation because they have been seen publicly as rivals for the same woman. Emily, the victim here, was, in fact, herself just teasing Tyrrel by agreeing to dance with Falkland. Whether or not they assume an erotic pose, Falkland's language is clear. He sees them locked in a relation that is "pregnant with death." Their dystopic bond, that is, is best represented culturally by the figure of death. Death haunts this relationship as it haunts the one between Caleb and Falkland later on.

This intimacy grows and deepens as the first volume of the novel develops. Once the innocent Emily has been sacrificed to the rivalry, it builds to a tragic climax. The consummation of the deeply conflicted, marriage-like bond takes place in two phases. The first encounter takes place at the assembly, public and ceremonial, with witnesses and a large group of friends in attendance. Tyrrel defies his official dismissal and marches into the assembly in spite of the protests of the master of ceremonies and others:

> His muscular form, the well-known eminence of his intellectual powers, the long habits to which every man was formed of acknowledging his ascendancy, were all in his favour. . . . Disengaged from the insects that at first pestered him, he paced up and down the room with a magisterial stride, and flashed an angry glance on every side. . . .
> At this critical moment, Mr. Falkland entered the room. . . . Both he [Falkland] and Mr. Tyrrel reddened at sight of each other. He advanced without a moment's pause toward Mr. Tyrrel and in a peremptory voice asked him what he did there. (97–98)

The public confrontation of these two rivals, the first meeting after the death of Emily Melville, is both emotional and ritualistic. Falkland speaks vow-like confirmation of his feelings of hatred—"Go, miserable wretch; think yourself too happy that you are permitted to fly the face of man! Why, what a pitiful figure do you make at this moment!" (99)—and it at first seems that

Tyrrel accepts this sentence and understands his own villainy. Soon, however, the mood of resignation turns to one of violence:

> In about an hour and a half he returned. . . . In a moment he was in a part of the room where Mr. Falkland was standing, and with one blow of his muscular arm levelled him with the earth. The blow however was not stunning, and Mr. Falkland rose again immediately. It is obvious to perceive how unequal he must have been in this species of contest. He was scarcely risen before Mr. Tyrrel repeated his blow. Mr. Falkland was now upon his guard, and did not fall. But the blows of his adversary were redoubled with a rapidity difficult to conceive, and Mr. Falkland was once again brought to the earth. In this situation, Mr. Tyrrel kicked his prostrate enemy, and stooped apparently with the intention of dragging him along the floor. (99–100)

The physically excessive and emotionally devastating encounter heralds the climax of the complex interaction between the two men. When, shortly later, Tyrrel is found dead, Godwin suggests that the final scene is even more emotionally complex. The nocturnal encounter at which Falkland carries his relation with Tyrrel to a physical climax also brings the "misery and guilt" that Clare had predicted. This "secret" becomes the heart of the novel; hiding and defending it becomes Falkland's dearest care.

Discovering it and confronting its significance is poor Caleb's curse. Whatever else is true, however, it is the structure of the secret that makes it all-powerful in the denouement of the novel. Caleb's "act of insanity" in peeking into Falkland's trunk is not mere idle curiosity, but neither is it a form of madness. Caleb wants to know the secret because he feels pushed to identify his employer. He wants to fix his identity because doing so will tell him what he needs to know about himself. He wants to give his abject relation to his arbitrary master the meaning that he feels it lacks. That lack, he will come to realize, is ineluctable and foundational.

The hideous extent to which Falkland tortures Caleb has everything to do with the terms of this identification and the nature of the secret. Falkland knows that identification means dissolution. Caleb can bring an end not only to Falkland's position or even his life but also to the entire system of heteronormative culture, of which he has pretended to be a part. In this sense the trial heralds the cataclysmic end of history, not only because the class system is threatened and one of the dispossessed succeeds in overwhelming his "master" but also because the erotic privacy of a man of means is revealed to his detriment. This threatens the fabric of culture more than anything else that transpires in volumes 2 and 3. At least it sets up a gothic configuration that becomes the basis of haunting in the nineteenth century. Falkland knows that his real enemy is the identity with which Caleb threatens him. For both Falkland and Caleb, that is, to fix identity is to confront absence, loss, and the abjection that heteronormativity implies.

Caleb's lament at the close of the novel, when he turns his prosecution against himself in a final gesture of powerlessness and abjection, measures that loss and gives it a peculiar shape: "I looked first at Mr. Falkland, and then at the Magistrate and attendants, and then at Mr. Falkland again. My voice was suffocated with agony. I began:—Why cannot I recall the last four days of my life? How was it possible for me to be so eager, so obstinate, in a purpose so diabolical. . . . No penitence, no anguish, can expiate the folly and the cruelty of this last act I have perpetrated" (331).

This crisis of confidence as Caleb's attempt to justify himself collapses into self-accusation reaches its inevitable climax in the final paragraph of the novel, where he laments to the memory of Falkland: "I began these memoirs with the idea of vindicating my character. I have now no character that I wish to vindicate: but I will finish them that thy story may be fully understood; and that, if those errors of thy life be known which thou so ardently desiredst to conceal, the world may at least not hear and repeat a half-told and mangled tale" (337).

Caleb's attempts to justify himself, to identify as an innocent subject, lead to the kind of dissolution that I have described. His attempt at vindication leaves him with "no character" at all. Whether because of a political system that uses identification for its own ends or a psychological impasse that makes identity a self-contradiction, Caleb is left with nothing. At the novel's end he is in a state of abject self-disgust, transfixed by the object of his misery and at odds with its subject. Trapped in the snare that culture has set for him, that is, Caleb closes with the kind of self-contempt that is rendered inevitable for the subject of male-male desire. In place of the self he had hoped to establish in relation to Falkland he finds a lack that can only be measured in terms of absence and loss.

In Mary Shelley's *The Last Man* this configuration is rewritten in a way that neither her earlier *Frankenstein* nor Godwin's *Caleb Williams* might lead one to expect. The book's politics, although repeatedly articulated in convincing public terms, are as deeply personal as those of any novel written in the early nineteenth century. In addition to concerns such as how a republic should handle a national emergency, Shelley concerns herself with family, personal relations, and the exigencies of desire among a small group of close friends. The male-male relations that are recounted do not fill the same contours that are familiar from *Caleb Williams* and other works of paranoid gothic. Instead, male friendship becomes the centerpiece of this analysis of the collapse of human civilization. The strength of the bond that emerges between Lionel Verney and Adrian, second Earl of Windsor, in this catastrophic novel is also a measure of loss that the final chapters of the novel spell out in increasingly poetic terms.

Morton D. Paley observes that *The Last Man* "denies the linkage of apocalypse and millennium that had previously been celebrated in some of the great works of the Romantic epoch, perhaps most fully in *Prometheus Unbound*."[11] For Paley, various imaginative realizations of a millennium are frustrated by the forces of nature that pull against any transformative resolution. "Close to the end," he writes, "Adrian, sailing with Lionel and Clara towards Greece, imagines an island paradise." Paley considers this to be a vision reuniting Mary Shelley (as Lionel Verney) with Percy Shelley (as Adrian) and Lionel's daughter Clara. "Here once more we see the rhythm by which the author raises the possibility of millennial bliss only to brutally disappoint both herself and the reader. Immediately the storm breaks, the boat is swamped, Adrian and Clara are drowned, and Lionel Verney survives as the Last Man."[12]

As reasonable as it is to see Lionel Verney as a version of the author, it is also fair to suggest that her choice of genders for the protagonists of her tale is meaningful as well. The women in her tale, like those in *Frankenstein*, are relegated to minor roles that are important—indeed, essential—to the development of the plot. Their roles are secondary, contingent, and dependent on the lives of the men they love, however, as Evadne's denunciation of Raymond and prediction of the plague suggests. In spite of all they offer in terms of personal consolation and deep, abiding friendship, these women fail to establish themselves except in loss. Their lives have meaning only in relation to the men, and when they lose them in a sense they lose themselves. Evadne dies on the battlefield, and Perdita commits suicide rather than continue living without her beloved. These dissolutions suggest that identity is a contradiction that leaves the women in a state of abjection. The men reserve their fullest expressions of love always for one another.

The novel begins with an account of Lionel's discovery by Adrian and their consequent devotion to one another. Because of his father's disgrace, Lionel begins life as a shepherd: "Thus untaught in refined philosophy, and pursued by a restless feeling of degradation from my true station in society, I wandered among the hills of civilized England as uncouth a savage as the wolf-bred founder of old Rome."[13] Very soon, however, he has learned the value of friendship, as Adrian represents it. When Lionel is caught poaching game on Adrian's estate, Adrian confronts him with grace and refinement:

> My garments were torn . . . my hair was matted; my face besmeared. . . . my whole appearance was haggard and squalid. Tall and muscular as I was in form, I must have looked like, what indeed I was, the merest ruffian that ever trod the earth. . . : [Then Adrian approaches]: he came up the while; and his appearance blew aside, with gentle western breath, my cloudy wrath: a tall, slim, fair boy, with a physiognomy expressive of the excess of sensibility and refinement stood before me; the morning sunbeams tinged with gold his silken hair, and spread light and glory over his beaming countenance. (19)

The erotically charged encounter forms the basis of a relationship that lasts until the last chapters of the book; indeed, in some ways the novel can be read as the history of a love affair between these two impressive youths. The rough country boy and the sophisticated aristocrat make an impressively complementary couple, and it is the devotion that they feel for one another that sustains the entire narrative. Lionel accounts for Adrian's effect on him in personal terms:

> It was not his rank . . . that, from the first, subdued my heart of hearts, and laid my entire spirit prostrate before him. Nor was it I alone who felt thus intimately his perfections: his sensibility and courtesy fascinated everyone. His vivacity, intelligence, and active spirit of benevolence, completed the conquest. Even at this early age, he was deep read and imbued with the spirit of high philosophy. . . . In person, he hardly appeared of this world; his slight frame was overinformed by the soul that dwelt within; he was all mind; "Man but a rush against" his breast, and it would have conquered his strength; but the might of his smile would have tamed an hungry lion, or caused a legion of armed men to lay their weapons at his feet. (20)

Critics who have reasonably made the point that in this description Mary Shelley is commemorating the particular attractions of her late husband Percy ignore the same-sex resonance of the exotic description.[14] Of course, it changes the mood of the work to shift gender in this way, and it does much, much more. The articulations of affection and admiration upon which the text is constructed have special resonance when one male character is talking about another. Even if it is easy to see Mary Shelley in the figure of Lionel Verney, the author's decision to work out the central drama of the tale between two men means that male-male love shapes the novel and gives it particular cultural meaning. If much of Mary Shelley's anxiety is contained in the image of two men who in their love for one another exclude the possibility of female companionship, then it might be possible to see special significance when the same couple faces the end of the world alone with one another and a single female child. As soon as this new family unit is defined, however, it is destroyed.

In a discussion of *Frankenstein* and *The Last Man,* Barbara Johnson observes about the former, "If Mary Shelley's novel constitutes a critique of humanism, that critique is directed not against the hubris of the humanist who takes himself for God, but against the blindness of the humanist who can't see himself." According to Johnson, "The *unknown* is not located in the object of humanism, but in the desiring humanistic subject. That which the humanist remains blind to in his efforts to know man is that nature of his own desire to know man."[15] Lionel Verney, like Victor Frankenstein, seems blind to the nature of his desire. His actions throughout the novel move him farther and farther from his first love, and it is only when Lionel and Adrian join forces at the final catastrophe that their bond is fully rekindled. Lionel's devotion to Adrian creates a mood in which male-male desire becomes an avenue for cultural survival. But, as the end of the novel demonstrates, Lionel instead chooses the unknown that identity finally signifies.

Of course, the novel tells of other loves: Adrian's frustrated love for the Greek girl Evadne, who is destined to give her love to the heroic and superhuman Lord Raymond; Raymond's for Lionel's sister Perdita (the little romantic love he has to share); and Lionel's for Adrian's sister Idris. The various challenges and frustrations of these relations give shape to the first half of the novel. Evadne's rejection of Adrian in favor of Lord Raymond causes the soft and sensitive hero to slip into near-madness, Evadne suffers Lord Raymond's rejection and flees to Greece, Perdita's love for Lord Raymond causes her increasing pain until she finally takes her own life, and Idris silently accompanies Lionel through the harrowing passages of decline that mark the beginning of the end.

When Lord Raymond is aiding Greece in its battle against the Turks he confronts the dying freedom fighter Evadne on the fields of Turkey. She rises and condemns him in terms that are significant:

> As her strength grew less, I lifted her from the ground; her emaciated form hung over my arm, her sunken cheek rested on my breast; in a sepulchral voice she murmured:—"This is the end of love!—yet not the end!"—and frenzy lent her strength as she cast her arm up to heaven: "there is the end! there we meet again. Many living deaths have I borne for thee, O Raymond, and now

I expire, thy victim! By my death I purchase thee—lo! the instruments of war, fire, the plague are my servitors. I dared, I conquered them all, till now! I have sold myself to death, with the sole condition that thou shouldst follow me—Fire, and war, and plague, unite for thy destruction—O my Raymond, there is no safety for thee!" (142)

Critics have read this scene as an announcement of the apocalyptic vision of the work.[16] Fire, destruction, and the plague follow this Cassandra-like outburst. Even more pointed, however, is Evadne's claim that "this is the end of love." The connection between the frustrations of desire that the novel has commemorated, the endless deferrals and dis-eases of love, are placed in relation to the physical destruction of the world. The end of love, Shelley seems to say, is the end of history. She also makes clear that the love her novel most clearly celebrates is the most impossible to realize. Even Lionel and Adrian can come together only through disease; their love threatens culture so palpably that plague can signify the power of its threat.

Perdita suffers at Raymond's death as well. She creates a kind of Grecian temple in which to bury him, and she wishes to join him there in her turn:

The platform on which the pyramid stood was enlarged, and looking toward the south, in a recess overshadowed by the straggling branches of a wild fig-tree, I saw foundations dug, and props and rafters fixed, evidently the commencement of a cottage; standing on its unfinished threshold, the tomb was at our right hand, the whole ravine, and plain azure sea immediately before us; the dark rocks, received a glow from the descending sun, which glanced along the cultivated valley, and dyed in purple and orange the placid waves; we sat on a rocky elevation, and I gazed with rapture on the beauteous panorama of living and changeful colours, which varied and enhanced the graces of earth and ocean. (164)

This lovely structure, which Perdita intends as a kind of honeymoon cottage, almost immediately becomes a tomb. The cottage and the tomb redefine desire and rewrite love in terms of desperation. This is the tomb of love. Perdita claims that she will live here forever with her lost love, but it soon turns out that rather than do that she will lie as a companion in death to Raymond. (After Lionel tricks her onto the boat that would take her back to England she throws herself into the water while clutching the instructions to return her to Athens and to Raymond's tomb.) The Grecian temple of love becomes a temple of loss as Perdita is ensconced there with her dear departed.

Adrian steps out from the shadows of the novel when a plague emerges from the East to threaten West European, especially English, civilization.

Adrian is the one character willing to lead the country in the moment of crisis, to take steps to prevent the spread of disease, care for those stricken, and lead and inspire those who survive. "I am now going to undertake an office fitted for me," he says. "I cannot intrigue, or work a tortuous path through the labyrinth of men's vices and passions; but I can bring patience, and sympathy, and such aid as art affords, to the bed of disease; I can raise from earth the miserable orphan, and awaken to new hopes the shut heart of the mourner. I can enchain the plague in limits, and set a term to the misery it would occasion; courage, forbearance, and watchfulness, are the forces I bring toward this great work" (194).

Adrian brings the talents of a priest, or a nurse, to a civilization in crisis. Patience, sympathy, and art are not the makings of a traditional hero. Adrian defies gender-coding to offer "feminine" traits that can sooth pain and ameliorate suffering. This is a new kind of hero. Rather than preen about his processes of response like a hero of sensibility would, Adrian acts in the world. He avoids the self-destructive heroic posturing of Lord Raymond, who storms into plague-infested Constantinople and says, "By my past labours, by torture and imprisonment suffered for them, by my victories, by my sword, I swear—by my hopes of fame, by my former deserts now awaiting their reward, I deeply vow, with these hands to plant the cross on yonder mosque" (152). Instead, Adrian offers "courage, forbearance, and watchfulness." Only seemingly passive and unheroic, these are the qualities that can preserve life rather than destroy it.

In answer to critics who find the politics of The Last Man apolitical or even nihilistic, Audrey A. Fisch notes that "Mary Shelley's grounds of critique have a special relevance today." In an essay that considers the politics of AIDS discourse, Fisch discusses the "slippage" between "our emphasis on the 'foreignness' of the disease, in terms of nationality but often coded racially, and an emphasis on the 'foreignness' within our society, often denoted as 'unnatural' sexuality, that allows the foreign disease access to us."[17] Similar "slippages" occur in The Last Man, of course. The plague enters the novel at a moment of imperial desire—Raymond insists on storming Constantinople as a way of proving his martial prowess—and is racially coded in a number of different ways. As Anne K. Mellor points out, Lionel contracts the plague from a black man, and the novel as a whole dramatizes the disease as a threat that emanates from the East and threatens the "civilized" world with the force of the utterly uncivilized.[18]

Like AIDS, the plague in The Last Man has a powerful political valence that is at least in part responsible for its epidemiological profile. As AIDS drugs are withheld from poorer countries and entire populations are infected with the illness today, health group warnings of future threats from the disease go largely unheeded. "About nineteen million people have been killed and an additional thirty-four million infected by the AIDS virus," one "millennial" newspaper report read in 2000, "wreaking social and economic devastation in the most stricken African nations—with the worst still to come." Moreover, "Unless action against the epidemic is scaled up drastically, the damage already done will seem minor compared with what lies ahead."[19] Responding to this epidemic, scaling up action against it, is a huge medical and political challenge that it is easy for first-world nations and multinational drug cartels to ignore. Cultural differences about sex education, for instance, are often used as an excuse for expressing dismay and doing very little. Shoddy healthcare facilities are also blamed, as is lack of will on the part of native populations.

In *The Last Man,* characters in northwestern Europe watch other civilizations collapse while reassuring themselves that their superior culture will remain untainted. After plague appears in Constantinople they measure their safety and assign geographic blame rather than attempt to deal with the horror of disease in the eastern world: "The plague at Athens had been preceded and caused by the contagion from the East; and the scene of havoc and death continued to be acted there, on a scale of fearful magnitude. A hope that the visitation of the present year would prove the last, kept up the spirits of the merchants connected with these countries" (175).

Trade takes precedence over a sensible program of health maintenance because England's cultural superiority depends on the indefatigability of its merchants as surely as big drug companies "cannot afford" to provide inexpensive treatment for AIDS in poorer countries or insist that unsophisticated populations will be unable to follow rigorous drug protocols. In Shelley's novel that attitude results in the rapid and systematic destruction of the world. The end of civilization, that is, results from imperial desires, racist cultural encounters, and refusal to check the forces of emerging capitalism.

Adrian and Lionel are consumed by these forces, and the tale of their love becomes a tale of woe: "Beware, tender offspring of the re-born world—beware, fair being, with human heart, yet untamed by care, and human brow, yet unploughed by time—beware, lest the cheerful current of thy blood be checked, thy golden locks turn grey, thy sweet dimpling smiles be changed to fixed, harsh wrinkles!" (341). Almost immediately after this, Shelley quotes from her husband Percy Bysshe Shelley's translations of Moschus ("When the winds that move not its calm surface sweep/ The azure sea, I love the land no more") as the little group sets sail for Greece.

Moschus is best known, of course, for his position in the classical elegy tradition, and Percy Shelley also translated a "Fragment of the Elegy on the Death of Bion": "Ye Dorian woods and waves lament aloud,— / Augment your tide, O streams, with fruitless tears, / For the beloved Bion is no more. / Let every tender herb and plant and flower, / From each dejected bud and drooping bloom, / Shed dews of liquid sorrow, and with breath / Of melancholy sweetness on the wind / Diffuse its languid love."[20] The author does not quote from this lament, but I think it is implied in the citation of Moschus at the moment of embarkation. The mood is one of loss. The love these men share is already constituted in elegiac terms.

The small alternative family—Lionel, Adrian, and Clara—sets sail for the unknown. Greece becomes the object of this journey, which might also be seen as a journey of self-discovery, a journey of identification for these two loving men. But the journey is doomed. The ship encounters a storm and capsizes in the dark. Adrian and Clara are both lost, and Lionel must go on alone. Paley says that the hope for millennial bliss is dashed with the death of Adrian and Clara.[21] But Lionel's solitary wanderings have a millennial quality all their own. He is realized in loss, and his love has become regret: "I was an untaught shepherd-boy, when Adrian deigned to confer on me his friendship. The best years of my life had been passed with him. All I possessed of this world's goods, of happiness, knowledge, or virtue—I owed to him. He had, in his person, his intellect, and rare qualities, given a glory to my life, which without him it had never known" (351). This romantic lament allows Lionel to rewrite love as loss just as generations of elegy writers had learned to do. Articulation of male-male desire as regret is the articulation that culture allows, and it seems appropriate that at this apocalyptic moment Lionel wanders on his own. He has been unable to realize the love for Adrian and has sought instead mere confrontation with himself. This is the absence that identification yields. If Lionel's wanderings take the outward form of a romantic quest, he nevertheless suffers from an emptiness within. Once again, a fundamental lack makes any myth of growth seem woefully inadequate.

A text from the later nineteenth century addresses the question of identity even more directly. In *Dr. Jekyll and Mr. Hyde* the conflict has been uncannily internalized, but the problem is the same. Utterson, the humorless but respectable lawyer from whose perspective the story is for the most part told, is obsessed with narrative. He tosses and turns through the night because he fears putting various strands of the narrative together. He fears some catastrophic conclusion from the history that he encounters, and, like Jekyll, he fears the conclusions that become increasingly obvious to those reading the tale: Dr. Jekyll and Mr. Hyde are the same person, and they will destroy each other.

Utterson's first conclusions are more fully suggestive of one of the signal undercurrents in this tale. He sees the relation between Jekyll and Hyde as "the ghost of some old sin, the cancer of some concealed disgrace; punishment coming, *pede claudo,* years after memory has forgotten and self-love condoned the fault."²² The uncanny discomfort he feels around Hyde he equates with Jekyll's guilt, and everything about the relationship that confuses him—the will, various odd coincidences, and the handwriting sample—all combine to suggest that Hyde is blackmailing Jekyll or in some other way binding him against his will. In a late-night conversation with Jekyll, he pushes this point home. "'Jekyll,' said Utterson, 'you know me: I am a man to be trusted. Make a clean breast of this in confidence; and I make no doubt I can get you out of it" (23).

Jekyll's response is measured and precise: "I would trust you before any man alive, ay, before myself, if I could make the choice; but indeed it isn't what you fancy; it is not so bad as that; and just to put your good heart at rest, I will tell you one thing: the moment I choose, I can be rid of Mr. Hyde" (23). The question of choice is a salient one, the significance of which becomes more vivid in Jekyll's narrative at the end of the volume. Notice here, however, the extent to which Utterson reaches out to Jekyll, his willingness to cope with any secret sin and help him escape it. Utterson assumes, that is, that Jekyll is hiding a particular behavior or behaviors, something that can be expunged by rewriting history. But Jekyll knows he is dealing with not a behavior so much as a feature of identity.

That such a distinction is articulated as clearly as it is at this stage in the history of sexuality should not be surprising. As Foucault and others have noted, sexological thinking codified the notion of homosexuality at this moment in history. As David Halperin suggests, "The term [homosexuality], which began life as a purely descriptive, conceptually empty category, so quickly absorbed from those who used it a number of quite specific substantive notions about the nature of same-sex sexual desire and behavior, thereby becoming a repository for a number of very different ideological perspectives."²³ Utterson approaches the problem of "secret sin" from the older conception of behaviors to be hidden. But given a context in which sexual secrecy is being given a different valence, it is not surprising that Jekyll experiments with a very different notion of identity, one closer in spirit to the work of sexologists in searching for personality types and that finally makes Utterson's kind of distinctions untenable.

For Sedgwick, the situation is far simpler. "In *The Picture of Dorian Gray*, as in, for instance, *Dr. Jekyll and Mr. Hyde*," she maintains, "drug addiction is both a camouflage and an expression for the dynamics of same-sex desire and its prohibition: both books begin by looking like stories of erotic tension between men, and end up as cautionary tales of solitary substance abusers."[24] This is a useful commentary for both stories, but it also tends to read means for ends in this case especially. As Jekyll later explains, it is a drug that allows him to shift between his Jekyll and Hyde personas. Still, according to Stevenson's biographer Graham Balfour, the powder was always considered an awkward effect. The family audience found it "too material an agency," but Stevenson was committed to it from the first.[25]

Rather than seeing same-sex implications as camouflaged by the drug dynamic it is helpful to consider the drug dynamic as a means for addressing questions of identity for which an alternative vocabulary was just beginning to emerge in 1886. In other words, Stevenson needed a drug in order to imagine the dual nature he tried to describe. If it is possible to see the dynamic, as Sedgwick and others do, in terms of same-sex desire and its prohibition, Stevenson seems to be pushing for a means of describing how this kind of desire and prohibition functions within a single psyche. The relation between Jekyll and Hyde is neither one of desire nor one of identity. Clearly, it is both. Jekyll pushes at his identity until he discovers it in the kind of absence that desire presupposes.

The terms of this relation become most vivid in Jekyll's harrowing account of his experimental life. In the first extended paragraph of the work he explains that he "concealed [his] pleasures" and that early on he "stood already committed to a profound duplicity of life" (60). Gradually, he says, "I thus drew steadily nearer to that truth, by whose partial discovery I have been doomed to such dreadful shipwreck: that man is not truly one, but truly two" (61). This notion of a dual consciousness is not a psycho-Machian struggle between good and evil but something more all-encompassing:

> I saw that, of the two natures that contended in the field of my consciousness, even if I could rightly be said to be either, it was only because I was radically both; and . . . I had learned to dwell with pleasure, as a beloved daydream, on the thought of the separation of these elements. If each, I told myself, could but be housed in separate identities, life would be relieved of all that was unbearable; . . . It was the curse of mankind that these incongruous faggots were thus bound together—that in the agonised womb of consciousness, these polar twins should be continuously struggling. How, then, were they dissociated? (61)

Jekyll here is obviously in a crisis of identity. He cannot face the fact that his identity might include elements that are not culturally sanctioned, and his remedy is to try to separate the "polar twins" of consciousness. The "incongruous faggots" that are "bound together" in the consciousness of Henry Jekyll are not just different patterns of behavior. They are different identities in the sense of "the condition or fact of a person or thing being itself and not something else," as the *OED* defines them. But they embody the contradiction inherent in identity as well. The violent and transgressive identity that is Hyde and the upright respectable identity of Jekyll are parts of the same process of abjection. The brutal, secretive acts of Hyde in the end condemn Jekyll to misery and frustration.

At first, Jekyll reports the transgressions of Hyde with barely disguised glee. He reports that Hyde is "smaller, slighter, and younger than Henry Jekyll" (63), which he explains by suggesting that "the evil side of my nature . . . was less robust and less developed than the good" (63). He also says that "evil . . . had left on that body an imprint of deformity and decay" (63). But he takes pleasure in Hyde's exploits and seems in awe of his abilities: "Men have before hired bravos to transact their crimes, while their own person and reputation sat under shelter. I was the first that ever did so for his pleasures. I was the first that could thus plod in the public eye with a load of genial respectability, and in a moment, like a schoolboy, strip off these lendings and spring headlong into the sea of liberty" (65).

Jekyll's relation with his "smaller, slighter, and younger" companion, as it suggestively seems, grows more and more intimate as his account progresses. "The pleasures which I made haste to seek in my disguise were, as I have said, undignified; I would scarce use a harder term. But in the hands of Edward Hyde, they soon began to turn toward the monstrous. When I would come back from these excursions, I was often plunged into a kind of wonder at my vicarious depravity" (65). As Sedgwick suggests, however, the tension between Jekyll and Hyde is an erotic one. Later, Jekyll and Hyde relate to each other as if they are two different people, Hyde destroying Jekyll's work and mocking his experiments and Jekyll protecting Hyde and trying to find a means of his survival. The horror Jekyll experiences when he realizes he is turning into Hyde without willing to do so is uncannily sexual:

> Some two months before the murder of Sir Danvers, I had been out for one
> of my adventures, had returned at a late hour, and woke the next day in bed
> with somewhat odd sensations. It was in vain I looked about me; in vain I
> saw the decent furniture and tall proportions of my room in the square; in

vain that I recognised the pattern of the bed curtains and the design of the mahogany frame; something still kept insisting that I was not where I was, that I had not wakened where I seemed to be, but in the little room in Soho where I was accustomed to sleep in the body of Edward Hyde. I smiled to myself, and, in my psychological way, began lazily to inquire into the elements of this illusion, occasionally, even as I did so, dropping back into a comfortable morning doze. I was still so engaged when, in one of my more wakeful moments, my eye fell upon my hand. Now the hand of Henry Jekyll (as you have often remarked) was professional in shape and size; it was large, firm, white and comely. But the hand which I now saw, clearly enough, in the yellow light of a mid-London morning, lying half shut on the bed clothes, was lean, corded, knuckly, of a dusky pallor and thickly shaded with a swart growth of hair. It was the hand of Edward Hyde. (66–67)

I quote this passage at length because it strikes me as one of the most intriguing bed scenes in all of gothic literature. In effect, Henry Jekyll finds himself in bed with the swarthy and seductive Edward Hyde. It reads like an account of finding oneself in a strange bed after a night of sexual transgression, including confusion at not knowing where he is upon waking, the even more pronounced sense that he is not who he thinks he is, and the almost luridly fetishistic representation of the hand as "lean, corded, knuckly, of a dusky pallor and thickly shaded with a swart growth of hair." In this case, though, Henry Jekyll has participated in a night of transgression as Edward Hyde, not with him. Does that distinction really matter? Jekyll is powerfully attracted by his darker side, attracted to it, and the revelation of Hyde's erotically coded hand begins to break down, for the reader as it does for Jekyll, the distinctions he has been struggling to make. The crisis is one of desire as well as identity. This confrontation "in the yellow light of a mid-London morning" makes the terms of that crisis ineluctable.

Very soon thereafter the terms of the crisis become impossible to ignore. "At all hours of the day and night," Jekyll reports, "I would be taken with the premonitory shudder; above all, if I slept, or even dozed for a moment in my chair, it was always as Hyde that I awakened. Under the strain of this continually impending doom and by the sleeplessness to which I now condemned myself, ay, even beyond what I thought was possible to man, I became, in my own person, a creature eaten up and emptied by fever, languidly weak both in body and mind, and solely occupied by one thought: the horror of my other self" (74).

The tale has been building to just this crisis of identity; it answers all questions the story seems to want to ask. But to identify Jekyll is also to destroy him. To push for this clarity leads to dissolution. Above I quoted Hegel's claim that "Identity, instead of being in its own self truth and absolute truth, is consequently the very opposite; instead of being the unmoved simple, it is the passage beyond itself into the dissolution of the self." "Half an hour from now," Jekyll says in his final comments, "when I shall again and forever reindue that hated personality, I know how I shall sit shuddering and weeping in my chair, or continue, with the most strained and fearstruck ecstasy of listening, to pace up and down this room (my last earthly refuge) and give ear to every sound of menace" (76). Jekyll is destroyed by the "hated personality" that haunts him, and he kills himself out of the fear the process of identification causes. Unlike Lionel Verney, he is never offered the possibility of love. In this novel love has ended before it began.

The three works that I have considered in this chapter take very different approaches to identity, dissolution, and even history. But they all show the ways in which apocalyptic thinking places male-male desire at the fulcrum of cultural collapse. Is this because of a fear of male love and its biblical associations with dissolution, or is it because of the desire for the escape from heteronormativity that male love offers? Or do fear and desire both make these accounts of male-male obsession culturally resonant? If works like Sarah Scott's *Millenium Hall* (1752) suggest the ways in which a female utopia can conquer time, the various works I have discussed here suggest that a male utopia is a cultural impossibility.[26] Male love, properly articulated and fully identified, can only mean the end of history.

PART 3

Gothic Fictions and the Queering of Culture

7

"Queer Company": *The Turn of the Screw* and *The Haunting of Hill House*

Henry James's *The Turn of the Screw* (1898) is the perfect gothic tale. Generations of critics have testified, either directly or indirectly, to its signal uncanniness.[1] Its position within the history of gothic fiction, however, is sometimes ignored. In the context of this study, where hystericized heroines are commonplace, the governess's uneasiness with her eerie surroundings is hardly surprising. What is more, the crisis James's heroine confronts, which concerns the haunting of children, Miles and Flora, under her charge, is not entirely unprecedented, but it brings into clear focus some of the central obsessions of the gothic literary tradition. Victimization of the young is, after all, a gothic staple, and concern for the safety of children has been there from the first.

Shirley Jackson's *The Haunting of Hill House* (1959) builds on some of James's insights and fashions a more fully "neurotic" gothic heroine. But there, too, house, haunting, and even ghostliness are familiar to readers of gothic fiction. Eleanor Vance, Jackson's heroine, does not know why she must obey the dictates of the house any more than James's governess knows why she must torment the children in her charge. In both cases a kind of debilitated female sexuality wreaks havoc in the intimate world of family and responsibility. Both heroines are neurotic in their different ways, but in both cases the novelists make the reader aware of more than simple female hysteria. In each we learn how the context feeds these neuroses and how even the most well-meaning friends hasten the (self-) destruction that this particular form of madness entails.

Together, these works show the ways in which twentieth-century gothic could begin to revise familiar tropes and give them new energy in the spirit of late-nineteenth- and early-twentieth-century developments in psychology and psychoanalysis. Seen within the context of the gothic tradition, moreover, they fulfill rather than reimagine gothic potential.

James was writing in a gothic tradition that made it perfectly reasonable to place a young woman in a "haunted" house and confront her with demons beyond her conscious control. As if to signal this connection, James has the governess ruminate after her first confrontation with what she takes to be the ghost of Peter Quint, once a valet at Bly: "Was there a 'secret' at Bly—a mystery of Udolpho or an insane, an unmentionable relative kept in unsuspected confinement? I can't say how long I turned it over, or how long, in a confusion of curiosity and dread, I remained where I had had my collision" (148).[2]

Like Ann Radcliffe's Emily in *The Mysteries of Udolpho*, James's governess must on her own confront the unknown, and the mysteries she faces are the mysteries of her deepest fears. Also like Emily, she is victim of the delusions into which her intelligence and sensibility lead her.[3] Confronted with partial knowledge, that is, she draws conclusions that are unwarranted and perhaps dangerous. In the first chapter of this study I quoted Claire Kahane, for whom the woman hidden in the recesses of Udolpho is "a victimizer victimized by her own desire." "Laurentini is presented as Emily's potential precursor," Kahane says, "a mad mother-sister-double who mirrors Emily's own potential for transgression and madness."[4] James's governess is both a victimizing victimizer and a "mother-sister-double" to the children under her care. But she is also the innocent Emily, who remains sane but seems at the same time potentially mad and dangerous.

No critic can challenge the structural integrity of the tale. The reader is limited to the perspective of the governess, and the uncertainty she faces concerns ambiguity and uncertainty about who can see the ghosts and who is being haunted by them. She challenges herself repeatedly with the fear of madness, as is clear when late in the tale, in the company of Flora and a servant, Mrs. Grose, she sees the ghost of Miss Jessel, her predecessor, across the lake: "She was there, and I was justified; she was there, and I was neither cruel nor mad" (213). The governess is uneasy about her sanity to the degree that she cannot prove the objective existence of the ghosts without threatening the children or challenging them directly. When she does come close to exposing them to her reality, they in each case deny seeing what she sees, and they curse her in the process, as Flora does immediately after the scene above ("'I don't know what you mean. I see nobody. I see nothing. I never *have*. I think you're cruel. I don't like you!'" [215]).

Of course it is possible to question the honesty of the children in scenes like this, and various passages can be cited to suggest that they must be involved with the infernal, just as various passages can be cited to suggest that they are victims of the governess's hysteria. But my argument is analogous to that made about "explained gothic": If what we imagined to be a ghostly presence—in Clara Reeve, say, or Radcliffe—turns out to be a corpse, even a waxen image of one, or if it reveals incest or sadistic incarceration, then the interest is even more pointed in a specifically human direction. In this case it hardly matters whether the ghosts have an objective existence in order to understand that the governess suffers. It takes no inversion of the tale to see her plight as harrowing and debilitating. Her confusion and desperate attempt to challenge the unknown is even more painful because they involve victimization of children under her charge. The tale does not allow us to determine whether she is correct or incorrect in her suspicions. It simply dramatizes—vividly, in fact—how much the suspicions matter.

James's governess has been the brunt of critical discomfort since Edmund Wilson first posited her victimization of the children and her compromised interest in them and their guardian. Ellis Hansen has observed that this reading, like other seeming alternative ones, all depend on an unassailable notion of childhood innocence:

> In all three approaches to the novella and film—as a ghost story, as a Freudian case study, as a self-conscious meditation on literary ambiguity—the allure of gothic children remains intact. If it is a ghost story, then the ghosts *are fiends who corrupt the children's innocence*. If it is a psychological case study of a paranoid woman, then the governess is *a fiend who corrupts the children's innocence*. If it is an irresolvable exercise in ambiguity, then the naïve reader entertains lecherous fantasies and suspicions resembling those of the *fiends who corrupt the children's innocence*. The predicate is always the same. Innocence was never so vulnerable, yet never so unassailable. It was never so sexy.[5]

The erotics of childhood are wittily suggested in this critical jeu d'esprit, but surely the trope of childhood complicity with adult desire is a familiar one to students of gothic fiction. Hansen's analysis, like so many readings of *The Turn of the Screw,* implies that James's greatest innovation is his insistence on involving children in the haunting. But gothic fiction has dealt in haunted children from the first. Poor Conrad has barely reached puberty when he is crushed by a gigantic helmet in *The Castle of Otranto;* William Beckford's

Vathek focuses on the erotics of childhood, understandably enough for this notorious pederast, and childhood innocence and its (not inevitable) demise are a central theme of the novel; Sophia Lee examines childhood and childhood memories at length in *The Recess;* the children Mary Shelly depicts in *Frankenstein* are haunted by the monstrous; Charlotte Dacre's characters in *Zofloya* begin their rapid decline because of the horrors of childhood; Ann Radcliffe considers her heroines as children and exposes violence upon children; Maria Regina Roche discusses the impossibilities of childhood; and Sheridan LeFanu articulates one of the most memorable hauntings of the nineteenth century when he introduces the eponymous Carmilla into the bedroom of Laura when she is still a little girl. Indeed, the examples are so numerous that one has to consider what sleight of hand led James to claim a distinction of this kind.

Hansen partly answers that question. Late-nineteenth and early-twentieth-century culture needed childhood innocence to fill out a certain kind of self-projection. Hansen adds that critics "scrutinize the children with a mixture of lasciviousness and impunity that is paradigmatic of the modern relation between adults and children: reading as child-loving without end, parental protection as paranoid pedophilia." James's children fall into this description in a way that Beckford's or Mary Shelley's do not, in part because he entered into a negotiation that renders their emerging sexuality as something always already taboo. Surely their "innocence" is the question that obsesses the governess. The ghosts she confronts, that is, are the specters of the possibility that these children are not as innocent as they seem. Their uncanny charm takes on a different, not to say nefarious, quality if the children have been consorting, in the past or in the haunted present, with the transgressive figures of Quint and Miss Jessel.[6]

From the very first the governess is trapped by the awkwardness of her situation at Bly. Unable to turn to her employer for help, she must rely on Mrs. Grose, an illiterate housekeeper; when the house starts to seem haunted, the governess is more and more harrowingly on her own. Having written herself into a romance that centers on her relation to her employer—"She was in love" (103) the narrator admits at the opening of the tale—she has no choice but to eroticize the details of her life at Bly and invest the children with this uncanny and unsettling power. The governess understands the situation as increasingly "queer." After the first encounter with Quint she muses, "Here it was another affair; for many days after, it was a queer affair enough" (149). What she means by "queer" is odd, strange, and uncanny, but as several critics have argued the term could also resonate with a hint of transgressive sexuality.[7] There is a queer mood in *The Turn of the Screw* to the degree that the governess is unable to confront the implications of what is going on around her.

When she talks to Mrs. Grose about their need to work together to protect the children from the ghosts, she makes the specific limits of her ability clear: "What was settled between us, accordingly, that night, was that we thought we might bear things together; and I was not even sure that, in spite of her exemption, it was she who had the best of the burden. I knew at this hour, I think, as well as I knew later what I was capable of meeting to shelter my pupils; but it took me some time to be wholly sure of what my honest ally was prepared for to keep terms with so compromising a contract. I was queer company enough—quite as queer as the company I received" (157).

The governess sees herself as queer because she has lost her footing in this bizarre world. She is not sure of the values that are implicit there, nor is she ready to interpret the goings-on in any way that criticizes her charges. In a sense, her desire to protect them queers her position more than any attack on their sensibilities. She becomes almost obsessed with the terms of their relations, and even their innocence she reads as uncannily complicated: "For if it occurred to me that I might occasionally excite suspicion by the little outbreaks of my sharper passion for them, so too I remember wondering if I mightn't see a queerness in the traceable increase of their own demonstrations" (173). There is something queer about the children, she is saying. There is something queer about their demonstrations of passion for her, and by implication there is something queer about their demonstration of affection for Quint and Jessel. These possibilities are described as queer because they are uncanny in a way the governess cannot fathom. Her tentative desire and frustrating isolation make it less likely that she will understand the erotics of childhood with anything but horror. When the governess confronts Miles about his behavior at school and his ultimate expulsion this motif becomes even more intense. She asks him to explain what happened:

> "Do you mean now—here?"
> "There couldn't be a better place or time." He looked round him uneasily, and I had the rare—oh, the queer!—impression of the very first symptom I had seen in him of the approach of immediate fear. It was as if he was suddenly afraid of me—which struck me indeed as perhaps the best thing to make him. (229)

Even here the governess discovers queerness in her impression of Miles's fear. She invokes queer as a modifier because Mile's fear is not something that she understands. She shifts from announcing a "rare" impression to announcing a queer one. What does that change imply? It seems to me that it articulates her deepest unspoken fear about Miles. She worries about his relation with Quint but does not know how to put it into words. An impression of queerness is the best she can do.

This queerness suffuses the text with a specific uncanniness the governess never fully understands. Her uneasiness fosters queer company; queer impressions; queer looks ("You looked queer," the governess tells Mrs. Grose when she is discussing the letter they received dismissing Miles from school; "I doubt if I looked as queer as you," the housekeeper retorts [171]); and queer elements ("I scanned all the visible shore while Mrs. Grose took again, into the queer element I offered her, one of her plunges of submission" [211]). This disquietude also forces her to act but makes it impossible for her to know how to do so.

Patricia White mentions Freud in her discussion of the film *The Haunting,* inspired by Shirley Jackson's *The Haunting of Hill House:* "Freud's essay on the uncanny draws on the literary gothic, particularly the work of E. T. A. Hoffman. In it he associates the sensation with the etymological overlap between definitions of the uncanny, *das Unheimliche,* and its apparent opposite *das Heimliche* (literally, the homey, the familiar), ultimately identifying this convergence with 'the home of all humans,' the womb. The woman provides the uncanny, her experience remains a shadowy area."[8]

The governess, like White's female spectator, "must undergo a constant process of transformation."[9] In her queer and uncanny world the familiar world of home and childhood is rendered unfamiliar because she cannot be sure that she is seeing what she thinks she sees. The potential "evil" of the children creates this uncanny context. As the governess tries to transform herself in order to come to terms with what is going on around her she is unequal to the demands the house has placed upon her. Like Eleanor Vance in *The Haunting of Hill House,* she finds herself drawn to its eeriness but is afraid of what that says about her.

One of the keys to her uneasiness is concern over what Miles did to be dismissed from school. She worries that his relations with Quint, either those of the past or those of a ghostly present, might have produced a quality in the boy that makes him dangerous to the others at the school, but she never discovers the nature of that behavior. When she confronts Miles, a confrontation that seems to be the cause of Miles's death, she refuses to understand him when he tries to answer her. She is in a realm that challenges all her assumptions, and that makes her react violently. Consider the encounter when she gets Miles to admit some sort of misbehavior at school:

> "What then did you do?"
>
> He looked in vague pain all round the top of the room and drew his breath, two or three times over, as with difficulty. He might have been standing at the bottom of the sea and raising his eyes to some faint green twilight. "Well, I said things."
>
> "Only that?"
>
> "They thought it was enough!"
>
> "To turn you out for?"
>
> Never, truly, had a person 'turned out' shown so little to explain it as this little person! He appeared to weigh my question, but in a manner quite detached and almost helpless. "Well, I suppose I oughtn't."
>
> "But to whom did you say them?"
>
> He evidently tried to remember, but it dropped—he had lost it. "I don't know!"
>
> He almost smiled at me in the desolation of his surrender, which was indeed practically, by this time, so complete that I ought to have left it there. But I was infatuated—I was blind with victory, though even then the very effect that was to have brought him so much nearer was already that of added separation. "Was it to everyone?" I asked.
>
> "No; it was only to— ." But he gave a sick little headshake. "I don't remember their names." (232–33)

Coming as it does right before the tragic conclusion of the tale, the conversation gives crucial insight into what has happened. This key passage manages to amplify the governess's confusion in direct relation to Miles's revelations. Miles is "sick," trapped in the implications of his crime and afraid of what this confrontation will mean, and that causes him to panic. "He might have been standing at the bottom of the sea and raising his eyes to some faint green twilight," an image that suggests compulsion, suffocation, and despair. "Some faint green twilight" is the hope the governess holds out, the hope she will be able to deliver him from his torment whatever it happens to be. But that is precisely what she cannot do. Instead, she turns the casual encounter into a gothic confrontation and forces Miles to confront some truth about himself.

"Saying things" does not seem a terrible transgression to the governess, and she struggles to come to terms with the few details of his confession. She has trouble making sense of it at all. Pushing Miles to give details of the things he

said and the people to whom he said them, the governess finds herself immediately out of her depth in this sea of truth. She seems to have him where she
wants him and thinks she might stop there. But even as she congratulates
herself, she tries to push things further: "But I was infatuated—I was blind
with victory, though even then the very effect that was to have brought him
so much nearer was already that of added separation" (233). That leads to the
final detail that leaves her confused and nearly helpless:

> "Were they then so many?"
> "No—only a few. Those I liked."
> Those he liked? I seemed to float not into clearness, but into a darker obscure,
> and within a minute there had come to me out of my very pity the appalling
> alarm of his being perhaps innocent. It was for the instant confounding and
> bottomless, for if he *were* innocent, what then on earth was *I*? (233)

As the governess floats into "a darker obscure," the source of the queer
uncanniness of the text starts to come clear. Miles is all along suspected of
some kind of unnatural relation with Quint. The governess has considered
the degree to which Miles occupies an unnatural place in her imagination.
She imagines that he could say to her, "'Either you clear up with my guardian the mystery of this interruption of my studies, or you cease to expect me
to lead with you a life that's so unnatural for a boy.' What was so unnatural
for the particular boy I was concerned with was this sudden revelation of a
consciousness and a plan" (197).

It does not take too much imagination to see the relation between Miles
and Quint as an erotic relation. Several critics have suggested this and often
take it for granted.[10] But it may simply be the erotics of language that Quint
has taught the boy. Miles does not say he did things with his schoolmates,
which would hardly have been a surprise. Public schools were a sexual workshop for many young boys and still are. But the difference between mechani-
cal sexual experimentation and "saying things" is profound. If Quint has
taught Miles erotic language—the language of love—such language can
threaten situations that are unemotionally sexual. Is that far-fetched? Well,
imagine if Miles confessed to saying things to little girls whom he "liked."
The erotically transgressive possibilities are immediately obvious. Because
Miles says things to boys he liked, the governess is at a loss. But how could
she not be? She is not prepared to understand Miles's position, nor is she able
to see where his confession will take her. By closing the possibility of hearing
what Miles is trying to say, by feeling lost in the darkness at his clear attempt
to satisfy her request, the governess chooses the haunting rather than the

simple reality of Miles articulating love for his friends. The famous ending of the tale vividly emphasizes this disjunction:

> "Is she *here?*" Miles panted as he caught with his sealed eyed the direction of my words. Then as his strange "she" staggered me and, with a gasp, I echoed it, "Miss Jessel, Miss Jessel!" he with a sudden fury gave me back.
>
> I seized, stupefied, his supposition—some sequel to what we had done to Flora, but this made me only want to show him that it was better still than that. "It's not Miss Jessel! But it's at the window—straight before us. It's *there*—the coward horror, there for the last time!"
>
> At this, after a second in which his head made the movement of a baffled dog's on a scent and then gave a frantic little shake for air and light, he was at me in a white rage, bewildered, glaring vainly over the place and missing wholly, though it now, to my sense, filled the room like the taste of poison, the wide, overwhelming presence. "It's *he?*"
>
> "Peter Quint—you devil!" His face gave again, round the room, its convulsed supplication. "*Where?*"
>
> They are in my ears still, his supreme surrender of the name and his tribute to my devotion. "What does it matter now, my own?—what will he *ever* matter? I have you," I launched at the beast, "but he has lost you for ever!" Then, for the demonstration of my work, "There, *there!*" I said to Miles.
>
> But he had already jerked straight round, stared, glared again, and seen but the quiet day. With the stroke of the loss I was so proud of he uttered the cry of a creature hurled over an abyss, and the grasp with which I recovered him might have been that of catching him in his fall. I caught him, yes, I held him—it may be imagined with what a passion; but at the end of a minute I began to feel what it was truly that I held. We were alone with the quiet day, and his little heart, dispossessed, had stopped." (234–35)

This passage is quoted at length because it unfolds in such fascinating a way and in doing so reveals the misunderstanding that costs Miles his life. The governess insists that Miles sees what she sees, feels what she feels, but it is obvious that he does not. Trapped and compelled as he has been all along, for him the air is empty and the window is blank. Why should Quint as a spectral presence appear to the governess and not to Miles? It may be precisely because the governess fears what Quint represents—adult sexuality, emotional maturity, and queer victimization of a kind she does not understand—but Miles understands the past not as a threat but as an opportunity. He has "said things" because Quint introduced him to a world beyond his years, perhaps, but that does not mean Miles sees any of this as evil. The governess can only imagine evil in such a relationship because her experience of emotional relations is so limited. She clearly prefers the tale of an otherworldly gothic haunting to the brutal reality of boyhood erotics that Miles comes so close to representing. Miles is confused to the point of torment because the governess wants to challenge him with a past that he sees as innocent. He did not say things to torment his friends; he said things because he liked them. Quint has not tormented him; he liked him. And the boy learned from Quint what it means for two males to be attached to each other emotionally. This may be more threatening that any sexual liaison they might have had. In the end, emotional bonds between men, love between men, is what is truly threatening. That kind of love looms up in this final scene, but the governess can see it only as evil. And as evil it has the power to destroy Miles, and that is exactly what it does.

Earlier in the tale the governess confronts Flora over her secret relation with Miss Jessel. In doing so she earns the child's undying hatred. Why would that be? In part the governess is guilty of literalizing a relation that is primarily emotional. Young girls who spend too much time together are hunted down, branded, and exposed.[11] Again the fear seems to be one of the girl's complicity. In the lakeside scene, where Flora plays at the side of the water while "Miss Jessel" glowers from the other side of the lake, the governess sees Jessel as "a figure of quite as unmistakeable horror and evil: a woman in black, pale and dreadful—with such an air also, and such a face!" (164). She feels this horror because her authority is threatened to be sure, but she also feels horror at the possibility that Flora sees and accepts this dark and threatening presence. That defies the governess's primary dictum: "I was there to protect and defend the little creatures in the world the most bereaved and the most loveable, the appeal of whose helplessness had become only too explicit, a deep, a constant ache of one's own committed heart" (161).

The governess's relation to the children is queer because she never fully admits the implicit erotics of her intense voyeuristic pleasure in their lives. Nor can she directly confront the erotic context of her original employment. She chooses to see ghosts—she is haunted, that is—because she is unwilling to confront the complex erotics of her position. She imagines these alternative competing sexual liaisons because they exonerate her in some way. At the same time, the possibility of what she has imagined haunts her. Rather than confront it directly, though, for her it is simply "queer." What torments her is being confronted by a world that exposes her limitations. As her anxiety grows so does the tension in the tale. "If he *were* innocent, what then on earth was *I*?" (233) is the story's central anxiety. What would constitute innocence in the world that James has described? It is impossible to tell. What could be more harrowing than that? And what could more clearly represent the basic tropes of twentieth-century psychoanalysis?

Shirley Jackson's *The Haunting of Hill House* tells a similar tale of a young single woman and the children who haunt her. In this case the children are ghosts in Hill House, the "deranged house" (70) in which Dr. Montague and his three assistants have gathered to pursue the unknown.[12] Eleanor Vance is central among those assistants. The reader gets to know her inner life directly and to experience Hill House primarily from her perspective. Like James's governess at Bly, Eleanor is out of her depth in Hill House, and the dwelling seems determined to undermine her sense of self and challenge her deepest fears. As the novel develops, these fears are articulated in three ways: the first is Eleanor's attraction to Theodora, the fashionable and self-possessed lesbian who has been invited to Hill House on account of her powers or ESP; the second is Eleanor's guilt over her mother's death; and the third is her identification with the house and the horrors that it reveals.

Theodora is as different from Eleanor as she could be: "Duty and conscience were, for Theodora, attributes which belonged properly to the Girl Scouts. Theodora's world was one of delight and soft colors" (8). Theo attracts Eleanor from the moment they meet. Just after unpacking, as they are dressing to spend some time outdoors, "Theodora came through the bathroom door into Eleanor's room; she is lovely, Eleanor thought, turning to look; I wish I were lovely. Theodora was wearing a vivid yellow shirt, and Eleanor laughed and said, 'You bring more light into this room than the window'" (47). Eleanor's attraction to Theodora's brightness often includes this hint of self-denigration and self-effacement. Part of the attraction she feels is to the difference between them. Theodora is beautiful, well-dressed, and self-assured, all things that suggest an ability Eleanor feels she lacks. Eleanor does not feel beautiful or self-assured, to say the least, and her clothes are an embarrassment to her. Her deficiencies are glaring, at least to herself, and at moments like these a kind of erotic relation emerges from the space between herself and Theodora. Eleanor turns the seemingly playful difference violently against herself as the novel proceeds.

Dr. Montague, the vague scholar of the paranormal, has rented the house and assembled the company. Luke Sanderson, a representative of the family that owns the house, with Eleanor and Theodora makes up the little group. Dr. Montague is an avuncular presence throughout. Making notes and trying to look at the larger picture, he keeps his distance from the other three. Young Luke, however, is a ladies' man, and he creates an odd dynamic by playing on the affections of both Eleanor and Theodora. The erotic dynamic among

Luke, Theodora, and Eleanor is a central feature of the narrative, but Luke's key function is to create tension between the women, which he manages to do without really trying.

The reader never gets any more than Eleanor's impressions of Theodora's feelings toward her. Eleanor's attraction is immediate and vivid: "she was always shy with strangers, awkward and timid, and yet had come in no more than half an hour to think of Theodora as close and vital, someone whose anger would be frightening" (49). At times, Theodora is sensitive and caring, and at others she is ruthless. In a scene just after Eleanor imagines Theodora's anger she is treated sweetly and Theodora seems to care about her: "Eleanor turned and stared, and then saw amusement on her face and thought, She's much braver than I am. Unexpectedly—although it was later to become a familiar note, a recognizable attribute of what was to mean 'Theodora' in Eleanor's mind—Theodora caught at Eleanor's thought, and answered her. 'Don't be so afraid all the time,' she said as she reached out to touch Eleanor's cheek with one finger. 'We never know where our courage is coming from'" (50). This intriguing scene measures the women's mutual desire in terms of Eleanor's fear and endless self-questioning. Theodora seems to understand in a way that allows her to care for her friend and offer her support. Eleanor's vulnerability is almost attractive to Theodora, at least it becomes the basis of their intimacy in this way. By reaching out to touch Eleanor's cheek, moreover, Theodora tries to instill some of her personal strength on the weak and soon-to-be suffering Eleanor.

This intimacy is repeated in the company of their two companions and in private moments. Sometimes Eleanor gets it wrong: "Theodora had abandoned any attempt at a chair and had put herself down on the hearthrug, cross-legged and drowsy. Eleanor, wanting to sit on the hearthrug beside her, had not thought of it in time and had condemned herself to one of the slippery chairs, unwilling now to attract attention by moving and getting herself awkwardly down onto the floor" (68). But at other times she and Theodora seem perfectly in tune.

"I went to private school where they made me learn to curtsy."

"I always had colds all winter long. My mother made me wear woolen stockings."

"*My* mother made my brother take me to dances, and I used to curtsy like mad. My brother still hates me."

"I fell down during the graduation procession."

"I forgot my lines in the operetta."

"I used to write poetry."

"Yes," Theodora said, "I'm positive we're cousins." (53–54)

The ease with which Eleanor and Theodora converse and share details of the past, the intimacy of the revelations, and the painful memories they reveal all suggest that the women want to find some common ground on which they may be able to construct an intimacy in which they can believe. The scene takes place before the women have met the others, and as a result it places them in a special relation to each other that continues throughout the novel. They are always aware of each other and can commune without speaking in the social setting as well as the paranormal one. The two are often the same. Even at this moment, for instance, they are threatened by the unknown. No sooner do they reach out to each other but they notice something odd move across the grass. They are momentarily "frozen, shoulders pressed together." Their fear of something they cannot see punctuates this moment of intimacy with the threat of the unknown. Indeed, the closer the two women move to one another, the more threatening the house becomes.

The growing intimacy between the women is hinted even at moments when they seem violently at odds. After the words "HELP ELEANOR COME HOME" (146) are found scrawled on the hallway walls, for instance, Eleanor nearly (and quite understandably) breaks down. Theodora taunts and teases her ("Maybe you wrote it yourself," [147]) until Eleanor retorts violently, "Maybe it was only addressed to me because no possible appeal for help could get through that iron selfishness of yours; maybe I might have more sympathy and understanding in one minute than—" (147). It is a tense moment until it becomes clear that Theodora's intention was to create an angry response in Eleanor in order to expel her fear. Everyone seems able to laugh off the tension—all, that is, except Eleanor, who is hurt and confused. The brutal truths used here are painful, to be sure, but they are couched in the care that Theodora has taken all along. Eleanor's fear of her friend seems justified at first, and it is difficult for Eleanor to get beyond that.

Much later, after they have endured a great deal, Theodora and Eleanor meet and almost break through the difficulties that surround them:

"Theo," Eleanor said awkwardly, "I'm no good at talking to people and saying things."

Theodora laughed. "What *are* you good at?" she demanded. "Running away?"

Nothing irrevocable had yet been spoken, but there was only the basest margin of safety left them; each of them moving delicately along the outskirts of an open question, and once spoken, such a question—as "Do you love me?"—could never be answered or forgotten. They walked slowly, meditating, wondering, and the path sloped down from their feet and they followed, walking side by side in the most extreme intimacy of expectation; their feinting and hesitation done with, they could only await passively for resolution. Each knew, almost within a breath, what the other was thinking and wanting to say; each of them almost wept for the other. They perceived at the same moment the change in the path and each knew then the other's knowledge of it; Theodora took Eleanor's arm and, ahead of them the path widened and blackened and curved. (174–75)

In the midst of the horrors of Hill House these women find each other. This scene makes it seem as if they are on the verge of expressing mutual love. The emphasis on expectation and knowledge, on meditation and meaning, and on walking in tandem on a path in the woods are all elements that suggest desire thwarted by circumstance, an intimacy that would be realized were it not for other developments that seem determined to destroy it. "Do you love me?" are the words never spoken. Hill House ensures that they are not.[13]

Hill House does so, it seems, by revealing the deeply buried guilt Eleanor feels about her mother's death. At the opening of the novel the reader is told that Eleanor had lived with her mother and cared for her until the older woman's death. The connection between that event and the horrors of Hill House becomes apparent the first time the group goes exploring. Dr. Montague stops them at the front door to show them the library that opens off the front hall: "Then the Doctor said, 'Now *here* is something none of you anticipated,' and he opened a small door tucked in beside the tall front door and stood back, smiling. 'The library,' he said, 'in the tower.' 'I can't go in there,' Eleanor said, surprising herself, but she could not. She backed away, overwhelmed with the cold air of mold and earth which rushed at her. 'My mother—' she said, not knowing what she wanted to tell them, and pressed herself against the wall" (163). Whether her sense of loss, her anger, her unresolved feelings about the death, or her fear of her mother or her mother's corpse, something causes Eleanor to connect the graveyard smell with the mother. Readers familiar with gothic fiction are forced to ask whether the mother is walled up in the house in some literal or figural way.

When supernatural events start to enliven things even further, which happens most dramatically when something starts pounding on all the bedroom doors in the middle of the night, these fears become more vividly realized. When Eleanor first hears the knocking and someone calling her name she assumes that it is her mother calling:

"Coming, mother, coming," Eleanor said, fumbling for the light. "It's all right, I'm coming." *Eleanor,* she heard, *Eleanor.* "Coming, coming," she shouted irritably, "just a *minute,* I'm *coming.*"
"Eleanor?"
Then she thought, with a crashing shock which brought her awake, cold and shivering, out of bed and awake: *I am in Hill House.*
"What?" she cried out, "What? Theodora?"
"Eleanor? In here." . . .
"Something is knocking on the doors," Theodora said in a tone of pure rationality.
"That's all. And it's down near the other end of the hall. Luke and the doctor are probably there already, to see what is going on." Not at all like my mother knocking on the wall. I was dreaming again. (127–28)

Eleanor connects the banging to her mother's knock and then feels that the fear she experiences is something alive. What she feels so intensely, however, is guilt that her mother's death has bequeathed her. The connection between Theodora and her mother is subtle but unmistakable. At first she thinks it is her mother when it is actually Theodora calling; even when she enters Theodora's room she is not sure what she is doing there. At the same time the women are thrown together violently to experience the banging, and as at other horrifying moments in the book they remain calm and in close touch.

Later, Eleanor expresses guilt about her mother more or less openly: "'It was my fault my mother died,' Eleanor said. 'She knocked on the wall and called me and called me and I never woke up. I ought to have brought her the medicine; I always did before. But this time she called me and I never woke up.' 'You should have forgotten all that by now,' Theodora said. 'I've wondered ever since if I did wake up. If I did wake up and hear her, and if I just went back to sleep. It would have been easy, and I've wondered about it'" (212). One source of the haunting of Hill House, then, is this tormenting guilt about her mother's death. Eleanor imagines this moment of transgression almost as if she needs guilt to give meaning to her existence.

When Mrs. Montague arrives to prepare everyone for communing with spirits, the planchette she uses spells out "Eleanor come home." Mrs. Montague is certain that she is hearing from a nun who must have been connected with Hill House, someone trapped in the house: "'I daresay she was walled up alive,' Mrs. Montague said. 'The nun I mean. They always did that, you know. You've no idea the messages I've gotten from nuns walled up alive'" (189). Invoking that same gothic tradition that James does in *The Turn of the*

Screw, in other words, Mrs. Montague understands what kinds of mysteries haunt the female imagination. The connection between a nun walled up alive and the messages to Eleanor suggest that the house calls her out of a private guilt and into itself.

Eleanor feels she is becoming part of the house—or the house is becoming part of her—from the beginning of her sojourn there. "I don't think we could leave now if we wanted to" she tells the group after their first conversation about the history of the house (75). Later, when she hears that two young girls grew up in the house, she has a hard time imagining children there. But her name is written on the wall and appears in other ways as well, so she feels the house is calling out to her. The most dramatic instance occurs when Eleanor finds her name splashed in blood on Theodora's bedroom walls and clothes:

> Moving quickly, Eleanor ran into the hall and to Theodora's doorway, to stop aghast, looking over Theodora's shoulder. "What *is* it," she whispered.
> "What does it *look* like, you fool?"
> And I won't forgive her *that,* either, Eleanor thought concretely through her bewilderment. "It looks like paint," she said hesitantly. "Except the smell is awful."
> "It's blood," said Theodora with finality. She clung to the door, swaying as the door moved, staring. "Blood," she said, "All over. Do you see it?" (153)

Soon after this first encounter, when Dr. Montague and Luke have joined them, they notice writing on the wall: "All of them stood in silence for a moment and looked at HELP ELEANOR COME HOME ELEANOR written in shaky red letters on the wallpaper over Theodora's bed. . . . The smell was atrocious, and the writing on the wall had dripped and splattered. There was a line of drops from the wall to the wardrobe—perhaps that was what had first turned Theodora's attention that way—and a great irregular stain on the green rug" (155). As gruesome as any image in this novel, this blood-spattered room suggests the violence of homicidal rage that smolders beneath the surface of relations here. Eleanor does not perhaps want to spatter Theodora's blood on the walls, but she does let jealousy and desire torment her to excess. Moreover, her relation to her mother and her sister was one of hatred: "Eleanor Vance was thirty-two years old when she came to Hill House. The only person in the world she genuinely hated, now that her mother was dead, was her sister. She disliked her brother-in-law and her five-year-old niece, and she had no friends" (6). Perhaps the familial intimacy of the plea for her return is written in blood because that is what the family represents to her. She thought that Hill House was an escape from that world, but it seems more and more to be a return to it.

In *Powers of Horror* Julia Kristeva describes this state as abjection, a term that describes Eleanor's demeanor. For Kristeva, "There looms, within abjection, one of those violent, dark revolts of being, directed against a threat that seems to emanate from an exorbitant outside or inside, ejected beyond the scope of the possible, the tolerable, the thinkable. It lies there, quite close, but it cannot be assimilated. It beseeches, it worries, it fascinates desire."[14] Here the house beseeches and worries and fascinates. It creates an abjection into which Eleanor fits like hand in glove. As the house calls to Eleanor she feels that she must answer:

> "Those letters spelled out *my* name, and none of you know what that feels like—it's so *familiar*." And she gestured to them almost in appeal. "Try to *see*," she said. "It's my own dear name, and it belongs to me, and something is using it and writing it and calling me with it and my own *name*. . . ." She stopped and said, looking from one of them to another, even down onto Theodora's face looking up at her, "Look. There's only one of me, and it's all I've got. I *hate* seeing myself dissolve and slip and separate so that I am living in one half, my mind, and I see the other half of me helpless and frantic and driven and I can't stop it, but I know I'm not really going to be hurt and yet time is so long and even a second goes on and on and I could stand any of it if only I could surrender— ."
> "*Surrender?*" said the doctor sharply, and Eleanor stared.
> "Surrender?" Luke repeated.
> "I don't know," Eleanor said, perplexed. I was just talking along, she told herself, I was saying something—what was I just saying? (160)

Eleanor wants to surrender to the house because she thinks she has no choice. She gives in to the voices calling her because she feels in her heart that she does not deserve the freedom she has started to feel. In this sense she is like James's governess and Miles or Flora. She is the one who is afraid of the implications of her desire. She both feels the desire and knows that she must stop doing so. A key moment in this transition is when Eleanor thinks it is Theodora's hand she grips as they hear voices in the night:

> Eleanor took a breath, wondering if she could speak now, and then she heard a little soft cry which broke her heart, a little infinitely sad cry, a little sweet moan of wild sadness. It is a *child,* she thought with disbelief, a child is crying somewhere, and then, upon that thought, came the wild shrieking voice she had never heard before and yet knew she had heard it in her nightmares. . . .

Now, Eleanor thought, perceiving that she was lying sideways on the bed
in black darkness, holding with both hands to Theodora's hand, holding so
tight that she could feel the fine bones of Theodora's fingers, now, I will not
endure this. They think to scare me. Well, they have. I am scared, but more
than that, I am a person, I am human. I am a walking reasoning humorous
human being and I will take a lot from this lunatic filthy house but I will not
go along with hurting a child, no, I will not; I will by God get my mouth to
open right now and I will yell I will I will yell "STOP IT," she shouted, and
the lights were on the way they had left them and Theodora was sitting up in
bed, startled and disheveled.

"What?" Theodora was saying. "What, Nell? What?"

"Good God," Eleanor said, flinging herself out of bed and across the room
to stand shuddering in a corner, "God God—whose hand was I holding?"
(162–63)

The child's voice seems to emerge from Eleanor's imagination in some way.
The familiar nightmare shrieking she hears seems to be something from her
own past as well. Is the suffering child herself in some way? Does she hear
the cry of a solitary child in pain because that is what she feels? These questions pale beside the central question that Eleanor asks, Whose hand was she
holding? The point seems to be that although she imagines she is gripping
Theodora tightly, she is actually gripping something out of the nightmare
of confused identity that the house has become for her. In other words, the
house emerges from her consciousness (subconscious?) to substitute itself as
an object of desire and lure her to her demise. Eleanor finds herself at home
because her repressed past returns in vivid clarity.

This end takes place in two parts. In the first, Eleanor sneaks out of her
room at night and makes her way down to the library and up the rickety
stairs to the top of the tower. Just before she makes her playful dash through
the house she hears the sound of children singing at their games: "Go walking through the valley. . . . Go in and out the windows. . . . Go forth and face
your lover, / As we have done before" (225–26). It is almost in the spirit of
this children's game that she runs around the dark house, seeking her mother
and avoiding her friends as they desperately search for her. "I have broken
the spell of Hill House," she tells herself, "and somehow come inside" (232).
When they finally find her at the top of the tower they panic, and as Luke
climbs up to help her down there is general disapproval of her behavior.

When the next morning she is told to go home, she panics. Not wanting
to leave, she pleads with the doctor to allow her stay: "The doctor took her
by the arm and, with Luke beside her, led her to the car and opened the door

for her. The carton was still on the back seat, her suitcase was on the floor, her coat and pocketbook on the seat; Luke had left the motor running. 'Doctor,' Eleanor said, clutching at him, 'Doctor.' 'I'm sorry,' he said. 'Good-bye.' 'You can't just *make* me go,' she said wildly. 'You *brought* me here'" (243). Her need to stay at Hill House is expressed by her desperate and successful attempt to crash her car into a tree along the drive and so kill herself. Even at the end, however, she is confused between the house and her need to become part of it and her new friends and her emotional and erotic attachment to them: "In the unending, crashing second before the car hurled into the tree, she thought clearly, *Why* am I doing this? Why am I doing this? Why don't they stop me?" (245–46).

The friends do not rush out to stop Eleanor because they know she does not belong in their world. Her solipsistic experience is brought into the fulfillment that the house has promised from the first. Eleanor accepts the hysteria that friends and family have assumed. At Hill House she is able to give it form. In hurtling herself at the tree she accepts what it means. Desire, for Eleanor, is nothing more than death.

The first two of Foucault's "four great strategic unities"—"1. *A hysterization of women's bodies*" and "2. *A pedagogization of children's sex*"—come into vivid focus here.[15] *The Turn of the Screw* and *The Haunting of Hill House* both reveal the relation between the first and second "unities" Foucault describes and the degree to which hysteria and gender emerge naturally from gothic works like these. Gothic fiction, in other words, participates in the formation of "specific mechanisms of knowledge and power." Or perhaps it is more correct to say that gothic fiction sees through these mechanisms and invokes them for affective force at the same time that it exposes their limitations.

The Turn of the Screw and *The Haunting of Hill House* suggest that gothic novelists were at least as adept as Freud at exposing the workings of hysterical response. Indeed, in some ways the novelists make the cultural terms of female victimization clearer than Freud did. James's governess and Jackson's Eleanor Vance are victims because they are put in situations that are outside of their control. The world of desire confounds them. Abject and isolated, they confront the darkness that haunts them, but in the end it consumes them. They cannot accept intimacy because intimacy is exactly what haunts them in the first place. In that sense they each understand intimacy as something that threatens to destroy them. Had Freud understood that, the history of twentieth-century psychiatric treatment might have been different. The almost overly familiar gothic trope of the persecuted female imbues these outwardly neurotic women with a depth and a complexity they would otherwise lack.

These are not "case studies" because both fictions invoke the richness of the gothic tradition, and in doing so they tell a more complex story than any that emerges from strict psychosexology. Both James and Jackson use the energy of the gothic tradition to confront their heroines with a world beyond themselves. The results are rich because so many gothic heroines have paved the way for these intrepid heroines. The novelists invoke contemporary psychological interpretations of the neurotic mind, and they also invoke a tradition that goes deeper than twentieth-century psychology could ever allow itself to go.

8

"Queerer Knowledge":
Lambert Strether and Tom Ripley

Early in Patricia Highsmith's *The Talented Mr. Ripley,* the title character is recommended to read "a certain book by Henry James."[1] That the book in question is *The Ambassadors* only becomes clear as Tom decides to look for it once he is onboard the *Queen Mary* in the first-class cabin that his sponsors, the Greenleafs, who have sent him to Europe looking for their son, have provided:

> "Have you Henry James' *The Ambassadors?* Tom asked the officer in charge of the first-class library. The book is not on the shelf.
> "I'm sorry, we haven't sir," said the officer.
> Tom was disappointed. It was the book Mr. Greenleaf had asked him to read. Tom felt he ought to read it. He went to the cabin-class library. He found the book on the shelf, but when he started to check it out and gave his cabin number, the attendant told him sorry, that first-class passengers were not allowed to take books from the cabin-class library. Tom had been afraid of that. He put the book back docilely, though it would have been easy, so easy, to make a pass at the shelf and slip the book under his jacket. (35)

Highsmith uses this scene to make an elaborate comment on Tom's class transgression. He seems to have ascended to the point that he has lost touch with material that could help him understand himself. He also seems to have moved into a world that cannot be bothered with the narrative complexities and high moral tone of Jamesian narrative. Perhaps the novel is marked, as Tom is later, as "bourgeois." *The Ambassadors* is, in any case, a strange title for Mr. Greenleaf to suggest. It tells, of course, an elaborate tale of the personal crisis that besets a middle-aged New Englander when he goes to Paris on a mission to bring a young man home to take up his responsibilities in the family business. That the hero, Lambert Strether, fails in his mission, fails so spectacularly that people at home have to send another group to take over the effort, is not the only reason Mr. Greenleaf's suggestion might seem odd. Another is the novel's insistently oblique take on issues that Mr. Greenleaf, at least, sees as tediously straightforward.

The Ambassadors is the queerest of James's novels. Strether finds himself in less and less secure circumstances, never sure where he stands or what he perceives, and the narrator finds that "queer" is the only term that captures this situation. He uses the term as a kind of mantra that accompanies Strether's gradual transformation, and it always resonates with uncanny significance. What is queer for Strether is his inability to control what is going on around him, the increasing sense that he is beginning to understand himself in a completely new way, and the transformation he feels in his response to people and events. In all of these experiences Strether is in confrontation with himself, and his ghosts loom in the soft Parisian twilight to challenge and undermine his sense of self-possession. What he sees so deeply affects Strether that he often seems utterly compromised and completely lost. At a climactic moment in the tale he says as much to his nemesis Sarah Pocock, who has come to pick up the pieces: "Everything has come as a sort of indistinguishable part of everything else. Your coming out belonged to my having come before you, and my having come was a result of our general state of mind. Our general state of mind had proceeded, on its side, from our queer ignorance, our queer misconceptions and confusions—from which, since then, an inexorable tide of light seems to have floated us into our perhaps still queerer knowledge."[2]

If the eerie darkness of ignorance ("queer ignorance") threatens him with a kind of psychological dis-ease, the glaring light of knowledge ("queerer knowledge") threatens even more. Strether's sense of his queer experience depends on this figure of collapse—"everything has come as a sort of indistinguishable part of everything else"—because his sense of proportion and powers of discrimination have been sacrificed in Paris to a sense of unlimited possibility. The quest for knowledge from a state of queer ignorance leads to awareness that knowledge itself is queer or "still queerer" as Strether would have it. The experience of Paris has suspended him from the world he knew in Woollett, Massachusetts, and for a long time he is not sure what it has put in place of that world.

That Paris—Europe, more generally—changes Strether utterly is one of the most insistent points of the novel. That this change has always to do with Chadwick Newsome and Strether's relation to Chad is also clear. That this relation is so intense as to seem almost like a haunting—the young man haunts the older one in the way a later hero is haunted to his death in Venice—is the queerer knowledge that Strether finally reaches. Its uncanny resolution, that is, puts Strether in possession of knowledge that finally dispossesses him and leaves him more than ever alone.

In *Epistemology of the Closet,* Eve Kosofsky Sedgwick pays only passing attention to *The Ambassadors,* choosing instead to focus on James's "The Beast in the Jungle," which was published in the next year. Her comments, nevertheless, have salience here. Discussing that tale, Sedgwick notes "the possibility of an embodied male-homosexual thematics [which] has . . . a precisely liminal presence. It is present as a—as a very particular, historicized—thematics of absence, and specifically the absence of speech. The first (in some ways the only) thing we learn about John Marcher is that he has a 'secret,' . . . a destiny, a something unknown in his future. . . . I would argue that to the extent that Marcher's secret has *a* content, that content is homosexual."[3]

Sedgwick's elaboration of these remarks helps rectify a long-standing critical silence on the issue of homosexuality in James. "For John Marcher," she observes, "the future secret—the secret of his hidden fate—importantly includes, though it is not necessarily limited to, the possibility of something homosexual. For *Marcher,* the presence or possibility of a homosexual meaning attached to the inner, the future, secret has exactly the reifying, totalizing, and blinding effect we described earlier in regard to the phenomenon of the Unspeakable."[4] Sedgwick is surely right to cast her observations in these terms, and her analysis of "The Beast in the Jungle" helps to answer some of the questions that have always surrounded the tale. That James was attentive to such concerns is clear in both his letters and his biography, but it is even more obvious in his fiction. The possibility of a "homosexual content" in works like "The Pupil" and *The Bostonians* is obvious. Less obvious, perhaps, is how *The Ambassadors* is structured similarly.

Strether's epiphany includes an even richer articulation of the "homosexual" possibility. The novel as a whole makes such an important point about the exigencies of male-male desire that to ignore it is to deprive twentieth-century gay culture of one of its foundational works. Of course, James would not have understood the language of homo/heterosexuality as readily as later generations. For him, a model of heightened sensitivity, feminine taste, and other signs of "inversion" would have typified his sexually indeterminate hero.[5] James is interested in the interior workings of this highly sensitive individual. The dynamic of his sensory responses singles him out as the special Jamesian type.

Sedgwick makes it clear that Strether is historically placed in a position that makes "newly formulated" terms of identification particularly revealing:

> To inscribe that vulgar classification supposedly derived from Freud on what was arguably the moment of the worldview and social constitution that he codified would hardly be enlightening. Still the newly formulated and stressed "universal" imperative/prohibition attached to male homosocial desire . . . required, of course, further embodiment and specification in new taxonomies of personality and character. These taxonomies would mediate between the supposedly classless, "personal" entities of the ideological fictions and the particular, class-specified, economically inscribed lives that they influenced; and at the same time, the plethoric and apparently comprehensive plurality of the taxonomies occluded, through the illusion of choice, the double bind that structured them all.[6]

Strether finds himself in this double bind as the narrative proceeds. It is the measure of his queer experience and the terms of the situation from which he can never extricate himself. It functions like a "closet," to be sure, but it is a closet that Strether feels he has learned to escape. Whether "homosexual," invert, or, as the garden imagery might suggest, a pansy, Strether is caught in the double bind that makes the desires he feels both impossible to resist and impossible to realize. He is caught, that is, between recognizing what he really wants and knowing that he can never achieve it. This is the uncanny, the queerer knowledge that he finally achieves.

When, some time before the scene in Gloriani's garden, which James makes central to his hero's development, Strether is wandering around Paris—the city itself represents a danger to him ("His greatest uneasiness seemed to peep at him out of the imminent impression that almost any acceptance of Paris might give one's authority away" [118])—he finds himself in front of "Chad's very house":

> High broad clear—he was expert enough to make out in a moment that it was admirably built—it fairly embarrassed our friend by the quality that, as he would have said, "sprang" on him. He had struck off the fancy that it might, as a preliminary, be of service to him to be seen, by a happy accident, from the third-story windows, which took all the March sun, but of what service was it to find himself making out after a moment that the quality "sprung," the quality produced by measure and balance, the fine relation of part to part and space to space, was probably—aided by the presence of ornament

LAMBERT STRETHER AND TOM RIPLEY · 155

as positive as it was discreet, and by the complexion of the stone, a cold fair grey, warmed and polished little by life—neither more nor less than a case of distinction, such a case as he could only feel unexpectedly as a sort of delivered challenge? Meanwhile, however, the chance he had allowed for—the chance of being seen in time from the balcony—had become a fact. Two or three of the windows stood open to the violet air; and before Strether had cut the knot by crossing, a young man had come out and looked about him, and lighted a cigarette and tossed the match over, and then, resting on the rail, had given himself up to watching the life below while he smoked. His arrival contributed, in its order, to keeping Strether in position; the result of which in turn was that Strether soon felt himself noticed. The young man began to look at him as in acknowledgement of his being himself in observation. (124)

This encounter, first with the house and then with the young man on the balcony—not Chad but his friend, Little Bilham—hints at all the loss, the gaping regret, that Strether is later to articulate ecstatically in Gloriani's garden. Here, the facade and the young man work together to cast their spell. Strether "feels" that he is being noticed before he sees the man above him. The sense that at this moment Strether is being given the answer to a question he has not known how to ask electrifies the scene. His queer uneasiness begins to have content. Paris and the "high broad clear" facade together create the perfect mood in which the young man can provide the answer to questions Strether has been asking, questions about what he risks in letting himself loose in Paris.

For Eric Haralson, "*The Ambassadors* both reflects and confronts the power of the modern sex/gender system in prescriptions and expectations for masculine performance."[7] The fact that Strether feels what he feels in this scene is a measure of the anxieties of masculine performance. In letting himself respond aesthetically, emotionally, and erotically to the scene before him, he takes a step away from Woollett and its values. It is a step that he will never retrace. He knows that as he moves toward the building, and he expresses it as a conflict between his new, young man and his older, old one: "It came to pass before he moved that Waymarsh, and Waymarsh alone, Waymarsh not only undiluted but positively strengthened, struck him as the present alternative to the young man in the balcony. When he did move it was fairly to escape that alternative. Taking his way over the street at last and passing though the *porte-cochère* of the house was like consciously leaving Waymarsh out" (125).

Waymarsh, a friend from Milrose, Connecticut, whose "sacred rage" (85) Strether repeatedly remarks, encounters Europe as an "ordeal" (71) and seems placed to threaten Strether with the moral purpose of Woollett in general and Mrs. Newsome in particular. And well he might, for Mrs. Newsome is not only the mother of the young Chad whom Strether has been sent off to fetch but also she is Strether's fiancée, his own wife and son having long since died ("He had married, in the far-away years, so young as to have missed the time natural in Boston for taking girls to the Museum; and it was absolutely true of him that—even after the close of the period of conscious detachment occupying the centre of his life, the grey middle desert of the two deaths, that of his wife and that, ten years later, of his boy—he had never taken anyone anywhere" [91]).

"Poor Strether had at this very moment," the narrator notes, "to recognize the truth that wherever one paused in Paris the imagination reacted before one could stop it" (123). This seems especially true as he approaches the figure of Chad, the quasi-prodigal son whom he has been sent forth to gather back into the American family and American business. Even before he meets him, however, he seems intrigued in a more intense way than his simple charge warrants. After he returns from his visit to the apartment on the Boulevard Malesherbes—the street name suggests another garden, in a sense, but this one vaguely threatening, more like Rappaccini's garden than Gloriani's—he reports:

> "I found his friend in fact there keeping the place warm, as he called it, for him; Chad himself being, as appears, in the south. . . . I might, you see, perfectly have waited a week; might have beaten a retreat; I did the opposite; I stayed, I dawdled, I trifled; above all I looked round. I saw, in fine; and—I don't know what to call it—I sniffed. It's a detail, but it's as if there was something—something very good—*to* sniff."
>
> Waymarsh's face had shown his friend an attention apparently so remote that the latter was slightly surprised to find it at this point abreast with him. "Do you mean a smell? What of?"
>
> "A charming scent. But I don't know."
>
> Waymarsh gave an inferential grunt. "Does he live there with a woman?"
> (130–31)

Strether's fascination with Chad takes on an almost fetishistic quality here, and Waymarsh's response, as if the act of sniffing around implies the presence of a female, suggests the reductive limitations of the New England view. The fact that Waymarsh is at least partly right—a woman involved, even if she doesn't live with Chad—is at this juncture beside the point. For what fascinates Strether, what he sniffs around to discover, is the transformation in Chad himself. ("The phenomenon that had suddenly sat down there with him was a phenomenon of change so complete that his imagination, had it worked so beforehand, felt itself, in the connexion, without margin or allowance. It had faced every contingency but that Chad should not *be* Chad, and this was what it now had to face with a mere strained smile and an uncomfortable flush" [154].)

The key figure in Chad's transformation is of course Madame de Vionnet, with whom Chad is involved in what Strether takes to be a "virtuous" relation (263). Strether likes her on their first meeting at Gloriani's party, and he grows to respect and value her as he gets to know her better. He is mesmerized by the changes she has wrought in Chad and feels devoted to her cause as a result. Strether's close female friend, Maria Gostrey, has helped him articulate this position: "Don't consider her, don't judge her at all in herself. Consider her and judge her only in Chad" (180). Strether does that, ecstatically, and as a result has nothing but appreciation for her effects.

A sense of the effect that Madame de Vionnet has on Chad causes the older man to reverse his position and urge the younger to stay in Paris. Chad meets with Strether and tells him that he is ready to leave, just after the latter has heard that another group is en route from Massachusetts: Chad's older sister Sarah Pocock, Sarah's husband Jim, and Jim's sister Mamie:

> Strether debated; he took another turn. "This last month I've been awaiting, I think, more than anything else, the message I have here."
> "You mean you've been afraid of it?" [Chad asks.]
> "Well, I was doing my business in my own way. And I suppose your present announcement isn't merely the result of your sense of what I've expected. . . ." [he then indirectly alludes to Madame de Vionnet].
> He had met again his companion's sufficiently searching look. "Are you tired of her?"
> Chad gave him in reply to this, with a movement of the head, the strangest slow smile he had ever had from him. "Never."
> It had immediately on Strether's imagination, so deep and soft an effect that our friend could only keep it before him. "Never?"
> "Never," Chad obligingly and serenely repeated.
> It made his companion take several more steps. "Then *you're* not afraid."
> "Afraid to go?"
> Strether pulled up again. "Afraid to stay."
> The young man looked brightly amazed. "You want me now to 'stay'?"
> (291)

It is hard to imagine a more intimate scene between the two men. They talk about Madame de Vionnet, of course, but she remains curiously absent from direct discourse. Instead, Strether watches Chad closely, notes his "deep and soft" effect, appreciates his comments as "serene," and challenges his young friend to stay in Paris. When Chad later asks more directly, "How much longer?" Strether responds, "Well, till I make you a sign. I can't myself, you know, at the best, or at the worst, stay for ever" (293). In effect, Strether wants Chad to stay only because he is so fascinated with the affairs of the younger man. He loves him, to be sure, and it seems that in scenes like these he starts to express his love more directly. It is not a possessive, destructive love, however, it is a love of admiration, appreciation, and wonder. "'You feel,' Chad asked in a tone of his own, 'the charm of life over here?' 'Immensely.' Strether faced it. 'You've helped me so to feel it that that surely needn't surprise you'" (293–94).

When the Pococks arrive in Paris they directly challenge Strether's author-ity and undermine his relation with his friends in Woollett. But the "queer truth" that strikes Strether—of "his having given from the first so much . . . and got so little" (333)—convinces him that he has moved beyond them, both in his devotion to the changed Chad, whom they officially deplore, and his appreciation of the woman they see as not "even an apology for a decent woman" (419). After his dramatic break with Sarah Pocock, Strether turns to Chad for reassurance and support. He visits the apartment on the Boulevard Malesherbes late one night and is left alone by the servant. "Strether found himself in possession as he never yet had been; he had been there alone, . . . but never at the witching hour and never with a relish quite so much like pang" (426–27). He wanders through the rooms and tries to confront himself with his failure. "He felt, strangely, as sad as if he had come for some wrong and yet as excited as if he had come from some freedom. . . . This was what it became for him at this singular time, the youth he had long ago missed—a queer concrete presence, full of mystery, yet full of reality, which he could handle, taste, smell, the deep breathing of which he could positively hear" (426).

Strether's elegiac mood, his emphasis on loss—lost youth, lost experi-ence—takes on special significance in this setting at this hour. The "queer concrete presence" that he evokes is the self he has never been and never allowed himself to be. This is the uncanny heart of Strether's tale. The love he feels—for himself, for Chad, and for his past—is love he had associated with loss. Paris has brought him out again, put him in touch with that lost youth. At the same time, his senses—touching, tasting, and smelling the loss—are renewed.

By invoking this elegiac tone Strether touches on a long elegiac tradition in English poetry, going back at least to the melancholy meanderings of the poet Thomas Gray, with whom Strether shares a sense of loss and unrealized possibility.[8] In both cases the loss is set in an erotic context, the regret tinged with the almost palpable sense of what might have been. That is what Strether is talking about, and it is directly connected to Chad's mysterious presence. He represents the youth that Strether has lost; he represents the possibility of fulfillment.

Strether wants in one sense to be Chad and in another sense he wants Chad himself, something he perhaps does not admit directly. Shortly after this, Chad comes up behind Strether, and they have an intimate conversation during which Strether observes, "I've come very much, it seems to me, to double up my fore legs in the manner of the camel when he gets down on his knees to make his back convenient" (429). This is a suggestive posture to be sure, but it also makes clear how much responsibility Strether is willing to take on himself. In fact, the two men bond over how much Strether has lost and how much Chad seems likely to lose if he does not return to Woollett. Strether finally understands that "it was in truth essentially by bringing down his personal life to a function all subsidiary to the young man's own that he held together" (427), and that it was "the striking truth about Chad . . . the truth that everything came happily back to his knowing how to live" (427). Strether at least clings to that.

How much more surprising then that Strether feels the ground fall away when he sees Chad and Madame de Vionnet together in a country village on a day when he has attempted to escape the confines of Paris. After a day of walking and musing, Strether chooses an inn for dinner. As he waits to be seated, he looks out over the river and sees a couple in a boat. And at the moment he recognizes that Madame de Vionnet and Chad are the couple in the boat, he feels a dis-ease that slowly overwhelms him:

> Chad and Madame de Vionnet were then like himself taking a day in the country—though it was as queer as fiction, as farce, that their country idyll could happen to be exactly like his; and she had been the first at recognition, the first to feel, across the water, the shock—for it appeared to come to that—of their wonderful accident. Strether became aware, with this, of what was taking place—that her recognition had been even stranger for the pair in the boat, that her immediate impulse had been to control it, and that she was quickly and intensely debating with Chad the risk of betrayal. He saw they would show nothing if they could feel sure he hadn't made them out; so that he had before him for a few seconds his own hesitation. It was a sharp

fantastic crisis that had popped up as if in a dream, and it had had only to last the few seconds to make him feel it quite horrible. (462)

This queer encounter, this strange scene of mutual distrust and suspicion, upsets Strether more than the secret liaison between his two friends that it reveals. "Betrayal" is an odd word for them to use, although they fear "betrayal" in the sense of "a revelation or divulgence of something which it is desirable to keep secret," as the *OED* defines the word.

The scene also implies a betrayal in the more familiar sense of "a violation of trust or confidence," also from the *OED*, and in that sense it is Strether who has been betrayed. The "fantastic crisis" that develops is not really the crisis of exposure that it has often been taken to seem. Harry Levin reminds us that F. R. Leavis found the novel disappointing on the grounds that "the subtle elaboration of its technique was disproportionate to the values and issues it held and presented. His objection was aimed at the very heart of the novel: 'What, we ask, is this, symbolized by Paris, that Strether feels himself to have missed in his own life? Has James himself sufficiently inquired? Is anything adequately realized?'"[9]

Part of the dissatisfaction, part of a sense that technique is disproportionate to values, emerges from a misunderstanding of the scene. If Strether is understood simply to be upset because Chad and Madame de Vionnet are having a tryst in the country or even because they have carried on their affair virtually under his nose, then the novel could seem disappointing. Instead, Strether is crushed because Chad has betrayed him in his love for Madame de Vionnet. Of course, that is not quite conscious on Strether's part, nor would it be particularly reasonable if it were. Although many features of the novel suggest that Strether is in love with Chad, many others make it clear that Chad is in love with Madame de Vionnet. Strether has imagined that this relationship could include himself as well, but this queer encounter seems to do nothing but exclude him. Strether's position is therefore a doubly false one. He can only fail in his mission because he has never understood himself well enough to know what the mission is.

Soon after his horrifying encounter, Strether walks out again in the direction of the apartment on the Boulevard Malesherbes, driven by the feeling that "he must see Chad" (496):

The windows of Chad's apartment were open to the balcony—a pair of them lighted; and a figure that had come out and taken up Little Bilham's attitude, a figure whose cigarette-spark he could see leaned on the rail and looked down at him. It denoted however no reappearance of his younger friend; it quickly defined itself in the tempered darkness as Chad's more solid shape; so that Chad's was the attention that, after he had stepped forward in the street and signalled, he easily engaged; Chad's was the voice that, sounding into the night with promptness and seemingly with joy, greeted him and called him up. (497)

This reworking of the earlier scene, this repositioning Strether in relation to Chad, who lights the dark night with his spark and calls out with joy, makes literal what has only been suggested in earlier scenes. It is a magical moment that has the quality of a dream. James insists on placing Chad in the position held by Little Bilham in the earlier encounter because by now Little Bilham has been superseded in the Parisian experience. Strether seeks, after all, Chad, alone and thoughtful, open to the careful ministrations of this older friend, joyful and welcoming.

Strether's inverted notion of himself, and his failure to assert the desire that he fears, leave him in a no-man's-land of sexological impossibility. James does not know how to break through the limits of his age and make the two men the lovers they so often seem. When, shortly after this, Chad reasonably asks his tired and panting friend (four flights without a lift) whether he would like to spend the night, Strether responds with a barely disguised expression of his deepest fantasy: "Our friend has in fact the impression that with the minimum of encouragement Chad would propose to keep him indefinitely; an impression in the lap of which one of his own possibilities seemed to sit. Madame de Vionnet had wished him to stay—so why didn't that happily fit? He would enshrine himself for the rest of his days in his young host's *chambre d'ami* and draw out these days at his young host's expense: there could scarce be greater logical expression of the countenance he had been moved to give" (498).

Chad never makes that extended proposal, and Strether never has to face the crisis of whether he would accept it. The fantasy is palpable, though, and almost reasonable. As Patricia Highsmith's novel on this theme will make clear, such offers are never as uncomplicated as they seem. Strether steers away from these difficult waters, however, by challenging Chad about his feelings for Madame de Vionnet: "You'll be a brute, you know—you'll be guilty of the last infamy—if you ever forsake her" (499). Later, when Chad shows that he has a real interest in (of all things) advertising, which Jim Pocock has been proposing as a job for him in the family firm, Strether panics.

In this last scene together, they come close and move farther apart. It is odd that money seems to come between them now, but then, of course, it always has. Chad is an heir and has the freedom to move in or out of any role or position. Strether is not and does not. That lack, that impossibility, makes this a bittersweet moment. Strether is as close to Chad at this moment as he ever is, but he knows there is a barrier he cannot cross. His love for Chad can never be expressed, nor can the terms of his desire be realized. If Chad's interest in advertising is "purely platonic," then his love for Strether might be described as platonic as well. Desire must be sacrificed as the two men part. For Strether, it is desire rather than a fortune or the hand of Mrs. Newsome that is a measure of what he no longer has in losing the support of Woollett. What he has lost is Chad.

In the novel that uses *The Ambassadors* as a model, Patricia Highsmith raises many of the same questions. Of course, *The Talented Mr. Ripley* does not make the same kind of discriminations that James makes in his novel. Highsmith's "ambassador" is, from one perspective at least, cruel, mean-spirited, and amoral. But those are the least interesting of his features when he is placed in this context. Like Strether, Tom Ripley is struggling to find a place in a world that seems to have excluded him. Although he fails even more spectacularly than James's hero in bringing home the wayward man he seeks, his attempts at creating a life for himself are no less intriguing.

Highsmith is more open—more open than Ripley himself, in fact—about the queer possibilities of her text. Throughout *The Talented Mr. Ripley* the hero's actions and his oddly amoral series of crimes are connected directly to his queer sensibility, carefully depicted if crudely imagined, which becomes the novel's central fascination. Tom Ripley never admits to being queer, but he dramatizes a kind of sexuality that would have been easily recognizable in the 1950s. Robert Corber has captured the mood of the period by suggesting that after World War II "the relation between homophobia and American national identity solidified. During the McCarthy witch hunts, homosexuals were compared to communists who were allegedly conspiring to overthrow the nation." Corber goes on to argue:

> The "homosexual menace" can in part be traced to the publication of the first Kinsey report in 1948, which showed that homosexuals did not differ significantly from heterosexuals. . . . But if sexual identity was not fixed, then homosexuals might be able to convert heterosexuals to their "perverted" practices. Kinsey's findings further contributed to the "homosexual men-ace" by calling into question the stereotype of the effeminate gay man. . . . Thus homosexuals could infiltrate the nation's centers of power without being detected and thus were akin to communists. In 1950, in response to mounting hysteria, Congress held widely publicized hearings on whether

homosexuals constituted a security risk. As a consequence of these hearings, more gays and lesbians were expelled from the federal government than were suspected communists.[10]

The instability and unreliability of "homosexuals" is surely at issue in Highsmith's novel, and so is the invisibility of the homosexual menace. The risk that the homosexual poses in this novel is obvious; he is violent, hysterical, and prone to brooding passions. He is also deceitful, uncentered, and unsure of his feelings. In short, he is a sociopath, or even a psychopath, who hides a dark and debilitating power behind his shy or self-effacing demeanor. This would seem to be a homophobic portrait, but I would like to bracket that response and look more closely at the text for two reasons. First, the novel is culturally revealing in ways that a more prohomosexual text like Gore Vidal's *The City and Pillar* cannot be. Second, Highsmith moves beyond the superficial disgust that a character like Tom Ripley might engender. For her, Ripley is not a villain or even a dark hero. She is so intent in looking into his motivations and explaining his behavior that he becomes in her hands a much more complex character than the facts of the case would suggest. That complexity is what I hope to explore.

The novel begins in a mood of paranoia from which it never escapes: "Tom glanced behind him and saw the man coming out of the Green Cage, heading his way" (3). That this man, Herbert Greenleaf, turns out to be Tom's unwitting benefactor is beside the point. Tom's feelings rarely have primarily to do with the immediate circumstances. A little later, walking into his apartment, he feels he is being followed ("If there was any feeling he hated, it was being followed, by *anybody*" [12]). Later, the sense that police are waiting to pounce on him "gave Tom the feeling he was being followed, especially when he walked though the long, narrow street to his house door" (217). This emotion wells up in him throughout the book, sometimes without warning.

His paranoia and his other phobias, among them misogyny and a fear of water, seem to emerge from a dark and only partly revealed past in which he lost his parents early and was forced to obey an aunt who barely tolerated him and whom he barely respected. The narrator says, for example, that Tom "hated water. He had never been anywhere on water. . . . His parents had died in Boston Harbour, and Tom had always thought that probably had something to do with it, because as long as he could remember he had been afraid of water, and he had never learned to swim" (25).

Tom is also "bored, God-damned bloody bored, bored, bored!" (8) as the novel opens. Tom resists when Herbert Greenleaf first employs him to go to Italy in search of his son, Richard (Dickie), in the hope that he might be able to persuade him to return home. Three things, however, convince him to take on the project. The first and most obvious is Greenleaf's offer to pay for Tom's trip. When Mr. Greenleaf asks if he could get leave from his job, "Tom's heart took a sudden leap. He put on an expression of reflection. It was a possibility. Something in him had smelt it and leapt at it even before his brain" (9).

That something might be the attraction/identification he feels for Dickie, the second reason he accepts the offer. "How old is Dickie now, by the way?" he asks in his first conversation with the father. Greenleaf answers, "He's twenty-five." "So am I, Tom thought. Dickie was probably having the time of his life over there. An income, a house, a boat. Why should he want to come home? Dickie's face was becoming clearer in his memory: he had a big smile, blondish hair with crisp waves in it, a happy-go-lucky face. Dickie was lucky. What was he himself doing at twenty-five? Living from week to week. No bank account. Dodging cops now for the first time in his life. He had a talent for mathematics. Why in hell didn't they pay him for it somewhere?" (7–8).

Tom's attraction for Dickie seems connected with his sense of frustration. Tom Ripley suffers a deeply rooted self-doubt that at times amounts to self-contempt. Dickie seems to offer Tom an imaginative and emotional escape from that sense of frustration, but the escape is also articulated in terms of desire. Tom does not quite articulate this to himself, but Highsmith makes it clear. When, for instance, the Greenleafs show Tom a photograph album, "The album was not interesting to him until Richard got to be sixteen or so, long-legged, slim, with the same tightening in his hair. So far as Tom could see, he had hardly changed between sixteen and twenty-three or -four, when the pictures stopped, and it was astonishing to Tom how little the bright, naïve smile changed" (19). Tom's subtle attraction to the figure of Dickie Greenleaf intensifies throughout the first half of the novel; for a time it seems as if his growing love and sexual attraction are its central concerns.

The third motivating force for Tom's European adventure is even more subtle than sexual attraction. It has more to do with Tom's past than his present and is evoked in scenes such as that which occurs just as Tom is about to leave the Greenleafs:

> Tom noticed that Mrs. Greenleaf was staring down at the rug in front of her. He remembered the moment at the table when she had said, "I wish I'd never heard of Europe!" and Mr. Greenleaf had given her an anxious glance and then smiled at him, as if such outbursts had occurred before. Now he saw tears in her eyes. Mr. Greenleaf was getting up to come to her.

> "Mrs. Greenleaf," Tom said gently, "I want you to know that I'll do every-
> thing I can to make Dickie come back. . . ."
> Mr. Greenleaf went out of the room with her. Tom remained standing, his
> hands at his sides, his head high. In a large mirror on the wall he could see
> himself: the upright, self-respecting young man again. He looked quickly away.
> He was doing the right thing, behaving the right way. Yet he had a feeling of
> guilt. When he had said to Mrs. Greenleaf just now. *I'll do everything I can
> . . .* Well, he meant it. He wasn't trying to fool anybody.
> He felt himself beginning to sweat, and he tried to relax. What was he wor-
> ried about? He'd felt so well tonight. (20)

This emotion is distinct from his feelings about Dickie and has more to do
with maternal love. It is love that Tom has not felt, and it overwhelms him
when he witnesses it. Tom wants a mother to cry for him; he wants to feel part
of a loving family. The family love he has not known strikes him as intense
and tender, something that would make him "upright and self-respecting."
In one sense that is what he would like to be. In another, of course, he would
like to take advantage of the Greenleafs and make the most of their offer.
Maybe he does not already know he will betray their trust, but that might
well be the source of the guilt Tom feels. After all, the position of the son, the
position into which he is so anxious to project himself, is also the position
most overdetermined in Freudian psychology. Tom is always already guilty
because his desires, as all desires must, defy the family and plot its destruction. It is perhaps not surprising that all three of these deep emotions come
together in the personality—indeed, the "sexuality"—of Tom Ripley.

The vague sense of identification that Tom feels, the immediate reaction
to an offer that improves his status, and an overwhelming experience of
mother-love all work conveniently to define a "homosexual" as the term was
understood in the 1950s when this sexuality was considered a perversion, an
illness, and, even when tolerated, an abnormality. Highsmith's interest in Tom
is surely influenced by this understanding of the homosexual and colored
by assumptions of the age. At the same time, Highsmith is deconstructing
these assumptions and working out a different version of the homosexual.
As that first encounter continues the emphasis changes:

> Tom straightened, glancing at the door, but the door had not opened. That
> had been the only time tonight when he has felt uncomfortable, unreal, the
> way he might have felt if he had been lying, yet it has been practically the
> only thing he said that was true: *My parents died when I was very small. I was
> raised by my aunt in Boston.*

Mr. Greenleaf came into the room. His figure seemed to pulsate and grow larger and larger. Tom blinked his eyes, feeling a sudden terror of him, an impulse to attack him before he was attacked. . . . A cold fear was running over Tom's body. (20–21)

Tom's fear—fear of exposure, fear he does not belong, and fear of being found out—is later associated with his desire, as it is, in a sense, here. The fear is all the greater because everything he wants has just been presented to him. He wants money, he wants family, and he wants Dickie—or, as it comes to seem, he wants to be Dickie. Is that the same thing? I do not think that Highsmith thinks it is. But the intensity of his desires also brings a physically debilitating fear that everything will be taken away. And in this novel such fear amounts to a kind of paranoia that not only is never overcome but also comes to seem more and more reasonable as the novel proceeds.

The common, quasi-Freudian understanding of homosexuality in the 1950s, the understanding expressed in the term *sexual pervert* that became a rallying cry for reactionary forces in church, government, and community, led to a debilitating system of public hatred and fear that makes a paranoid response, like that of Tom Ripley, both cogent and sensible. As John D'Emilio describes the situation:

The widespread labeling of lesbians and homosexuals as moral perverts and security risks gave local police forces across the country a free rein in harassment. Throughout the 1950s gays suffered from unpredictable, brutal crackdowns. Men faced arrest primarily in bars and cruising areas such as parks, public restrooms, beaches, and transportation depots, while women generally encountered the police in and around lesbian bars. But even the homes of gay men and women lacked immunity from vice squads bent on increasing their arrest records.[11]

Highsmith steers her character through the waters of such opinion, never proving that Tom is not some sort of pathological figure but then never treating him as anything other than some version of normal. Tom's paranoia may be simply the result of police harassment at establishments like the Green Cage, or it may be more deeply rooted in private fears. In either case, the nightmare that D'Emilio outlines was all too real in the 1950s to expect that Tom could completely have escaped its power.

Once Tom has accepted the Greenleafs' offer and set sail on his European adventure some of the terms of his particular nightmare become clearer:

He thought suddenly of one summer day when he had been about twelve, when he had been on a cross-country trip with Aunt Dottie and a woman friend of hers, and they had got stuck in a bumper-to-bumper jam somewhere. It had been a hot summer day, and Aunt Dottie had sent him out with this thermos to get some ice water at a filling station, and suddenly the traffic had started moving. He remembered running between huge, inching cars, always about to touch the door of Aunt Dottie's car and never being quite able to, because she had kept inching along as fast as she could go, not willing to wait for him a minute, and yelling, "Come on, come on slowpoke!" out the window all the time. When he had finally made it to the car and got in, with tears of frustration and anger running down his cheeks, she had said gaily to her friend, "Sissy! He's a sissy from the ground up. Just like his father!" (37–38)

Tom's treatment at the hands of Aunt Dottie, in this passage at least, seems both sadistic and taunting. The picture of her inching the car forward as she needles him with his inability to catch up is strikingly vivid, and the feelings of frustration that well up in Tom are understandable. The accusation that she hurls in his direction, a castrating gesture of contempt, of course, puts his masculinity into question, and by bringing his father into the accusation she undermines that masculinity even further and dashes one of the boy's few ideals. His response is about his father rather than himself, his only defense: "And just what, he wondered, made Aunt Dottie think his father had been a sissy. Could she, had she, ever cited a single thing? No." (38).

The term *sissy* does not apply to Tom as he is now, but clearly it undermines who he is and creates the kind of residual anger that in different situations leads him to violence: "Tom writhed in the deck-chair as he thought of it. . . . he remembered the vows he had made, even at the age of eight, to run away from Aunt Dottie, the violent scenes he had imagined—Aunt Dottie trying to hold him in the house, and he hitting her with his fists, flinging her to the ground and throttling her, and finally tearing the big broach off her dress and stabbing her a million times in the throat with it. He had run away at seventeen and had been brought back, and he had done it again at twenty and succeeded" (39).

Dottie has instilled the violence and is at least partly responsible for the anger that rages within him. The form the violence takes, even in mere imagining, is out of proportion only from without, for Tom feels the discomfort physically and harbors homicidal feelings. From his perspective that is what Aunt Dottie deserves. What Tom Ripley shares with gothic villains who are his progenitors is this oblique relation to family, this implicit abuse at the hands of a victimizing stepmother. At the same time, a gothic plot is not necessary to see this configuration as deeply upsetting to the sensitive young Tom Ripley, who is always already transgressing the limits placed on him and guilty for the desire to transgress. Slavoj Žižek says, "There is no subject without guilt, the subject exists only in so far as he is ashamed because of the object in himself, in its interior. This is the meaning of Lacan's thesis that the subject is originally split, divided: he is divided as to the object himself, as to the Thing, which at the same time repels him."[12] Tom is so ashamed of the object within that he never allows himself to know it fully.

Tom's first response to the situation in Mongibello, Italy, like Strether's in Paris, is to want to be liked. He states it simply. After meeting Dickie and his girlfriend Marge and overexposing himself to the sun, Tom muses on his situation: "He'd let a few days go by, he thought. The first step anyway, was to make Dickie like him. That he wanted more than anything else in the world" (53). This simple desire creates anxiety that colors all dealings between the two men. During the first days that Tom spends in Mongibello he remains in cordial contact, but soon he decides that he must take a step closer to Dickie or risk losing him altogether. He does so by risking everything and mentioning the deal he has struck with Dickie's father. "'What do you mean?' Dickie frowned. 'Paid your way?' 'Yes.' It was his one last chance to amuse Dickie or to repel him, to make Dickie burst out laughing or go out and slam the door in disgust. But the smile was coming, the long corners of his mouth going up, the way Tom remembered Dickie's smile" (56). As Dickie breaks into a smile, Tom laughs with him in elated relief. Like Strether, in other words, Tom betrays the parent and transfers his duty and affection to the son. Also like Strether, he does so as he finds his devotion to the son more complex than the simple terms the parental project demands. The mood that begins with a smile builds to a kind of hilarity that leads Tom to self-revelation:

> Dickie sat down in a wicker chair and swung his legs over one of the arms. "Tell me more," he said, smiling. "What kind of work do you do? You said you might take a job."
>
> "Why? Do you have a job for me?"
>
> "Can't say that I have?"
>
> "Oh, I can do a number of things—valeting, baby-sitting, accounting—I've got an unfortunate talent for figures. No matter how drunk I get, I can always tell when a waiter's cheating me on a bill. I can forge a signature, fly a helicopter, handle dice, impersonate practically anybody, cook—and do a one-man show in a nightclub in case the regular entertainer's sick. Shall I go on?" Tom was leaning forward, counting them off on his fingers. He could have gone on. (58)

Tom's quiet desperation comes through in this speech, for all his exuberance, as does his need to be liked. He reveals that he is ready to settle for anything and would jump at a job offer from his new friend. Even worse, the string of talents Tom ingenuously reels off—it sounds genuine enough, after all—is a list more suitable for a spy or government agent or even a petty crook, which Tom in fact is, than for the aspiring friend of a shipping heir. But Tom responds to Dickie's easy familiarity even at the risk of exposing himself. In his attempt to be amusing, moreover, he lists talents, such as accounting, forging, and impersonating, which he will later use to impersonate Dickie. Dickie then asks Tom whom he can impersonate:

> "Well—" Tom sprang up. "This for example." He struck a pose with on hand on his hip, one foot extended. "This is Lady Assburden sampling the American subway. She's never even been in the underground in London, but she wants to take back some American experiences." Tom did it all in pantomime, searching for a coin, finding it didn't go into the slot, buying a token, puzzling over which stairs to go down, registering alarm at the noise and the long express ride, puzzling again as to how to get out of the place . . . walking through a door which could only be the door to the men's room from her twitching horror of this and that, which augmented till she fainted. Tom fainted gracefully on to the terrace glider. (58–59)

The success of the impersonation is almost ruined by Marge's entrance before it is finished. For Dickie, however, it is a great success. It would be hard not to imagine that this is a camp performance and that Tom, by parading around the terrace as Lady Assburden, has begun the process that will lead to him being challenged about his sexual intentions. His performance is naïve camp in the sense that he is unaware of its full ironic potential. He wants to amuse Dickie, and he knows that his Lady Assburden can get a laugh. He is not, however, in full control of the effects of what he does.[13] Marge's entrance and refusal to understand what is going on ("Marge didn't seem to get it and asked, 'What?'" [58]) suggest that she sees the pantomime as a kind of self-exposure and already suspects Tom of being more a rival than a friend.

The rivalry becomes more vivid as the days pass in Mongibello. Admittedly, the reader is mostly treated to Tom's resentment of Marge, his wish to avoid her, and his frustration when she is included in plans that he has made with Dickie. Tom's misogyny is so blatant, even clumsy, that Marge's resentment continues to grow, but that does not stop Tom from making plans for a future that he and Dickie will share: "Tom sat on the broad window-sill in Dickie's studio and looked out at the sea, his brown arms folded on his chest. He loved to look out at the blue Mediterranean and think of himself and Dickie sailing where they pleased. Tangiers, Sofia, Cairo, Sevastopol. . . . By the time his money ran out, Tom thought, Dickie would probably be so fond of him and so used to him that he would take it for granted they would go on living together. He and Dickie could easily live on Dickie's five hundred a month income" (74).

Tom's fantasy of escape, mutual trust, and cohabitation is, of course, too good to be true, and he does not recognize the degree that he is willing to take advantage of Dickie. Nor does he understand himself enough to admit the erotic implications of this scenario. But as he dreams, Marge and Dickie are arguing below. The implications of Tom's fantasies are not lost on Marge, and before long he sees her as the only bar to happiness with Dickie.

At first Tom only notices that Dickie seems somewhat strained. To cheer himself he tries on Dickie's clothes and dances around their apartment, playing with tones of voice that are close to Dickie's. In this madcap impersonation of Dickie he also threatens Marge: "Tom turned suddenly and made a grab in the air as if he were seizing Marge's throat. He shook her, twisted her, while she sank lower and lower, until at last he left her, limp, on the floor. He was panting" (78). Playing out his murderous rage against Marge, even though in the guise of Dickie, is ironic. He pretends that her breaking the "bond" between them has caused Dickie's rage, but this is Tom's rage. Marge is his enemy, not Dickie's. In fact, she has already calculated how to destroy him. She uses Tom's odd ways to get her revenge in a particularly virulent way.

Tom's choice to channel his desire into identification, his need to be Dickie rather than want him, is clearly an attempt to redirect his desire in Freudian terms. Like the young boy who must redirect polymorphous desires along clearly established cultural lines—desire for the mother, identification with the father, as Freud describes—Tom uses identification to short-circuit a trajectory of desire that is culturally unacceptable. Of course, identification and desire are not always neatly separated in the unconscious, and Tom's identification can also be understood as an expression of his desire. Kaja Silverman notes, for instance, that "Freud establishes in *The Ego and the Id* that object-cathexis and identification are initially 'indistinguishable,' in that oral sexuality internalizes its object much as the ego does. The same text suggests that throughout life the subject is able to relinquish the love-object only by incorporating it—that 'identification is the sole condition under which the id can give up its objects.'"[14] Tom's ecstatic dance in Dickie's clothes suggest that he is erotically engaged in this impersonation and it somehow expresses the love he feels for his friend.

When Dickie walks in and catches Tom in his clothes he is angry and quickly makes it clear that he understands Tom's behavior in the terms I have described:

Dickie looked at Tom's feet. "Shoes, too? Are you crazy?"

"No." Tom tried to pull himself together as he hung up the suit, then he asked, "Did you make it up with Marge?"

"Marge and I are fine," Dickie snapped in a way that shut Tom out from them. "Another thing I want to say, but clearly," he said, looking at Tom, "I'm not queer. I don't know if you have the idea that I am or not."

"Queer?" Tom smiled faintly. "I never thought you were queer."

Dickie started to say something else, and didn't. He straightened up, the ribs showing in his dark chest. "Well, Marge thinks you are."

"Why?" Tom felt the blood go out of his face. He kicked off Dickie's second shoe feebly and set the pair in the closet. "Why should she? What've I ever done?" He felt faint. Nobody had ever said it outright to him, not this way.

"It's just the way you act," Dickie said in a growling tone, and went out the door. (80)

In articulating the suspicions about Tom in this way, Highsmith is doing something James could never have done. The queer quality of his work resides in the inability to put a name to the odd sensation that lingers in the text. Terms would have been available for James at the turn of the century, of course, but none—*invert, sodomite,* even *homosexual*—precisely captures the elusive mood that James creates around his central figure.

Sedgwick's study helps explain why this indeterminacy might be particularly powerful for James.[15] For Highsmith the term *queer* is irresistible for various reasons. As an epithet of abuse it is analogous to "sissy" in the cruelty and condescension implicit in its use, but at the same time that it shifts its force, the mere notation of childhood effeminacy. It implies a kind of sexual irregularity that it does not precisely name. It includes notions of both moral pervert and political liability, as in the "moral pervert/security risk" model that D'Emilio articulates. In other words it does not register merely sexual behavior, like an earlier term *sodomite* might do, or a personality trait, like the earlier term *invert.* Instead it ruthlessly labels a sexual/political social outcast who cannot be loved, trusted, or even befriended.

At the same time the word *queer* does here what it does throughout James's text as well, open an area of "strangeness" in the text that no attempt at simple sexual definition can ever contain.[16] *The Talented Mr. Ripley* is queer in the way *The Ambassadors* is—queerer perhaps—because Highsmith does not want merely to label her character a "queer" the way he might be labeled a spy, as an end point to her investigation of his character. In a sense, that is where she begins.

Tom and Dickie cannot address the question of homosexuality without invoking Marge, whom Dickie uses as the source of the accusation because to have noticed anything himself would have been a little queer. Tom is taken aback by the accusation because for all his desire to be close to Dickie and spend time with him, he has not articulated to himself what that would imply. As the passage continues he remembers annoying his friends by joking repeatedly, "I can't make up my mind whether I like men or women, so I'm giving them *both* up" (81). The implication is that he does not know where his feelings might lead. "As people went," Tom tells himself, "he was one of the most innocent and clean-minded he had ever known. That was the irony of this situation with Dickie" (81).

The irony is that he could have carried on a Jamesian relationship with Dickie without addressing the question directly. As Highsmith puts it, "He had been half concealing himself from Dickie from behind the closet door." He uses the closet to hide from himself as well. For all his outright denials, once pulled out of that closet ("Dickie, I want to get this straight. . . . I'm not queer either, and I don't want anybody thinking I am" [80]) things will never be the same for Tom. Sedgwick says that "the closet is the defining structure for gay oppression in this century." Moreover, "A lot of the energy of attention and demarcation that has swirled around issues of homosexuality since the end of the nineteenth century . . . has been impelled by the indicative relation of homosexuality to wider mappings of secrecy and disclosure, and of the public and private that were and are critically problematical for the gender, sexual, and economic structures of the heterosexist culture at large."[17]

Tom Ripley is trapped in multiple closets of his own construction. If the sexual closet is the most obvious, as in this scene, it is only slightly more prominent than the "class closet" and the "crime closet" that function in different ways throughout the novel. The novel addresses the increasingly claustrophobic experience of these closets, and it might be possible to separate them. But "so permeative has the suffusing stain of homo/heterosexual crisis been that to discuss any of these indices in any context, in the absence of antihomophobic analysis, must perhaps be to perpetuate unknowingly compulsions implicit in each." As Sedgwick puts it more simply, "Vibrantly resonant as the image of the closet is for many modern oppressions, it is indicative for homophobia in a way that it cannot be for other oppressions."[18]

For D'Emilio in the 1950s "the dominant view of homosexuality as sin, sickness, or crime accustomed homosexual men and women to seeing their situation as a personal problem, not as a cause of political action."[19] Tom is uneasy about who he is and unwilling to risk what he has already established with Dickie. He is also defensive ("Who was making an issue of it anyway? Dickie was. Tom hesitated while his mind tossed in a welter of things he might have said, bitter things, conciliatory things, grateful and hostile" [81]). He says nothing, however, and tries to bring the situation "back to normal" (83), which he does in a few hours. At least he thinks he does.

After the relationship between Tom and Dickie is strained, Tom does what he can to salvage the intimacy that has been lost. Meanwhile, Herbert Greenleaf is understandably impatient and starts to write letters that suggest Tom is being cut off. Tom tries to hold Dickie to a plan for visiting Paris, and when that falls through Tom settles for a trip to San Remo, although he is far from happy at the finality in which it is cast.

Tom decides to murder Dickie during this trip, immediately after another incident that seems to reveal the dark secret of Tom's sexuality. He and Dickie slip over the border to Cannes while they are in San Remo and walk on the beach. There Tom becomes absorbed in the performance of some acrobats ("'They must be professionals,' Tom said, 'They're all in the same yellow g-strings'" [98]). When the acrobats complete their pyramid, a boy on top, Tom shouts "Bravo!":

> The boy smiled at Tom before he leapt down, lithe as a tiger.
> Tom looked at Dickie. Dickie was looking at a couple of men sitting on the beach.
> "Ten thousand saw I at a glance, nodding their head in sprightly dance," Dickie said sourly to Tom.
> It startled Tom, then he felt that sharp thrust of shame, the same thrust of shame he had felt in Mongibello when Dickie had said, *Marge thinks you are.* All right, Tom thought, the acrobats were fairies. Maybe Cannes was full of fairies. So what? Tom's fists were clenched tight in his trouser pockets. He remembered Aunt Dottie's taunt. *Sissy! He's a sissy from the ground up. Just like his father!* Dickie stood with his arms folded, looking out at the acrobats again, though they were certainly more amusing to watch than the ocean. "Are you going in?" Tom asked, boldly unbuttoning his shirt, though the water suddenly looked cold as hell. (98–99)

Highsmith evokes surging feelings effectively through Dickie's quote of Wordsworth ("I Wandered Lonely as a Cloud" [1807]) as a way of taunting Tom. Wordsworth is talking about "a host of golden daffodils," and Dickie may be alluding to the yellow g-strings of the acrobats, but he is also using flower imagery to note his awareness of the "fairies" on the beach. Tom understands this, and it causes the rage of shame that he felt before. Invoking Aunt Dottie's taunts, Highsmith connects Tom's fascination with the acrobats and his desire for Dickie with his hatred for the inner betrayals that leave him so exposed. That is why, as in earlier accounts, Tom's shame leads to rage and the rage to violence: "Damn him anyway, Tom thought. Did he have to act so damned aloof and superior all the time? You'd think he'd never seen a pansy! Obvious what was the matter with Dickie, all right! Why didn't he break down, just for once? What did he have that was so important to lose?" (99). As they ride back to San Remo on the train the tension builds:

> Tom sat opposite him, staring at his bony, arrogant, handsome face, at his hands with the green ring and the gold signet ring. It crossed Tom's mind to steal the ring when he left. It would be easy. . . . Tom stared at Dickie's closed eyelids. A crazy emotion of hate, of affection, of impatience and frustration was swelling in him, hampering his breathing. He wanted to kill Dickie. It was not the first time he had thought of it. Before, once or twice or three times, it had been an impulse caused by anger or disappointment, an impulse that vanished immediately and left him with a feeling of shame. (99–100)

Tom can only deal with love by means of violence. The welter of emotion he feels—hate, affection, impatience, and frustration—suggests the pain of desire that cannot be realized. Violence, the desire to kill Dickie, is so clearly connected to his desire to make love to Dickie that it becomes a form of love-making in Tom's mind. Freud suggests that "the impulse to cruelty arises from the instinct to mastery" and that the "sexuality of most male human beings contains an element of aggressiveness—a desire to subjugate."[20] Tom needs to "master" Dickie in order to give himself value. His love can finally only be expressed in violence, which is why it evokes shame in this way. But his frustration has become so intense that even shame does not stop him:

> Now he thought about it for an entire minute, two minutes, because he was leaving Dickie anyway, and what was there to be ashamed of any more? He had failed with Dickie, in every way. He hated Dickie, because, however he looked at what happened, his failing had not been his own fault, not due to anything he had done, but due to Dickie's inhuman stubbornness. And his blatant rudeness! He had offered Dickie friendship, companionship, and respect, everything he had to offer, and Dickie had replied with ingratitude and now hostility. Dickie was just shoving him out in the cold. If he killed him on this trip, Tom thought, he could just say that some accident had happened. He could—He had just thought of something brilliant: he could become Dickie Greenleaf himself. He could do everything that Dickie did. . . . He could step into Dickie's shoes. He could have Mr. Greenleaf, Sr. eating right out of his hand. The danger of it, even the inevitable temporariness of it which he vaguely realized, only made him more enthusiastic. He began to think of *how*. (100)

"What was there to be ashamed of any more?" Tom is ashamed before Dickie, and killing him can bring his desire to fulfillment at the same time that he destroys the object of desire and with it the source of shame. He hates Dickie because he cannot be the partner Dickie wants. He feels, in other words, that he has failed Dickie, which implies that what he hates about Dickie is the impression he has made on him. He hates himself for failing, and he hates Dickie because he can only imagine that Dickie has caused him to fail. He also imagines that his offerings of "friendship, companionship, and respect" have not been received with gratitude. They have been devalued. His love has been rejected. To kill Dickie would remove the cause of that contempt. To become Dickie would enable him to reimagine himself in a guise that Dickie could not help but respect. This is an enormously elaborate ruse for overcoming his feeling of rejection, but it is precisely what Tom does. The "how" with which he ends the passage becomes the mainspring of the remainder of this fascinating text.

Most details fall into place once Tom sets his mind on killing Dickie and taking his place. The murder itself, although brutal and bloody, takes place in a motorboat out in the bay at San Remo. Tom finds it exhausting but relatively easy to dispose of the body by throwing it overboard, hide the evidence by scuttling the boat, and present himself as Dickie Greenleaf merely by walking through the town in Dickie's jacket, his head held high. He handles Marge and the elder Greenleafs with letters and forgeries that are completely convincing, and although he has to kill Dickie's friend Freddie Miles more or less cold-bloodedly, he carries off his imitation of Dickie impeccably. He dresses in Dickie's clothes, uses his jewelry, withdraws his money, and for all practical purposes does what he had threatened in his reverie.

Throughout the later sections of the novel Tom seems to court danger. At one point late in the book he reminds himself that risk is what he enjoys: "The police would certainly look for Tom Ripley around Dickie Greenleaf. It was an added danger—if they were, for instance, to think that he was Tom Ripley now, just from Marge's description of him, and strip him and search him and find both his and Dickie's passports. But what had he said about risks? Risks were what made the whole thing fun" (179).

This is partly pure bravado, but it also begins to explain Tom's motivations and give another explanation for his boldfaced impersonation of his friend. Tom is not really worried that he will be discovered as Dickie Greenleaf and accused of the murder of Freddie Miles. Far more worrying is the decision to avoid suspicion in the most obvious way available, by becoming Tom Ripley again. The only crisis comes when he has to abandon the new identity and take up his old self: "He hated becoming Thomas Ripley again, hated being nobody, hated putting on his old set of habits again, and feeling that people looked down on him and were bored with him unless he put on an act for them like a clown, feeling incompetent and incapable of doing anything with himself except entertaining people for minutes at a time. He hated going back to himself as he would have hated putting on a shabby suit of clothes, a grease-spotted, unpressed suit of clothes that had not been very good even when it was new" (192).

Hating Tom Ripley is after all the motivation behind the action in the novel. This is self-hatred to be sure as well as hatred of the contemptible sissy Aunt Dottie created with her condemnatory tone and whom Tom castigated with his accusatory "I'm not queer." Tom is happy living with the danger but does not want to live with himself, as identified in these ways. Later, when he presents himself to the police, he adds that "identifying himself as Thomas Phelps Ripley was going to be one of the saddest things he had ever done in his life" (200).

It seems at first that the return to Thomas Ripley is a matter of class. He feels himself incompetent, incapable, shabby, unpressed, and not good even when new. This would seem tantamount to failure, but it is the odd success of *The Talented Mr. Ripley* that Tom can return to being his incompetent former self and find not just competence but an extravagant ability to be himself in a new way. Dickie, at least his impersonation of Dickie, has given him new ability that leads him from triumph to triumph over unimaginable odds until he stands at the end of the novel healthy, free, and independently wealthy. His talents are not to be underestimated. "Tom Ripley had never really been despondent, though he had often looked it. Hadn't he learned something from these last months? If you wanted to be cheerful, or melancholic, or wistful, or thoughtful, or courteous, you simply had to *act* those things with every gesture" (193).

Tom Ripley learns that his feeling will destroy him and those he loves. Desire is destructive by nature, and its full expression brings only shame. Instead, he learns that feelings can be faked and that the emotions the feelings represent are ushered in by the gestures they employ.

At the same time, this triumph is also a measure of failure. After all, Tom has not just killed the man he loved. He has sacrificed genuine emotion and moved into a world in which every emotion is faked. If this seems to work like a charm it is only because the world has already learned the danger of true emotion and mastered the technique of disguise. Tom is not alone in this. Marge has insisted on feelings that have no basis; Freddie Miles seemed more friendly than he was; and Herbert Greenleaf dismisses the question of his son's whereabouts: "Apparently Mr. Greenleaf's attitude was that Dickie was either dead or to hell with him. During that telephone call the to-hell-with-him attitude seemed to be the uppermost" (273).

Tom triumphs by accepting terms that the 1950s demand for a queer. He accepts his shame and seems to inhabit it, abject and filled with self-contempt. He turns it into an advantage by faking who he is, just as the repressive culture of the time wished him to fake it. If Highsmith's contemporaries in the 1950s were founding the Mattachine Society as a way of resisting the negative stereotype, with "a vision of a homosexual culture with its own positive values," Tom Ripley is trapped by a sense of being a sexual pervert who has used violence to cope with that knowledge and must remain in flight in order to keep his house of cards from collapsing.[21] If Tom asks for the best hotel in Athens at the end of the novel, then it is with the knowledge that he can never go home again. He no longer has a home, nor does he have a self. At the end of the novel he is a simulacrum, the simulacrum that culture has demanded from the young sissy/queer who feels only shame and cannot realize the love he feels. If Strether must return home a failure, without Chad, with Maria, and, of course, with Mrs. Newsome, at least he has discovered something about himself. Tom, however, has foreclosed the possibility of self-knowledge in this flight from himself. He succeeds but at a greater cost than Strether could even imagine.

Anthony Minghella's screenplay (1999) for a film version of Highsmith's novel puts both trajectories together in a fascinating reorganization of the plot and economical account of the novel's insistent perversions. In Minghella's version, Dickie is a jazz enthusiast and sometime performer, and Tom is a rather talented pianist who, when the film begins, is attempting to teach himself the basics of jazz. There are vast differences between the film and the novel, and it is not my purpose to enumerate them in any detail. Minghella has impressively managed to capture something about the novel, but he has created something new. My concern is the degree to which what is new concerns sexuality and gender and the degree to which he rewrites the queer narrative as a gay one or a queerer one.

The first sign that Tom has become involved in a complex relation to the young man he has been sent to find comes in a scene with Meredith Logue, whom he meets while in a queue for customs. When Meredith asks his name he inexplicably says "Dickie Greenleaf."[22] It seems as if he is already trying on a different persona, as if he is embarrassed to be traveling as Tom Ripley. This could seem an innocent joke, but when he arrives in Mongibello the terms of this "joke" become more explicit:

A SAILBOAT has slid into view, now drops anchor, drops the sail. A couple dive off and swim towards the shore.

ALL OF THIS FROM THE POINT OF VIEW OF RIPLEY, who's watching the vents through binoculars from his tiny balcony in the Miramare Hotel. An Italian Vocabulary Book is perched on his knees and during this he continues his study, mouthing the Italian words.

Ripley [looking at a long lean girl about to dive]. La fidanzata a una faccia. The fiancée has a face. La fidanzata e Marge.

[Her partner, Dickie Greenleaf dives too. They're brown, beautiful, perfect.]

Questo e la mia faccia. . . . This is my face. This is my face.

[The golden couple emerge from the sea. Dickie shakes off the water, grins.]

Questa . . . e la mia facca. Questa e la faccia di Dickie. (11)

Minghella finds this a useful technique for getting Tom to express his interest in Dickie. Just as he is learning the language he seems to be learning how to express a possessive attraction. He does not say "this is the face I want" but rather "this is my face." It is this confusion of desire and identification that Minghella develops from the novel. Minghella's Tom is more aware of his desires, readier to put them into words. The effect, at first, is the same.

Minghella is deft when it comes to dealing with the issue of sexual attraction between the men. Instead of using Marge to articulate Dickie's fear of Tom, Minghella dramatizes the growing intimacy and (almost?) mutual attraction in a series of powerful scenes. In a crowded Naples jazz club, for instance, they sing "Tu vuo' fa' L'Americano" together in boisterous high spirits, and clearly both of them enjoy the moment intensely. By the end of the song the entire club has joined in enthusiastically. Flushed with their success, Dickie leans over and kisses Tom, who is almost overjoyed (23; the kiss is not in the screenplay). Soon after this, Tom sings "My Funny Valentine" "in a flawless imitation of Chet Baker" as Dickie accompanies him on the saxophone. Again Dickie "beams at Ripley," and their intimacy continues to intensify. Marge has already told Tom that "My Funny Valentine" was the song Dickie used to court her. But the Rogers and Hart ballad, like so many others the closeted, homosexual Hart wrote for his always indulgent composer-friend to set, resonates with a queer undertone that would have been familiar in the New York of the Green Cage and other bars that Tom frequented as well as in hipper jazz clubs, even in Naples.[23]

When Dickie uses Tom's money to buy a refrigerator, we see Dickie hugging the appliance and saying "I could fuck this icebox I love it so much" (32). This is in the midst of such scenes and another in which Dickie stares at Tom without his glasses and says, "Without the glasses you're not even ugly" (33). In other words a feeling of erotic intensity subtly grows between the two men in a series of scenes that could easily lead to a same-sex encounter.

The mood culminates in a carefully constructed scene in which "Dickie is in the bath. Ripley, dressed, sits on the stool next to the bath. They're in the middle of playing chess, the board propped on the bath tray. Ripley puts his hand in the water, checking the temperature. He turns on the faucet for a burst of hot. Ripley is absurdly happy" (34). They talk about being only children, and when Dickie asks, "What does that mean?" Tom takes his chance. "Means we never shared a bath," he responds. "I'm cold. Can I get in?" (35). Dickie's "No!" is emphatic enough. But when Tom saves face by saying "I didn't mean with you in it," Dickie offers the bath and gets out, almost unselfconsciously naked but also aware of Tom looking at him: "Ripley looks, then Dickie turns, holds his look momentarily before clicking him with his towel" (35).

There is no such scene in the novel, of course, but Minghella uses it as a substitute for Marge's accusations and Dickie's aggressive "I'm not queer." The difference is significant. First, Tom more actively expresses desire for Dickie, as if he were fully aware of his desires and prepared to act on them, and, second, the scene between Tom and Dickie is much more erotic than the scene in the novel. Tom could hardly be blamed if he understood Dickie's "no!" as a "yes!" As a result, the configuration of desire seems less "queer," in the fifties sense, than "gay" in a post-Stonewall sense. Tom suppresses desires that need to be liberated, and Dickie may harbor gay feelings he does not recognize. It is not the "sexual pervert" model that seems to fascinate Highsmith, but a more liberated "repressed gay man" model that circulated most extensively in the 1970s—post-Stonewall and pre-AIDS—generation.

All this changes not because of anything Marge says. She seems unfailingly kind to Tom even though her name is later evoked in Dickie's blanket attack on Tom's character. Instead, it is the character Freddie Miles who changes everything. He assesses Tom, "Tommy" he calls him, and quickly dismisses him. Freddie sees through Tom's class pretensions and attempts at remaking himself and, seemingly, through his sexuality as well. In the film this is brought out by Freddie's repeated contemptuous stares in Tom's direction, as if he can see through him, and it culminates in a scene on Dickie's boat, where Freddie sees Tom "mesmerized, aroused, and absolutely betrayed" by a sexual encounter between Dickie and Marge: "Tommy—how's the peeping! Come on Tommy, you were looking. Tommy, Tommy, Tommy." At this Tom is "shamed" (47). Shame emerges once again in a specifically sexual context, and Tom feels shame at his own erotic response. Of course the shame is exacerbated when he is caught looking, which is different from the shame that Highsmith's Ripley feels. Freddie becomes the fulcrum of shame, and Tom's intense fear of exposure seems more like a fear of "coming out" than does anything in Highsmith.

Immediately after Freddie's appearance Tom tries on Dickie's clothes and dances around his room to the accompaniment of Bing Crosby's "May I?". It is an exciting, an exhilarating moment, and it may not strike the viewer that Tom is transforming himself into Dickie. He seems to be having the time of his life. For a moment he seems almost thrilled with the new self he is creating, but when the dance is interrupted abruptly by Dickie's entrance guilt washes over Tom's face and the mood plummets. The scene makes it clear that the magic between the two has ended, yet something even more ominous is in the air. "I wish you'd get out of my clothes," Dickie says as he turns off the music (43). Tom's apologies are abject, and his long decline in Dickie's affections has begun. Little by little he is closed out of Dickie's life. Dickie seems weary of him, fed up, and when several days later they plan a trip to San Remo Dickie calls it "our last trip before you leave" (51).

They go to San Remo and momentarily rekindle their affection. Dickie challenges Tom about his identity. Did he attend Princeton? Does he really like jazz? Tom "[conceding, without guile]" (54) uses the moment to confess his many deceptions in the hope of growing closer to Dickie. But Dickie is loud and aggressive in a way that might suggest to Tom that the playboy is bored with him. Tom does seem to realize that something is not quite right about the mood, but the next day, when they are on the bay in a motorboat, the awkward mood does not stop Tom from articulating a "plan" whereby he can return to Italy and share a future with Dickie in some way. Dickie rejects him energetically: "Oh God, I don't think so." He adds, "Marge and I are getting married" (55). When Tom protests and questions the "I love Marge" with "you love me and you're not marrying me," Dickie responds, "Tom, I don't love you."

The exchange erupts into the scene in which Tom and Dickie fight and Dickie is killed. It begins with Tom accusing Dickie of hiding his feelings. When Tom alludes to the chess-playing evening and Dickie responds, "What evening?" Tom attacks: "Sure—I know, that's too dangerous for you, fair enough, hey! We're brothers, fine, then you do this sordid thing with Marge, fucking her on the boat while we all have to listen, which was excruciating, frankly, plus you follow your cock around you like a—and now you're getting married! I'm bewildered, forgive me . . . you're lying to Marge then getting married to her, you're knocking up Silvana, you've got to play sax, you've got to play drums, which is it, Dickie, what do you really play?" (57).

Before considering Dickie's violent response, consider whether Highsmith's character would have been capable of such an outburst. That the answer must be no does not mean Minghella has failed. In fact, with his decision to give Tom the outburst, to make him this aware of his needs and demands, and to liberate him from shame enough to allow him this outburst he is creating a different kind of gay character, one obviously middle class and with strictly middle-class values. Just a short time later, for example, Freddie will condemn Tom's interior decor: "Did this place come furnished? It doesn't look like Dickie. Horrible, isn't it?—so bourgeois" (82). Tom is betrayed as the man who thinks that a certain degree of intimacy equals a similar degree of commitment; he seems ready to come out of the closet and confront with Dickie the reality of his love.

Dickie is appalled by the accusations as well as by the terms in which they are cast. There is a certain amount of truth in what Tom says, but Dickie is not "bourgeois" enough to listen to him. Even if he were "gay," in other words, he is not in love with Tom. His response is to attack Tom "I can't move without 'Dickie, Dickie, Dickie'—like a little girl. You give me—." At that point, "Ripley smashes him across the head with the oar. Dickie slips off the wooden seat, his eyes rolling in groggy surprise" (57–58).

A battle ensues, and when Dickie recovers from the attack he lurches at Tom with "I'll kill you!" The two struggle with the oar, which Tom finally grabs and uses to pound Dickie to death. They have a love scene at last: "[Ripley] starts to sob, sprawls there, sobbing next to Dickie, horrified by what he's done." Then, "Nobody's in sight. The boat rocks, gently, the sun sparkling indifferently on the waves. Ripley lies by Dickie in the bottom of the boat, in the embrace he's always wanted" (58).

Tom's act amounts to little more than manslaughter in this version. Much more sympathy is available for someone like this Tom Ripley, who pours himself out to his friend and then finds himself dismissed and threatened. There is much more potential sympathy for this crime of passion, the despairing response of a rejected lover, than there could ever be for Highsmith's Ripley, the premeditating murder who kills his friend out of frustration, hatred, and affection. By devising this murder and its briefly glimpsed but powerfully affecting aftermath, the would-be lovers in each other's arms, lying in the hull of the boat, Minghella creates a gay tragedy that avoids the queer politics of Highsmith's novel.

This is not the shameful sexuality of the Highsmith novel but the sordid closet of the post-Stonewall generation, grotesque in its inability to be expressed and violent in internalized homophobia. Dennis Altman captures the early post-Stonewall mood in his classic *Homosexual Oppression and Liberation:* "The sublimation of homosexual desire into both aggression and mateship between men seems a particular characteristic of frontier societies. ... Violence seems on the whole remarkably absent among self-accepting homosexuals, while particularly prevalent among those who have strong homosexual desires that they seek to repress."[24]

Similarly, the important subplot with Peter Smith-Kingsley shifts the focus from a queer grotesque to a tragic gay character. In the novel Peter is a minor figure, but Minghella enlarges his role considerably and makes his relationship with Tom the centerpiece of the final section of the film. Peter steps in as another gay man who seems ready to love Tom and accept him as he is. He first appears at the opera with Marge, but his interest in Tom is obvious from the first. When later he repeats an invitation to Tom to visit Venice, Tom accepts in an attempt to escape from the character of Dickie back into that of Tom Ripley. Because it is Tom Ripley whom Peter loves, or seems to love, this makes perfect sense.

In one touching scene in Peter's apartment he sets the table for supper and Tom plays Vivaldi's *Stabat Mater* on the piano. The maternal continues to haunt him, and the misery of loss is expressed in the moody chords. Peter wonders what Dickie must feel if he did kill Freddie: "What that must be like? To wake up every morning" with such knowledge. At that Tom goes into a reverie:

> Ripley. Whatever you do, however terrible, however hurtful—it makes sense, doesn't it? inside your head. You never meet anybody who thinks they're a bad person or that they're cruel.
>
> Peter. But you're still tormented, you must be, you've killed somebody . . .
>
> Ripley. Don't you put the past in a room, in the cellar, and lock the door and just never go in there? Because that's what I do.
>
> Peter. Probably. In my case it's probably a whole building.
>
> Ripley. Then you meet someone special and all you want to do is toss them the key, say *open up, step inside,* but you can't because it's dark and there are demons and if anybody saw how ugly it was. . . . (105–6)

At this remarkable moment it almost seems as if Tom has learned to trust Peter and is ready to let him into the dark secrets of his soul. Peter is the friend Dickie could never be, and it almost seems that he could understand and forgive the horrors Tom could pour forth. He seems to love Tom in a way no one else has. He seems to embrace Tom with a security and an independence that defies everything about male-male couples as Dickie portrayed them. Peter is a healthy homosexual who seems to understand that two men can love one another in a way that makes them stronger together than either is apart. Minghella structures this as a possible coming-out because his is a coming-out narrative. If Tom could come out to Peter, it almost seems, all would be well. He cannot, however, allow himself the relief of letting Peter "inside," and that is his tragedy.

When this bond has endured the horrors of Marge's nearly hysterical accusations and finally firm conviction that Tom has murdered Dickie—something that never quite happens in the book—and when Herbert Greenleaf and his private investigator have left Tom with some past secrets about Dickie and with a guarantee of financial support, Tom and Peter sail away for Athens in a seeming escape into a world where their love can sustain them.[25] "'Ask me what I want to change about this minute?' Tom asks Peter." And when Peter asks, he replies, "Nothing." This is the happiest and most relaxed Ripley we have seen. Peter Kingsley-Smith seems to have brought him joy.

What a shame then that Meredith appears when Tom is alone on deck, recognizing him as "Dickie" and causing Tom's final crisis. He knows that there is no way out and stands before Peter, nearly broken: "I suppose I always thought—better to be a fake somebody than a real nobody" (130). "What are you talking about?" Peter answers. "You're not a nobody! That's the last thing you are." Tom realizes that this is a man who truly loves him for who he is. But because he knows the real Tom Ripley, because he loves the real Tom Ripley, he must die. In a final love scene, they list Tom's virtues: "Tom is talented. Tom is tender . . . Tom is beautiful. . . . Tom is musical. Tom is not a nobody. Tom has secrets he doesn't want to tell me, and I wish he would" (130–31). But instead of telling Peter his secrets Tom kills him in this final embrace, using his bathrobe cord to strangle him as he lies on top of him. "I love you," he seems to say in the film as he gasps his final breaths. Tom is in tears, sobbing; his one chance of love is gone.

The film ends as it began, with an image of Tom staring blankly into space. We know why he stares, what he has lost—"Ripley alone in a nightmare of his own making" (131). He has no faith in himself and therefore cannot believe Peter's love would be strong enough to bear the truth. Of course

Peter may have been able to handle the real truth. His final comments seem to suggest the tragedy—the gay tragedy—is that Tom has so internalized his homophobia that he cannot believe Peter loves him. The person Peter loves is someone Tom holds in contempt, and the result is that Peter's love is the measure of his worthlessness. The film concludes on that note of gay tragedy. Because Tom cannot come out as who he really is, he destroys those he loves and sacrifices real happiness to the demands of a heteronormative culture. The nightmare into which he is plunged is not entirely of his own making. His culture has participated in convincing him that as Tom Ripley he has no talent worth mentioning.[26]

In his preface to the screenplay of *The Talented Mr. Ripley* Minghella maintains that "the novel is about a man who commits murders and is not caught. And so the film is about a man who commits murders and is not caught. But it departs in one crucial sense by concluding that eluding public accountability is not the same thing as eluding justice. The film has a moral imperative: you can get away with murder, but you don't really get away with anything. Ripley, always looking for love, always looking to love and be loved, has to kill his opportunity for love."[27] This "moral imperative" is foreign to the amoral tale Highsmith tells. In her telling, Ripley's "success" is eerily ironic, utterly guiltless, and queer. For Minghella, he must be guilty. He must suffer for his inability to realize this love in an open and healthy way. Strether fails but at least discovers something about himself. Highsmith's Mr. Ripley, however, forecloses the possibility of self-knowledge in a final flight from himself. Minghella's Ripley fails in his success as devastatingly as Strether fails, and his self-knowledge at the end of the novel is a measure of that failure.

9

Anne Rice and the Queering of Culture

At the climax of her novel *Memnoch the Devil*, Anne Rice dramatizes her witty arch-enemy's fall from grace. Unlike any codified story of Satan's rebellion, however, Memnoch falls because of his desire for things human— indeed, his desire for a human female. This may strike the readers of Rice's *Vampire Chronicles* as a surprising turn. More surprising, even shocking, is this creature's celebration of the family. This is Memnoch's challenge to God: "I went down and I looked into the family . . . I saw the family as a new and unprecedented flower, Lord, a blossom of emotion and intellect that in its tenderness was cut loose from the stems of Nature from which it had taken its nourishment, and was now at the mercy of the wind. Love, Lord, I saw it, I felt Love of Men and Women for one another and for their Children."[1] Rather than feel that the chronicler of the darkness has betrayed her vision with this hymn of praise to the family, readers might look into those earlier volumes to consider how her "Savage Garden" could be transformed into conservative urban, or rather suburban, American values.

The *Vampire Chronicles* of Anne Rice have long managed an uneasy relation with conservative politics and the cult of glamour. If not the record of the cultural experience of the United States since the 1980s, they at least offer a précis of some of the nation's most deeply held cultural assumptions and an overview of the banality of transgression in the later twentieth century. The novels have all the topical urgency of popular fiction as well as the peculiar air of decadence in which Rice specializes. The sine qua non with which Rice mesmerizes readers, however, is homoerotic desire. *Interview with a Vampire* begins in the gay district of San Francisco, and the scene between

186 · QUEER GOTHIC

the vampire Louis and the gay "boy" who interviews him after they have met in a "bar" is a straightforward parody of a queer seduction. That cannot be accidental. Rice is interested in male-male desire and uses the imagery of gay life to give characters substance and texture. She makes Lestat culture's prototypical gay predator, roving in the darkness with an insatiable appetite that is usually satisfied by the blood of a troubled but beautiful male. Rice has more than once expressed her attraction for this wildly transgressive hero, a super-human blond who moves with the grace of a dancer and takes his prey with a lusty abandon that fulfills—violates—every cultural taboo.

Lestat and Louis, the vampiric couple from *Interview;* Lestat's devoted friend Nicholas from *The Vampire Lestat;* and Armand, Daniel, and David, the central characters who emerge throughout the *Chronicles*—all these dazzling young men can be read as gay. To understand the *Chronicles,* in fact, they must be read as gay, and their relations can only be understood in terms of male-male desire. The front-page attention that greeted the filming of one of these novels was a symptom of their availability for the identifactory purposes of readers and viewers that Rice's works have long commanded. What they offer, however, is not exactly clear. One might paraphrase a collection of critical essays and ask "whose homoeroticism" is it that Rice so richly articulates in *Vampire Chronicles?* In her study of vampires in film and fiction, Nina Auerbach makes an important point: "The fraught ménage of Louis and Lestat is a return to vampire beginnings. Their irritable mutual obsession recovers literary vampires' lost origin: the homoerotic bond between Byron and Polidori."[2] Byron and Polidori were not themselves vampires, however, and this slippage between characters and writers exonerates Rice of any voyeuristic interest in the homoerotic and assumes that vampires have almost naturalized homoerotic origins.

Rice may well be tapping the vampiric past in her delightfully lurid tales, and she is also tantalizing the homophobic present with her sleek and sultry undead. The homoerotics of Rice's vampires are at least as culturally telling as anything that happens in Byron, or Sheridan LeFanu, or even Bram Stoker. Rice makes her vampires homoerotic for reasons that tell more about their moment of creation than about historical precedents, however rich these might be. What interests me is how the homoerotic bonds that surface everywhere in Rice's *Vampire Chronicles* function as part of the self-consuming culture that has produced them. For Auerbach, "Rice's infraction of this final Stoker-instigated taboo brings a special electricity to *Interview with a Vampire,* giving its predators a glamour more socially engaged vampires lack."[3] Glamour is part of what these vampires are about, but a more complex relation exists between Rice's gorgeous creatures and the late-twentieth-century's cultural conservatism.

How do we explain the eroticization of Rice's figures of the night? What is it about the male-male seductions of Rice's work that places them on best-seller lists and makes them the staple of shopping malls and supermarket check-out lines? What makes these tales of pulsing bodily fluids the hottest topic in suburban as well as urban U.S. culture? For those of us who are gay it may seem almost too good to be true that these queer figures are able to pop out of their darkened hiding places and into the hearts of millions. It *is* too good to be true. Rice's vampires express culture's secret desire for, and secret fear of, the gay man, the need to fly with him beyond the confines of heterosexual convention and bourgeois family life to explore unauthorized desires and at the same time taste his body and his blood, to see him bleed and watch him succumb to death in life.

In *Bodies That Matter,* Judith Butler maintains that "much of the straight world has always needed the queers it has sought to repudiate through the performative force of the term."[4] The vampire also fulfills the needs of the straight world that attempts to repudiate the lure of darkness. In our twenty-first century cynicism, heroism gives way to superheroic posturing and masculinity becomes self-consciously iconic (rather than authentic) in ways that render it distant, unapproachable, dangerous, and straight. What could be straighter than the grotesquely muscled and gruffly inarticulate heroes of popular film and fiction? Elegant, powerful, thoughtful, and queer, Lestat offers a different version of masculinity. He starts as a rock star in the 1970s, the time of the publication of *Interview with a Vampire,* and then travels back and forth through history and culture to find himself a suave, self-assured international financier who, in a later volume of the *Chronicles,* is invited to witness and pass judgment on heaven and hell. The Dorian Gray of the 1990s, he remains witty, beautiful, and forever young. At the same time, for all his stature Lestat is the passive, the bloodied, and the castrated male.[5] He represents the 1990s' hope that masculinity can survive the emasculation that terminal straightness finally represents, as well as its fear that every man is always already castrated by desire. Lestat is queer, that is, because heterosexist culture needs him as a reflection of its own dark secret.

The deep complicity between vampirism, sexuality, and culture is played out most vividly in the theater the vampires inhabit and open early in the *Chronicles.* The concept behind the "Theatre of the Vampires" is, after all, similar to the early rationale of gay liberation, partly rearticulated in the credos of Act Up and Queer Nation. "We will make a mockery of all things sacred," Nicholas says. "We will lead them to ever greater vulgarity and profanity. We will astonish. We will beguile. But above all, we will thrive on their gold as well as their blood and in their midst we will grow strong" (265). This defiant speech, reminiscent of so much of the politics of the "gay revolution," suggests just how threatened culture can become by the secret it hides. Culture's most cherished features can be used to defy its dictates. What Nicholas preaches is the invisibility of the gay man, the ease with which he can work his way into the hearts and pocketbooks of the society that takes him for one of its own. This is a bold stance, and again and again in *The Vampire Chronicles* the ease with which Rice's vampires coexist with the mortal world around them is both startling and fully convincing. Of course, the vampires pay a price for the open mockery of culture that the open secret of their desire represents. For them, the price is a sell-out to the tormented immortality the vampire world represents.[6]

The Theatre of the Vampires is like a trendy gay disco of the 1970s, fascinating, thrilling, and deadly. It beckons with the call of desire and threatens with the curse of the unnatural. In her essay "Tracking the Vampire," Sue-Ellen Case suggests what is so threatening about queer desire: "Unlike petitions for civil rights, queer revels constitute a kind of activism that attacks the dominant notion of the natural. The queer is the taboo-breaker, the monstrous, the uncanny. Like the Phantom of the Opera, the queer dwells underground, below the operatic overtones of the dominant; frightening to look at, desiring, as it plays its own organ, producing its own music."[7] Case's prose, brimming with double entendre, approximates the gay or lesbian experience in culture. The queer moves in and out of culture as an undertow of the uncanny, the slow burn of desire, and the iceberg of the real cutting into the breathless air of cultural self-satisfaction with its lethal edge. The vampire can hide or she can perform her difference; he can lurk in the shadows or he can burst forth in a blaze of counterfeited glory.

Lestat always chooses to blaze with a performance of narcissism that knows no bounds. Later in the *Chronicles,* in *The Tale of the Body Thief* for instance, Lestat must repossess his body, and the scene in which he pushes the wicked body thief from himself is the climax of the book. In order to achieve his end he must see himself as the object of desire, and in doing so he places the terms of his existence in vivid relief:

> And as a volley of oaths came from the being, I made for him once more, panic driving me as surely as courage and plain mortal will. The first hot ray of the sun cut across the water! Dear God, it was now or never and I couldn't

fail. I couldn't. I collided with him full force, feeling a paralytic electric shock as I passed through him and then I could see nothing and I was being sucked as if by a giant vacuum down and down into the darkness, crying, "Yes, into him, into me! Into my body, yes! Then I was staring directly into a blaze of golden light." (336)

The erotic thrill of actually taking himself in the early morning light is expressed in the violent desperation of the act. Lestat uses all his power to reenter the darkness, to take possession of himself, and to be Lestat once more. This is his most revealing act of preternatural violence. It shows him to have no greater desire than the desire for the self that prevents him from ever breaking out of vampiric isolation.

Readers of *The Vampire Chronicles* are offered a conflicted relation to Lestat and his posturing. Like the audience in the Theatre of the Vampires, they desire voyeuristic participation in something they want to believe and disbelieve at the same time. Their attraction to these creatures of the night is also repulsion. They need to witness the homoerotics of this world and reject its power at the same time. This is an uncanny relation but also a tremendously powerful one.

Slavoj Žižek helps to explain why late-twentieth-century culture would need the homosexual as its particular fetish. In articulating Lacan's account of the symptom in terms that help to explain the workings of ideology Žižek has occasion to explain that cultural signification involves foreclosure of its key determinate: "Whenever we have a symbolic structure it is structured around a certain void, it implies the foreclosure of a certain key-signifier."[8] Culture, then, according to Žižek's reading of Lacan, is structured around the void left by a "key signifier" that explains the structure at the same time that it must be "foreclosed." The void that exists at the center is therefore symptomatic of the structure of culture itself, and as Žižek goes on to suggest here and elsewhere, sexuality can be understood to function in this way. If "what was foreclosed from the Symbolic returns in the Real of the symptom," then Žižek's argument explains not just why, in his words, woman returns as the symptom of man but also why the predatory homosexual, foreclosed from the symbolic, would return as the symptom of a culture so caught up in its own sexuality that it cannot see its sexual obsessions for what they are.

To the woman as culture's symptom, that is, it is possible to add the homosexual, that threat of the sexual relation that cannot be symbolized, the impossible fact of desire, and the final antagonism. The homosexual is the figure who is foreclosed in the Symbolic and returns as a symptom of the culture that would reject him.[9] The vampire represents the return of the repressed in a culturally significant way. Both inside culture and outside, both a charmingly honest man and a wickedly deceptive one, both the phallic aggressor and the always already penetrated one, the vampire represents everything the culture desires and everything it fears.

Žižek says that "we must not obliterate the distance separating the Real from its symbolization: it is this surplus of the Real over every symbolization that functions as the object-cause of desire."[10] What is the Real to which these vampires hold with uncanny tenacity? What do they do to become the "object-cause" for this culture's desire? They defy the death drive and turn radical negativity into the originary commodity, life itself—well, death in life, but the simulation is exactly the point. Rice's vampires bring this surplus of the real back into the symbolic as its desired objects. In doing so they expose the terms of the symbolic structure that would exclude them. Another way of saying this is that the vampire exposes the roots of bourgeois ideology in his ability to represent its desires and its fears. The vampire Lestat functions as the traumatic real kernel from which social reality is constantly trying to escape. Žižek claims that ideology "is not a dreamlike illusion that we build to escape insupportable reality; in its basic dimension it is a fantasy-construction which serves as a support for our 'reality' itself: an 'illusion' which structures our effective, real social relation and thereby masks some insupportable, real, impossible kernel. . . . The function of ideology is not to offer us a point of escape from our reality but to offer us the social reality itself as an escape from some traumatic, real kernel."[11]

In *The Vampire Chronicles* Rice is aware of the vampire as the surplus of the real in Western culture. The vampire moves with the suave invisibility of the prototypical gay man. He offers companionship, friendship, and even love before revealing his true and deadly nature; appears silently and takes his pleasure ruthlessly; and suffers for his sexual transgression by being shut out from the light and condemned to an eternity of darkness. The dark world is a transcendent world, and culture exacts this simple price in exchange for the freedom that Lestat and his friends feel they can exercise.

Cultural anxiety was at fever pitch as the 1990s began to realize their fully victimizing potential, as fights over gays in the military, the militarization of the country's borders, the politics of bigotry, and the institutionalization of misogyny and homophobia all suggest. But the novels emerge from specific historical circumstances, three of which are the AIDS crisis, the crisis over "family values," and the collapse of the war on drugs, with its attendant militarization of civilian life and war on male potency. Rice's *Vampire*

Chronicles address the anxiety surrounding all of these issues in a way that poses the gay man both as the solution to this problem and indicts him as its cause. Ann Rice's characters bear their symptomatic relation to culture with bravado. Lestat especially creates a public space for himself in which he seems symptomatic of an age both demonic and dispossessed. Rice and her readers find Lestat attractive because he is as much a creature of this age as a representative from any other. He lives by the exchange of body fluids, he defies the family at the same time he repeatedly reconstitutes it, and he moves with ease through a drugged-out culture as its inspiration and rationale.

In the late twentieth century the male became the sexualized object in a range of popular forms. Lauren Berlant and Elizabeth Freeman argued that "at present the nation suffers from *Americana nervosa,* a compulsive self-gorging on ritual images."[12] The sexually active male body is one of these images. It graced the pages of magazine advertisements and the frames of films as never before, and it still does. Indeed, the desired object is the male body itself. He represents the healthy alternative to the body weakened by AIDS, the always already coupled family man, and the captain in the silent army against drugs. At the same time he also threatens to be gay. A model or actor might just defy all the demands placed on him and love another man. What is desired in this dynamic of representation and what is feared are the same. Culture wants its young heroes to defy convention; to escape demands on health, family, and sobriety; and to move with the freedom of the night. At the same time culture must condemn such movement as unhealthy, immoral, and deadly.

The cultural secret here is this desire for the man, this homoerotics of secularity that make male-male desire the only desire that the culture can support. The culture gorges itself on the ritual image of the eroticized young man in order to construct its most cherished masculinity. Berlant and Freeman observe that "mainstream national identity touts a subliminal sexuality more official than a state flower or a national bird."[13] Late-twentieth-century culture fed on the eroticized gay man because he, in the popular imagination, is his sexuality. He alone can reanimate the "national identity" with the virility it so powerfully lacks. That is why this desire is at the heart of popular fiction, but it is also why it is so feared. What it says about those who desire is, in Auerbach's terms, a cherished taboo. Homophobia was intense in the later twentieth century precisely because this desire is so intense and so evident. The homosexual is a symptom for that cultural situation because he reflects culture's deepest desires and therefore must bear the brunt of its systematic hatred in the form of homophobia.

192 · QUEER GOTHIC

A microscopic version of the issues I raise can be glimpsed in the controversy that surrounded the establishment of an interdisciplinary minor in
lesbian, gay, and bisexual studies at the University of California, Riverside,
where I teach. Riverside is an open-minded community surrounded on all
sides by fundamentalist and strongly conservative communities whose rep-
resentatives to state government were appalled that public funds could be
used in this way. "Gee," one assemblyman said, "send somebody off to San
Francisco for six months and let them learn there." Another asked, "Do
you want to have a degree in child molesting just because people who don't
happen to be child molesters might want to know more about what they're
missing?" "They just keep pushing their lifestyle and their agenda. . . . It's
all part of the liberal social agenda." And, "We're having trouble preparing
students for the real world and here we're trying to fog up their minds with
all this stuff that goes on around society. It just makes no sense to me."[14] The
substance of these responses constitutes an impressive litany of late-twentieth-century homophobia: Gay people need to be isolated in specific urban
settings, gay men are child molesters, the liberal social agenda is a plot against
family values, and the real world and the world of sexuality are somehow
separate. Rice plays with homophobic responses like these and uses them
to challenge contemporary values. At the same time, she reinscribes them
because of her own uneasiness about the desire she depicts.

"This is my Body, this is my Blood," Magnus tells Lestat just before the
coup de grace that carries him into the darkness (*The Vampire Lestat,* 99).
This moment of Lestat's vampire origin is central to the *Vampire Chronicles,*
and Rice is suitably sacramental in her depiction of the transformation. It
is not an accidental use of Christian imagery. Magnus understands that he
is literalizing the transubstantiation of the Catholic Mass both as a way of
suggesting the brute physicality of the image that is central to Christianity,
the image of the crucified figure of Christ, and as a way of hinting that Lestat
will challenge Christ himself. After he is made, and Magnus abandons him,
Lestat crawls through a "narrow dark passage" in order to reach the "inner
room" in which Magnus's legacy lies hidden. This movement through a narrow passage into Magnus's dark interior is sexually suggestive to be sure, just
as Magnus's desire for Lestat was a palpably homoerotic longing that could
fulfill itself only in his own dissolution. In order to give Lestat all the life and
all the power that he possesses, that is, he must die.

What Lestat finds in the deepest hollows of his new abode, however, are
not just the riches and the wealth of Magnus's long reign as a master vampire
but also the mangled corpses of all the gorgeous young blondes who did not

quite measure up to the demands of Magnus's mighty longing. Lestat sees them and shudders at what they represent:

> In a deep prison cell lay a heap of corpses in all states of decay, the bones and rotted flesh crawling with worms and insects. Rats ran from the light of the torch, brushing past my legs as they made for the stairs. And my nausea became a knot in my throat. The stench suffocated me.
>
> But I couldn't stop staring at these bodies. There was something important here, something terribly important, to be realized. And it came to me suddenly that all these dead victims had been men,—their boots and clothing gave evidence of that—and every single one of them had yellow hair, very much like my own hair. The few who had features left appeared to be young men, tall, slight of build. And the most recent occupant here—the wet and reeking corpse that lay with its arms outstretched through the bars—so resembled me that he might have been a brother. (*The Vampire Lestat,* 107)

Lestat finds himself in the presence of his victim-brothers, a heap of corpses who shared with him youth, beauty, and delicate power. Yet they are enjoying the process of putrefaction that will forever be denied him. They have died in order that he might live. The gay male is the chosen son, the one who can fulfill the destiny of a condemned race. Dozens die for not being quite right. It is almost as if Lestat knows that they are there, knows that he must confront them, and knows that by seeing his resemblance to them he can free himself from the last attraction of mortality. Lestat vomits in horror at what confronts him, but then he laps of the blood that has spewed from his mouth because the thirst is stronger than the disgust. The need to feed on others overpowers his lament for what he has lost and what has been sacrificed so that he might succeed.

The pile of corpses haunts Lestat with its decay, insects, and worms. It haunts him with its familiarity. Youth, in this case Aryan in its features, is the ultimate sacrifice in Western culture. Rice racializes Magnus's quest in order to emphasize Lestat's white—increasingly enameled—identity. This whiteness reminds us of other races and the various ways in which culture has managed to sacrifice its youth. Inner-city drug and gang wars fulfilled that role in the 1990s in ways earlier decades relegated to KKK and random lynchings. This uncanny familiarity emerges in war coverage, whether from feature films or the evening news that haunts daily life. But culture hides other piles of bodies as well, those of the dispossessed and undernourished, the bodies of the victims of racial violence, the bodies wasted by ethnic "cleansing," and of course the bodies of AIDS victims in various communities throughout

194 · QUEER GOTHIC

the world, the gay community in particular. The communion that Magnus initiates is a communion with the dead, and culture's repression of its own carnage is represented in this putrefying vault. Each boy has crawled though the narrow passage to Magnus's inner chamber. For them it was an end, but for Lestat it is only the beginning.[15]

The pile of blond corpses is important to the structure of *The Vampire Chronicles*. This massacre of the innocents determines the limits of the brash and magisterial reign of Lestat; there is no power without a pile of rotting corpses to generate it. The putrefying heap also represents culture's deepest fear of the male relations that structure it. Writers such as Eve Kosofsky Sedgwick have theorized homosocial relations in Anglo-American culture as displacing desire into the violence of rivalry in the classic male-male bond around which culture is organized. She sees "a special relationship between male homosocial (*including* homosexual) desire and the structures for maintaining and transmitting patriarchal power."[16]

Sedgwick's suggestive use of parenthesis implies that homosexual desire is included within the structures of patriarchal power and violence against gay men is part of this. What this violence masks, of course, is the desire that culture must repress in order to function as a coherent system in which men bond in order to effect the exchange of women.[17] What the vampire world threatens to do is to expose the erotic basis of male-male relations in culture. The thirst of the vampire, in other words, is the symptomatic reality of desire itself. What Magnus's heap of corpses suggests, however, is that male-male desire must be compulsive, repetitive, and fatal. This is the secret around which the *Chronicles* are built. For all the love they express they also threaten with a kind of male-male desire that is victimizing and destructive.

At the opening of the *Chronicles,* the first scene in which an unnamed interviewer, a boy from the streets of San Francisco, talks to an unnamed vampire, the first event recounted is the death of a brother: "'There was a tragedy' . . . the vampire started. 'It was my younger brother. . . . 'He died'" (*Interview with the Vampire,* 4). Dead brothers abound in these novels. Rice seems to find in these deaths the source of imaginative life, the beginning of the tale, its generative force. Life and death are mirrored in this way, and the surviving brother always finds himself inexplicably drawn to the grave of his dead sibling. Louis the eighteenth-century plantation owner who begins the story walks through the novels in the shadow of death. His respect for life has a depressing quality, as if his refusal to kill is a refusal to face adult responsibilities or the consequences of adult sexuality. He tells of his making in a wistful mode, as though still clinging to the life he so longed to leave and never quite satisfied with the amazing powers he has acquired. His stance is one of loss. Even in coming to Lestat he knows he has already lost him: "He stepped close to my bed and leaned down so that his face was in the lamp-light, and I saw that he was no ordinary man at all. His gray eyes burned with an incandescence, and the long white hands which hung by his sides were not those of a human being. I think I knew everything in an instant, and all that he told me was only aftermath. What I mean is, the moment I saw him, saw his extraordinary aura and knew him to be no creature I'd ever known, I was reduced to nothing" (*Interview with the Vampire*, 13).

Louis succumbs to the power of Lestat, and for doing so he never forgives himself or his creator. The love Louis feels for Lestat is refigured as "noth-ing" here because the emotional and erotic climax of their encounter would expose the homosocial terms of their bond as thoroughly homoerotic, and Rice needs to play this distinction very carefully. It is the measure of the homophobia of the work that Lestat and Louis can never really make love. They can only play at making house.

Lestat tempts Louis into the dark world of his desire in order to replace friends he has lost, to create a partner with whom he can share the watches of the night, and to be "kept" by the friend who has money to support his every whim. He can hardly admit this desire or show his love because Louis is already trapped within the rhetoric of loss that has domesticated his desire for his brother as mourning and placed him in a position vulnerable to the power of Lestat's seduction but immune to the consequences of his desire. He knows the moment of passion, though, and his flesh feels "a shock of sensation . . . that was not unlike the pleasure of passion" as Lestat sucks the blood from his body. Later, Lestat realizes that he has forgotten to prepare a proper bed for Louis, who must spend his first vampiric day in the same coffin as Lestat. "'You will get in on top of me if you know what's good for you.' And I did," he tells us, as if to consummate the intimacy that the early pages of the book so deftly avoid (*Interview with the Vampire*, 18, 24).

Rice makes it immediately clear, however, that this world of male-male desire cannot be satisfying. For all the homoerotics of these volumes, Rice seems unable to create a bond between two men that is more than the symp-tom of a corrupt and corrupting culture. Even in creating moments of the most intense intimacy or of unbridled sexual attraction, Rice insists on the repulsion that homosexuality regularly breeds in the minds of fundamen-talist politicians and other members of the extreme right. For all the sexual freedom that Rice's heroes experience, in other words, her novels work to ensure that her representation of homosexuality is culturally determined, as if it could be anything else.

Rice loves her creatures—their bravado and their contempt for convention, their physicality and their sensuousness, and their love for one another as well as their hatred. But she also makes them easy to loathe. They avoid the kinds of commitments that make human beings human; they betray human relations with the kiss of everlasting life that is death itself; and they slip among, between, and even within ordinary mortals and bring them grief. Their pleasure is narcissistic, and narcissism is performed with abandon throughout these texts.

The homosexual, cunning and lethal, figures as a kind of symptom of everything that is most thrilling but also most deadly about contemporary culture. In a climactic scene of *Interview with the Vampire,* after the Theatre of the Vampires has been destroyed, Louis and Armand find themselves confronting the possibility of their love for one another. As Louis recounts the moment:

> "Yes," I said softly to him, "that is the crowning evil, that we can even go so far as to love each other, you and I. And who else would show us a particle of compassion or mercy? Who else, knowing us as we know each other, could do anything but destroy us? Yet we love each other."
>
> And for a long moment, he stood there looking at me, drawing nearer, his head gradually inclining to one side, his lips parted as if he meant to speak. But then he only smiled and shook his head to confess he didn't understand. (319)

Louis understands that it is their love that is finally the "crowning evil." He also understands that nothing matters as much in this culture, and it is this love that is the ultimate transgression. This is what culture finally represses, not sexual desire but love. "Love and love and love in the vampire kiss," Armand feels as a boy when Marius takes him in the night. "It bathed Armand, cleansed him, *this is everything,* as he was carried into the gondola and the gondola moved like a great sinister beetle though the narrow stream into the sewers beneath another house" (*The Vampire Lestat,* 292). The image of the dark beetle of love moving through the sewers of Venice, slipping beneath the homes of its victims, and sliding stealthily through the darkness, powerful but secret, is everything as Armand feels now and nothing as he later learns. This child of darkness waits silently for the secret kiss of his master and burns with a quiet flame of love that is not merely desire and therefore infinitely more deadly than the rakish profligacy of Lestat or even the poetic melancholy of Louis. He says silently to Lestat, "Love me. You have destroyed everything! But if you love me, it can all be restored in a new form. Love me" (281). Of course, Lestat cannot love in this way. His narcissism traps him in a relationship only with himself.

David Talbot, the aged superior of Talamasca, the human society that comes closest to understanding Lestat and his breed, almost breaks through the narcissism. In *The Tale of the Body Thief,* David finds himself trapped in a younger and more powerful body than his own. Just as he is relishing the new vigor he feels, he understands that Lestat will take it from him: "I'm going to do it to you, David. I'm going to bring you to me" (412). This violent act of sexual aggression brings *The Vampire Chronicles* to a fitting climax. The scene that ensues is as violent as any act of vampiric penetration in *The Chronicles.* David struggles to resist and pleads with Lestat to let him live. Lestat shows no mercy, however, and transforms his act of brutal victimization into an act of love:

> I grabbed him by the neck before he reached the porch. I let my fingers massage the flesh as he struggled wildly, like an animal, to tear my grip away and pull himself loose. Slowly I lifted him, and cradling the back of his head effortlessly with my left hand, I drove my teeth through the fine, fragrant young skin of his neck, and caught the first bubbling jet of blood.
>
> Ah, David, my beloved David. Never had I descended into a soul I knew so well. How thick and wondrous the images that enveloped me: the soft beautiful sunlight slicing though the mangrove forest, the crunch of the high grass on the veldt, the boom of the great gun, and the shiver of the earth beneath the elephant's pounding feet. It was all there: all the summer rains washing endlessly through the jungles, and the water swimming up the pilings and over the boards of the porch, and the sky flashing with lightning—and his heart pounding beneath it with rebellion, with recrimination, you betray me, you betray me, you take me against my will—and the deep rich salty taste of the blood itself. (415)

With the taste of the blood comes life—the life that Lestat has loved and wanted to possess. He takes in an entire culture, of course, its colonial past as well as its rebellious present. His fantasy is one of possession; he wants to be David as much he wants to have him. It is as much about himself, that is, as it about the man whose blood he tastes. As if to emphasize this, his love can only be expressed in draining life, absolute possession.

David does not give in easily. He struggles and curses as best he can. His

new, strong, young body fights off the violence of Lestat's assault, but he
must succumb, as must anyone whom Lestat desires:

> The heart was slowing. The moment had almost come. One more little
> drink, my friend.
>
> I lifted him and carried him up the beach and back into the room. I kissed
> the tiny wounds, licking them and sucking them with my lips, and then let-
> ting my teeth go in again. A spasm passed through him, a little cry escaped
> his lips.
>
> "I love you," he whispered.
>
> "Yes, and I love you," I answered, words smothered against the flesh, as the
> blood spurted hot and irresistible once again. (417)

David is taken against his will and yet his expression of love seems to
suggest that Lestat has given him what he really wanted. The lurid exchange
of endearments as the blood spurts and the sucking continues hints at the
deepest fear behind the vampire's kiss, not that victims are taken against their
will but rather that the kiss releases the hidden desires that the will would
repress. The kiss steals masculinity from itself, as in this scene, and refigures
it as homoerotic desire. David has been recruited to the race of vampires, as
it were, and he enjoys the new death in life he finds there. "The carnival starts
tomorrow in Rio," he says when Lestat next finds him in New Orleans. The
athletic young man has become a giddy queen; the dark trick has begun to
work its magic. What could be more threatening to a culture afraid of the
implications of its own darkest secret?

Christopher Craft discusses the almost maniacal penetration of Lucy in
one of the climactic scenes of *Dracula* that "disperses a specifically homosexual threat, and consolidates the male homosocial community." He goes
on to argue that the "vigor and enormity of this penetration (Arthur driving
the 'round wooden stake,' itself 'some two and a half or three inches thick
and about three feet long' . . .) do not bespeak Stoker's merely personal or
idiosyncratic anxiety, but suggest as well a whole culture's uncertainty about
the fluidity of gender roles."[18] No such phallic reassurance takes place in
Rice's novels. She is about undoing the homosocial and reeroticizing male
relations so as to reawaken the sleeping homosexual threat that at the turn-
of-the-century was just being laid to rest, as Craft argues.

Rice is as little idiosyncratic as Stoker in this project because it seems that
culture now needs the homosexual to answer anxieties about its makeup,
to explain its unabating violence, and to be a scapegoat to its most violent
forms of self-abuse. In the 1970s and 1980s Rice might have been ahead of

her time. What better moment could there be for Lestat to become a cultural icon? He can draw the blood of this corrupt culture and take from it the power to do the only evil culture acknowledges: the dark trick that would lead us from ourselves and into the world of our desires. If this culture can embrace Lestat as its transcendent figure, think of the numbers that can be sacrificed in his name.

The last volume of this cycle of Vampire Chronicles appeared in 1998. *The Vampire Armand* concerns the arrogant, boyish character who had an important role in the early volumes of the chronicles but has since nearly disappeared. Now he emerges with a story of his own, one that allows Rice to offer some of her most sumptuous descriptions of Renaissance Italy, Italian art, and, of course, male-male love. The love between Armand and his master Marius is retold in rich emotional and physical detail. After one nearly brutal beating, Marius licks the boy's wounds: "I closed my eyes, and there came his lips on my leg. He kissed one of the bruises. I thought I would die. . . . Beneath me, my groin was alive with thankful and desperate and isolated strength. The burning blood flowed over the bruise. The slightly rough stroke of his tongue touched it, lapped at it pressed it, and the inevitable tingling made a fire in my closed eyes, a blazing fire across a mythical horizon in the darkness of my blind mind" (82–83). If it is at first difficult to see culture in this moment of private ecstasy, then we need to remember that the broken male form around which this volume most insistently revolves is the figure of Christ on Calvary. Armand uses Christ's body and blood in order to reconstitute a family configuration, with a woman and a young boy, that is, before the novel reaches it heady vampiric close. What began as theatrics has ended—or nearly ended, there are several series of volumes to follow—as religion. The gay man is sacrificed so the family can be preserved. It is a familiar story.

And so I return to the "family values" with which I began this chapter. The "Love of Men and Women for one another and for their Children" is the measure against which all the transgressive desire of these works must finally be measured. This is the love that could cause Memnoch to sacrifice his happiness and bring God into the experience of mortality. This is all that Lestat has been missing for his centuries of nightly ventures into the homoerotic world of darkness and desire. The family has hovered behind all the action of these chronicles, and it emerges in *Memnoch the Devil* as if to mock those who imagined that Rice might really give credence to alternative sexualities. At last she has made her position most painfully clear, or I suppose I should say that God's plan is finally worked out to the satisfaction of those who have used him to assert the family at the expense of every attempt at difference.

Afterword

In this study I have considered a range of gothic fiction and drama from the eighteenth, nineteenth, and twentieth centuries. I have shown how early gothic works anticipate the family romance of late-nineteenth-century psychology and how later works extend and deepen the possibilities of psychological analysis. We can never overestimate the value of this literary material in helping explain a topic as undefined as "the history of sexuality." In some ways there is no such history unless we consider the literary representation of personal relations. Freud himself relied on literary examples in describing the uncanny, the Oedipus complex, sadism, and masochism, as most of these titles express unmistakably. At the end of chapter 1, I suggested a revision of sexological thinking: "Gothic novels articulate more complex 'sexualities.' Theories of sexuality that depend on the gothic—whether Walpole-Lewisism, or Lewis-Maturinism, or Radcliffe-Lewism—would be more varied, more sexually complex, less heteronormative and more polymorphously perverse than any thus far considered."

At the conclusion of this work that claim may seem less facetious. Gothic novels challenge the narrow definitions that psycho-sexology has offered, and they help redefine familiar sexological categories. If Walpole and Lewis rewrite the family romance as brutal and victimizing, if Radcliffe reimagines the homoerotics of maternal bonds, and if Shelley posits the monstrous construction of subjectivity, then all these writers contribute to what we now understand as sexuality. If James, Jackson, Rice, and Minghella force reconsideration of some of the basic terms of twentieth-century "homosexuality," and if they dramatize personal neuroses in terms Freud never imagined, then they, too, expand understanding of what we thought we already knew. In his essay "How to Do the History of Male Homosexuality," David Halperin complains about the way homosexuality functions in twentieth-century discourse: "The very notion of homosexuality implies that same-sexual feeling and expression, in all their many forms, constitute a single thing, called 'homosexuality,' which can be thought of as a single integrated phenomenon, distinct and separate from 'heterosexuality.' 'Homosexuality' refers to *all* same-sex sexual desire and behavior, whether hierarchical or mutual, gender-polarized or ungendered, latent or actual, mental or physical."[1]

Halperin's lament is welcome, especially because it comes at the end of his long discussion of earlier forms and behaviors. Gothic fiction and drama offer opportunity to rediscover the complexities that Halperin argues the term *homosexuality* obscures. Throughout this study, gothic works defy limits and preconceptions of behavior and offer a usefully uncategorized range of personal, sexual, and emotional behaviors and attitudes. In doing so they add to an understanding of the sexual past and enrich understanding of the culture of which they are a part.

Some years ago, an eighteenth-century scholar suggested that fiction was relatively unimportant when what was being addressed was a history of ideas. I think we have only started to move beyond that antifictional prejudice. Few come to the early conclusion that gothic novelists were breaking important ground with their lurid tales of dysfunctional and incestuous families, of paranoid personal relations and sadistic practices. But the importance of what they were doing is striking, before the sensationalism, before the sentimentality, before the cataclysmic endings, and even before the marriages, deaths, and disappearances. Gothic novels teach more than critics have been ready to recognize. *The Failure of Gothic,* as one critic puts it, is more vivid than its success.[2] But even gothic failure is a kind of success if it challenges the status quo and insists on behaviors otherwise invisible in eighteenth- and nineteenth-century cultures. Cultural studies allows seeing beyond the limitations of a "history of ideas" approach to the cultural past, and as a result novels and plays offer as rich a source of historical material as any other body of material. As George Rousseau maintains:

> What counts to those among us who would understand the deepest levels, the most original ideas, which made the cult of sensibility possible in the first place—whether in the novel or elsewhere in imaginative literature—it is a simple fact (and it is so simple that we have never bothered to notice it) that no novel of sensibility could appear until a revolution in knowledge concern-

ing the brain, and consequently its slaves, the nerves, had occurred. If Sterne or Smollett, or even Jane Austen with *Sense and Sensibility,* had chronologically preempted Richardson by writing for the first time about the delights of moral sentiments of charitable sensibility, it would make no substantive or impressionable difference to the historian of ideas.[3]

Rousseau wrote that in 1976. I can imagine him revising that sentence now in the same ways that I would like to revise it, for scientists do not always precede novelists, as I hope I have shown. In the case of sensibility, of course, it matters that Richardson, Sterne, and Austen wrote what they did when they did. In fact, they tell us more than the physiologists do about how feeling was coded in the later eighteenth century. Gothic fiction and drama, even more profoundly, anticipate developments in the history of sexuality, at times by a few years, at times by a few generations, and at times by nearly a century.

Notes

Acknowledgments

1. Eve Kosofsky Sedgwick, *Between Men: English Literature and Male Homosocial Desire* (New York: Columbia University Press, 1985); Judith Halberstam, *Skin Shows: Gothic Horror and the Technology of Monsters* (Durham: Duke University Press, 1995); G. S. Rousseau, "The Pursuit of Homosexuality in the Eighteenth Century: Utterly Confused Category and/or Rich Repository?" *Eighteenth-Century Life* 9 (1985): 132–68; Lee Edelman, *Homographesis: Essays in Gay Literary and Cultural Theory* (New York: Routledge, 1994); Andrew Elfenbein, *Romantic Genius: The Prehistory of a Homosexual Role* (New York: Columbia University Press, 1999); Claudia L. Johnson, *Equivocal Beings: Politics, Gender, and Sentimentality in the 1790s* (Chicago: University of Chicago Press, 1995); Kristina Straub, *Sexual Suspects: Eighteenth-Century Players and Sexual Ideology* (Princeton: Princeton University Press, 1992).

Introduction

1. E. J. Clery and Robert Miles, *Gothic Documents, a Sourcebook, 1700–1820* (Manchester: Manchester University Press, 2000); Edward H. Jacobs, *Accidental Migrations: An Archaeology of Gothic Discourse* (Lewisburg: Bucknell University Press, 2000); see also Kelly Hurley, *The Gothic Body: Sexuality, Materialism, and Degeneration in the Fin de Siècle* (Cambridge: Cambridge University Press, 1996).

2. George E. Haggerty, *Gothic Fiction/Gothic Form* (University Park: Pennsylvania State University Press, 1989), 14–35.

3. The word *Gothic* is usually capitalized when referring to a literary movement or aesthetic style. I think it useful to retain a lower-case *gothic* when referring to a literary trope. Most gothic fiction refers to itself rather than to any specific Gothic

age. *Gothic effects, gothic conventions, gothic writing, gothic anxieties*—these are terms that I prefer to leave in lower case.

4. Joseph Bristow, *Sexuality* (London: Routledge, 1997), 1–11.

5. Horace Walpole, *The Castle of Otranto*, edited by W. S. Lewis and Joseph N. Reed Jr. (1764, repr. New York: Oxford University Press, 1982, 1996), 27.

6. See, for instance, Eve Kosofsky Sedgwick, *Between Men: English Literature and Male Homosocial Desire* (New York: Columbia University Press, 1985); and Judith Halberstam, *Skin Shows: Gothic Horror and the Technology of Monsters* (Durham: Duke University Press, 1995); see also George Haggerty, "Literature and Sexuality in the Later Eighteenth Century: Walpole, Beckford, and Lewis," *Studies in the Novel* 18 (1986): 341–51.

7. For the concept of "dominant fiction," see Kaja Silverman, *Male Subjectivity at the Margins* (New York: Routledge, 1992).

Chapter 1: Gothic Fiction and the History of Sexuality

1. I have discussed gothic conventions in an earlier study, *Gothic Fiction/Gothic Form* (University Park: Pennsylvania State University Press, 1979), 1–14.

2. Slavoj Žižek, *The Sublime Object of Ideology* (New York: Verso Press, 1989), 169.

3. David Punter explains the gothic in similar terms. He says that "Gothic . . . provides an image language for bodies and their terrors, inhabits a point of undecidability in the area of the growth of self-awareness." Punter, *Gothic Pathologies* (New York: St. Martins Press, 1998), 14.

4. Tzvetan Todorov made a similar argument about "the fantastic" in his book with that title. For Todorov, however, everything depended on whether or not the supernatural was explained. See *The Fantastic: A Structural Approach to a Literary Form*, translated by Richard Howard (Cleveland: Case Western Reserve University Press, 1973).

5. Žižek, *The Sublime Object of Ideology*, 169.

6. Kaja Silverman, *Male Subjectivity at the Margins* (New York: Routledge, 1992), 17, 21; see also Žižek, *The Sublime Object of Ideology*, 34.

7. Linda Bayer-Berenbaum sees this as a question of repression: "Gothic literature continued to portray all states of mind that intensify normal thought or perception. Dream states, drug states, and states of intoxication have always been prevalent in the Gothic novel because repressed thoughts can surface in them; under their influence inhibitions are minimized, and thus the scope of consciousness widened. Gothic novelists are particularly fond of hypnotic trances, telepathic communications, visionary experiences, and extrasensory perceptions, for these reveal the secret recesses of the mind or powers of increased mental transmission and reception." *The Gothic Imagination: Expansion in Gothic Literature and Art* (Rutherford: Fairleigh University Press, 1982), 25. As I argue in the pages that follow, gothic fiction also dramatizes the surfacing of repressed thoughts and repressed behaviors.

8. The best account of this process remains that presented in Claudia L. Johnson, *Equivocal Beings: Politics, Gender, and Sentimentality in the 1790s* (Chicago: University of Chicago Press, 1995); see also Felicity A. Nussbaum, *Torrid Zones: Maternity, Sexuality, and Empire in Eighteenth-Century English Narratives* (Baltimore: Johns Hopkins University Press, 1995).

9. Haggerty, *Gothic Fiction/Gothic Form,* 1–14.

10. Matthew G. Lewis, *The Monk: A Romance,* edited by Howard Anderson (1796, repr. New York: Oxford University Press, 1973), 304; further references in the text are to this edition.

11. Stephen Bruhn, *Gothic Bodies: The Politics of Pain in Romantic Fiction* (Philadelphia: University of Pennsylvania Press, 1994), xvii.

12. Claude Lévi-Strauss, *The Elementary Structures of Kinship,* translated by James Harle Bell and Richard von Sturmer, edited by Rodney Needham (1949, repr. Boston: Beacon Press, 1969), 44–45; see also Emile Durkheim, *Incest: The Nature and Origin of the Taboo, together with "The Origins and the Development of the Incest Taboo"* by Albert Ellis, Ph.D., translated by Edward Sagarin (1898, repr. New York: Lyle Stuart, 1963), 84–86. For a feminist response to these arguments see Gayle Rubin, "The Traffic in Women: Notes toward a Political Economy of Sex," in *Toward an Anthropology of Women,* edited by Rayna Reiter (New York: Monthly Review Press, 1975), 157–210.

13. George E. Haggerty, *Unnatural Affections: Women and Fiction in the Later Eighteenth Century* (Bloomington: Indiana University Press, 1998), 27, see also 26–32.

14. Michel Foucault, *The History of Sexuality,* vol. 1: *An Introduction,* translated by Robert Hurley (New York: Vintage-Random House, 1980), 109, 105; see also Joseph Bristow, *Sexuality* (London: Routledge, 1997), 168–74.

15. For Robert Miles, she is "the great enchantress." Miles, *Ann Radcliffe: The Great Enchantress* (Manchester: Manchester University Press, 1995).

16. Ann Radcliffe, *The Mysteries of Udolpho,* edited by Bonamy Dobrée (1794, repr. New York: Oxford University Press, 1966), 226–27; further references in the text are to this edition.

17. Fred Botting, *Gothic* (London: Routledge, 1996), 38–39.

18. Vijay Mishra, *The Gothic Sublime* (Albany: State University of New York Press, 1994), 33.

19. Miles, *Ann Radcliffe,* 123.

20. For a comparison of this novel to Radcliffe's other efforts, see Miles, *Ann Radcliffe,* 129–48.

21. Punter, *Gothic Pathologies,* 10.

22. Claire Kahane, "The Gothic Mirror," in *The Mother Tongue: Essays in Feminist Psychoanalytic Interpretation,* edited by Shirley Nelson Garner, Claire Kahane, and Madelon Springnether (Ithaca: Cornell University Press, 1985), 339.

23. Cynthia Griffin Wolff, "The Radcliffean Gothic Model: A Form for Female Sexuality," *Modern Language Studies* 9 (1979): 98–113, quotation on 102–3.

24. Susan C. Greenfield, "Veiled Desire: Mother-Daughter Love and Sexual Imagery

in Ann Radcliffe's *The Italian*," *The Eighteenth Century: Theory and Interpretation* 33 (1992): 73–89, quotation on 74; see also Johnson, *Equivocal Beings,* 162–63, 134–35.

25. Haggerty, *Unnatural Affections,* 88–102.

26. Ann Radcliffe, *The Italian; or, The Confessional of the Black Penitents,* edited by Frederick Garber and E. J. Clery (1797, repr. New York: Oxford University Press, 1968, 1998), 369–78.

27. Susan Wolstenholme, *Gothic (Re)Visions: Writing Women as Readers* (Albany: State University of New York Press, 1993), 25, 30.

28. Judith Butler, *The Psychic Life of Power: Theories in Subjection* (Stanford: Stanford University Press, 1997), 135.

29. Diane Long Hoeveler, *Gothic Feminism: The Professionalization of Gender from Charlotte Smith to the Brontës* (University Park: Pennsylvania State University Press, 1998), 23.

30. Bayer-Berenbaum discusses this novel at length (*The Gothic Imagination,* 75–106); see also Eve Kosofsky Sedgwick, *The Coherence of Gothic Convention* (New York: Methuen, 1986), 15–18; and Bunting, *Gothic,* 91–112.

31. Stephen Bruhm, *Gothic Bodies* (Philadelphia: Pennsylvania University Press, 1994), 33.

32. Charles Robert Maturin, *Melmoth the Wanderer,* edited by Douglas Grant (1820, repr. New York: Oxford University Press, 1968, 1988), 192; further references in the text are to this edition.

33. Punter, *Gothic Pathologies,* 17.

34. Botting, *Gothic,* 6.

35. Cindy Hendershot, *The Animal Within: Masculinity and the Gothic* (Ann Arbor: University of Michigan Press, 1998), 1, 9.

36. David M. Halperin, "Forgetting Foucault: Acts, Identities, and the History of Sexuality," *Representations* 63 (Summer 1998): 93–120.

Chapter 2: Gothic Fiction and the Erotics of Loss

1. Quotations are from Horace Walpole, *The Castle of Otranto: A Gothic Story,* edited by W. S. Lewis and E. J. Clery (1764, repr. New York: Oxford University Press, 1996), 19; further references in the text are to this edition.

2. I borrow the term from Kaja Silverman, *Male Subjectivity at the Margins* (New York: Routledge, 1992), 15–51.

3. David M. Halperin, "Forgetting Foucault: Acts, Identities, and the History of Sexuality," *Representations* 63 (Summer 1998): 93–120, quotations on 96, 97, 98, 107–8, and 109.

4. Judith Butler, *The Psychic Life of Power: Theories in Subjection* (Stanford: Stanford University Press, 1997), 7.

5. Butler, *The Psychic Life of Power,* 9.

6. Leo Bersani, *The Freudian Body* (New York: Columbia: University Press, 1986), 41. Bersani sees this as the "counterargument" in Freud's *Three Essays on Sexuality.*

7. Bersani, *The Freudian Body*, 39.

8. In an article about "Desire in *The Monk*," Wendy Jones argues that "Ambrosio's unquenchable sexual desire is a displacement of his desire for his mother" and that Matilda and Antonia are in various ways mother substitutes for the breast-deprived hero. Jones, "Desire in *The Monk*," *ELH* 57 (1990): 134.

9. Matthew G. Lewis, *The Monk: A Romance*, edited by Howard Anderson (1796, repr. New York: Oxford University Press, 1973), 420; further references in the text are to this edition.

10. Butler, *The Psychic Life of Power*, 179.

11. Leo Bersani, "Foucault, Freud, Fantasy, and Power," *GLQ: A Journal of Lesbian and Gay Studies* 2 (1994): 31.

12. She asks her friend to "teach [her] to bear with fortitude this sudden transition from misery to bliss. So lately a Captive, opprest with chains, perishing with hunger, suffering every inconvenience of cold and want, hidden from the light, excluded from society, hopeless, neglected, and as I feared, forgotten" (416–17). The conventual experience can barely release into the protocol that her "exquisite" "happiness" feebly articulates.

13. Michelle A. Massé and Tania Modleski, among others, have written about female masochism in gothic fiction, but something else is going on in these and other examples. Michelle A. Massé, *In the Name of Love: Women, Masochism, and the Gothic* (Ithaca: Cornell University Press, 1992); Tania Modleski, *Loving with a Vengeance: Mass-Produced Fantasies for Women* (New York: Routledge, 1988).

14. Bersani, "Foucault, Freud, Fantasy, and Power," 29.

15. Important discussions of "female gothic" include Modleski, *Loving with a Vengeance*; Claudia L. Johnson, *Equivocal Beings: Politics, Gender, and Sentimentality in the 1790s* (Chicago: Chicago University Press, 1995); Anne Williams, *Art of Darkness: A Poetics of Gothic* (Chicago: University of Chicago Press, 1995); and Susan Wolstenholme, *Gothic (Re)Visions: Writing Women as Readers* (Albany: State University of New York Press, 1993).

16. Johnson, *Equivocal Beings*, 117.

17. Ann Radcliffe, *The Italian; or, The Confessional of the Black Penitents*, edited by Frederick Garber and E. J. Clery (1797, repr. New York: Oxford University Press, 1998), 234; further references in the text are to this edition.

18. For a discussion of the homoerotics of this scene see Susan C. Greenfield, "Veiled Desire: Mother-Daughter Love and Sexual Imagery in Ann Radcliffe's *The Italian*," *The Eighteenth Century: Theory and Interpretation* 33 (1992): 73–89; see also Johnson, *Equivocal Beings*, 117–37.

19. Robert Miles, *Ann Radcliffe, The Great Enchantress* (Manchester: Manchester University Press, 1995), 159, see also Miles, "Radcliffe's Politics: *The Italian*," 149–73.

20. Butler, *The Psychic Life of Power*, 133–34; see also Sigmund Freud, *The Ego and the Id*, in *The Standard Edition of the Complete Psychological Works of Sigmund Freud*, edited and translated by James Strachey (London: Hogarth Press, 1953–74), 19: 29.

21. See, for instance, Kim Ian Michasiw, Introduction, in Charlotte Dacre, *Zofloya, or the Moor,* edited by Kim Ian Michasiw (1806, repr. New York: Oxford University Press, 1997), xx–xxi; further references in the text are to this edition.

22. George E. Haggerty, *Unnatural Affections: Women and Fiction in the Later Eighteenth Century* (Bloomington: Indiana University Press, 1998), 173–77.

23. Butler, *The Psychic Life of Power,* 193, 195.

24. Michasiw, Introduction, xxiv–xxv.

25. Percy Bysshe Shelley, *Zastrozzi, A Romance* [and] *St. Irvyne; or, The Rosicrucian, A Romance,* edited by Stephen C. Behrendt (1810, 1811, repr. New York: Oxford University Press, 1986), 8; further references in the text are to this edition.

26. Percy Bysshe Shelley, *Adonais* (1821), in *Shelley's Poetry and Prose,* edited by Donald H. Reiman and Sharon B. Powers (New York: W. W. Norton, 1977), 398.

27. Roger Lonsdale, ed., *The Poems of Gray, Collins, and Goldsmith,* (London: Longman, 1969), 328; translation (adapted) 332. George E. Haggerty, "O lachrymarum fons: Tears, Poetry, and Desire in Gray," *Eighteenth-Century Studies* 30 (1996): 81–95, quotation on 91; George E. Haggerty, "Love and Loss: An Elegy," *GLQ* 10 (2004): 385–406.

28. Butler, *The Psychic Life of Power,* 84; see also Michel Foucault, *Discipline and Punish: The Birth of the Prison,* translated by Alan Sheridan (New York: Random House, 1979), 203.

Chapter 3: "Dung, Guts, and Blood": Sodomy, Abjection, and the Gothic

1. Quoted in *The Phoenix of Sodom; or, The Vere Street Coterie* (London, 1813), facsimile reprint in *Sodomy Trials: Seven Documents* (New York: Garland Publishing, 1986), unnumbered pages; further references in the text are to this edition. Christopher Z. Hobson explains that "the events described [here] were reported in at least four London newspapers: *The Times* and *Morning Chronicle,* both dailies; *Bell's* published Sunday"; and the unidentified source from *The Phoenix of Sodom.* Hobson, *Blake and Homosexuality,* (New York: Palgrave, 2000), 213n4 and 114–15.

2. A discussion of sodomy as a version of bad taste is to be found in John Beynon, "Men of Mode: Taste, Effeminacy, and Male Sexuality in Eighteenth-Century England," Ph.D. diss., University of California, Riverside, 2000; see also Joseph Litvak, *Strange Gourmets: Sophistication, Theory, and the Novel* (Durham: Duke University Press, 1997).

3. Jonathan Swift, *Complete Poems,* edited by Pat Rogers (New Haven: Yale University Press, 1983), 114.

4. Peter Linebaugh, *The London Hanged: Crime and Civil Society in the Eighteenth Century* (New York: Cambridge University Press, 1992), esp. 402–41; see also Douglas Hay et al., *Albion's Fatal Tree: Crime and Society in Eighteenth-Century England* (New York: Pantheon, 1975).

5. Julia Kristeva, *Powers of Horror: An Essay on Abjection,* translated by Leon S.

Roudiez (New York: Columbia University Press, 1982), 109; see also Judith Butler, *Bodies That Matter: On the Discursive Limits of Sex* (New York: Routledge, 1993), 71.

6. Kristeva, *Powers of Horror,* 109; see also Butler, *Bodies That Matter,* 1–12, 243n2. For an extended discussion of abjection, see George E. Haggerty, *Men in Love: Masculinity and Sexuality in the Eighteenth Century* (New York: Columbia University Press, 1999), 126–35.

7. Haggerty, *Men in Love,* 126–35.

8. Slavoj Žižek, *For They Know Not What They Do: Enjoyment as a Political Factor* (New York: Verso Press, 1991), 17–18.

9. Žižek, *For They Know Not What They Do,* 19. By "quilting," Žižek is discussing the way heterogeneous materials are folded into a "unified ideological field" (18).

10. Ibid., 19.

11. For a discussion of sodomites in earlier eighteenth-century culture, see, for instance, Cameron McFarlane, *The Sodomite in Fiction and Satire* (New York: Columbia University Press, 1997); and *Secret Sexualities: A Sourcebook of Seventeenth and Eighteenth Century Writing,* edited by Ian McCormick (New York: Routledge, 1997).

12. Jonathan Goldberg, *Sodometries: Renaissance Texts, Modern Sexualities* (Stanford: Stanford University Press, 1992), 119; see also Alan Bray, "Homosexuality and the Signs of Male Friendship in Elizabethan England," *History Workshop: A Journal of Socialist and Feminist Historians* 29 (1990): 1–15; and Haggerty, *Men in Love,* 23–43

13. Mary Shelley, *Frankenstein; or, The Modern Prometheus,* edited by M. K. Joseph (1818, repr. New York: Oxford University Press, 1983), 37, 39, 47; further references in the text are to this edition.

14. Bette London connects the representation of the male body to the cultural production of Mary Shelley's literary authority. London suggests "the ways conventionalized operations of gender have foreclosed access to *Frankenstein*'s exploitation of masculinity." London, "Mary Shelley, *Frankenstein,* and the Spectacle of Masculinity," *PMLA* 108 (1993): 253–67, quotation on 256.

15. George E. Haggerty, *Gothic Fiction/Gothic Form* (University Park: Pennsylvania State University Press, 1989), 49–55.

16. For London, "Normative readings [of the description of the creature], focusing on its horrific aspects, disguise its participation in the Petrarchan convention of (female) dismemberment: in the representation of the loved one as a composite of details, a collection of parts." London, "Mary Shelley, *Frankenstein,* and the Spectacle of Masculinity," 261.

17. Judith Butler, *The Psychic Life of Power: Theories in Subjection* (Stanford: Stanford University Press, 1997), 171.

18. For a fascinating discussion of *Frankenstein* and technology, see Judith Halberstam, *Skin Shows: Gothic Horror and the Technology of Monsters* (Durham: Duke University Press, 1995), 28–52.

19. Ellen Moers, "Female Gothic," in Moers, *Literary Women: The Great Writers*

(New York: Oxford University Press, 1985), 90–100; see also Barbara Johnson, "My Monster/My Self," *Diacritics* 12 (1882): 2–10.

20. William Veeder, *Mary Shelley and Frankenstein: The Fate of Androgyny* (Chicago: University of Chicago Press, 1986), 81–102.

21. For a discussion of the concept of the unnamable in *Frankenstein* see Haggerty, *Gothic Fiction/Gothic Form*, 37–64.

22. London, "Mary Shelley, *Frankenstein*, and the Spectacle of Masculinity," 260.

23. James Hogg, *The Private Memoirs and Confessions of a Justified Sinner,* edited by John Carey (1824, repr. New York: Oxford University Press, 1990), 21, 45; further references in the text are to this edition.

24. Eve Kosofsky Sedgwick, *Between Men: English Literature and Male Homosocial Desire* (New York: Columbia University Press, 1985), 114; for an earlier version of this reading of Hogg see George Haggerty, "Gothic Fiction, 1764–1824," in *The Columbia History of the British Novel* (New York: Columbia University Press, 1994), 220–46.

25. Dennis A. Foster, *Confession and Complicity in Narrative* (New York: Cambridge University Press, 1987), 7.

26. Foster, *Confession and Complicity,* 9. For Peter Brooks, "The confessional subject . . . is obliged to perform a scrupulous self-examination and to submit the results, in a verbal transaction, to an examiner who holds the power to absolve and, in absolution, to acknowledge and legitimate the individual as a valid part of the community." Brooks, *Troubling Confessions: Speaking Guilt in Law and Literature* (Chicago: University of Chicago Press, 2000), 100.

Chapter 4: The Horrors of Catholicism: Religion and Sexuality in Gothic Fiction

1. Horace Walpole, *The Castle of Otranto: A Gothic Story,* edited by W. S. Lewis and E. J. Clery (1764, repr. New York: Oxford University Press, 1996), 50; further references in the text are to this edition.

2. Walpole, "Preface to the First Edition," in *The Castle of Otranto,* 9–14.

3. David Halperin notes that the "word *homosexuality* appeared in print for the first time in German (as *Homosexualität*) in 1869." Halperin, "Homosexuality," in *Gay Histories and Cultures: An Encyclopedia,* edited by George E. Haggerty (New York: Garland Publishing, 2000), 450–52.

4. This is not the last moment in the history of sexuality when such as connection is possible. See, for instance, Ellis Hansen *Decadence and Catholicism* (Cambridge: Harvard University Press, 1997): "How, after all, is the transcendental nature of God made known? How does the Church make its fascination palpable? Inevitably, the answer is through language, through the symbol, through the brilliant lie that is great art. Sexuality, or more precisely the art of sexuality, is also part of the answer" (21). For a political account of this phenomenon, see Robert Miles, "Europhobia: The Catholic Other in Horace Walpole and Charles Maturin," in Miles, *European Gothic: A Spirited Exchange* (Manchester: Manchester University Press, 2002), 84–103.

5. I have discussed the details of this novel elsewhere. George E. Haggerty, "Literature and Homosexuality in the Late Eighteenth Century: Walpole, Beckford, and Lewis," *Studies in the Novel* 18 (1986): 341–51.

6. See, for instance, Samuel Taylor Coleridge, "Review of *The Monk: A Romance*," *The Critical Review* (Feb. 1797): 194–200, reprinted in *Coleridge's Miscellaneous Criticism,* edited by Thomas Middleton Raysor (Cambridge: Harvard University Press, 1936), 370–78. For Coleridge, "The whole work is distinguished by the variety and impressiveness of its incidents; and the author everywhere discovers an imagination, rich, powerful, and fervid" (371). When he does the criticize the work—and he finds a lot to criticize—he largely discusses novelistic technique. But when he does turn to the lurid sexual energy of the work, he says, "Not without reluctance then, but in full conviction that we are performing a duty, we declare it to be our opinion, that the Monk is a romance, which if a parent saw in the hands of a son or daughter, he might reasonably turn pale" (374). He finds something to complain about in the handling of the Bible but never mentions an injustice to monks, nuns, or Catholics in general.

7. Colin Haydon, *Anti-Catholicism in Eighteenth-Century England, c. 1714–1780* (Manchester: Manchester University Press, 1993), 204–44; for an opposing explanation of the riots, see George Rudé, "The Gordon Riots: A Study of the Rioters and Their Victims," *T.R.H.S.* 5th series, 6 (1956): 93–114.

8. Haydon, *Anti-Catholicism in Eighteenth-Century England,* 206.

9. This quotation from Bishop Sherlock was used on the title page of the popular *Appeal from the Protestant Association to the People of Great Britain* (1779), 59 (ibid., 210).

10. Ibid., 234.

11. See, for instance, Gary Kelly, *The English Jacobin Novel* (New York: Oxford University Press, 1976), 7. Kelly discusses a group of novelists who "opposed tyranny and oppression, be it domestic, national, or international, spiritual or temporal" in the spirit of English Jacobinism (7).

12. The classic statement of this horror is that expressed by Edmund Burke, *Reflections on the Revolution in France* (London, 1790).

13. *Satan's Harvest Home* (1749), in *Hell upon Earth; or, The Town in an Uproar and Satan's Harvest Home,* edited by Randolph Trumbach (New York: Garland Publishing, 1985), 51–52. This section of the work appeared earlier as *Plain Reasons against Sodomy* (London, 1730).

14. John C. Beynon, "Men of Mode: Taste, Effeminacy, and Male Sexuality in Eighteenth-Century England," Ph.D. diss., University of California, Riverside, 2000; see also Bernard de Mandeville, *A Modest Defence of Public Stews* (London, 1724), 7–8.

15. Cameron McFarlane, *The Sodomite in Fiction and Satire, 1660–1750* (New York: Columbia University Press, 1997), 55, 80.

16. Charles Churchill, "The Times," 1764, reprinted in *The Poetical Works of Charles Churchill,* edited by Douglas Grant (New York: Oxford University Press, 1956), 2:

177–84; further references in the text are to this edition; see also *Secret Sexualities: A Sourcebook of Seventeenth and Eighteenth Century Writing*, edited by Ian McCormick (New York: Routledge, 1997), 169.

17. E. J. Clery, "Attitudes to Italy," in introduction to Ann Radcliffe, *The Italian; or, The Confessional of the Black Penitents*, edited by Frederick Garber and E. J. Clery (1797, repr. New York: Oxford University Press, 1998), x.

18. Simon Richter, "Winkelmann, Johann Joachim (1717–1768)," in *Gay Histories and Cultures: An Encyclopedia*, edited by George E. Haggerty (New York: Garland Publishing, 2000), 956. Richter also says that "Winckelmann's major work, the *History of the Art of Antiquity*, was published in 1764. Showing the fruits of his sustained daily engagement with ancient artifacts and texts, *History* is a compendium of numerous individual artworks, placing them in the service of aesthetic, art-historical and cultural observation and theorization. Whereas *Reflections* featured Laocoön as its centerpiece, *History* more openly describes an eroticized ideal of male beauty" (957). See also Simon Richter and Patrick McGrath, "Representing Homosexuality: Winckelmann and the Aesthetics of Friendship." *Monatshefte* 86 (1994): 45–58.

19. Tobias Smollett notes that young English travelers "are seized with the ambition of becoming connoisseurs in painting, music, statuary, and architecture." He continues, "I have seen in different parts of Italy, a number of raw boys, whom Britain seemed to have poured forth on purpose to bring her national character into contempt; ignorant, petulant, rash, and profligate, without any knowledge or experience of their own, without any director to improve their understanding, or superintend their conduct." Smollett, *Travels through France and Italy*, edited by Frank Felsenstein (1766, repr. New York: Oxford University Press, 1981), 241. In a novel like *Peregrine Pickle* (1751) Smollett is more specific about the dangers of Italian love. George E. Haggerty, *Men in Love: Masculinity and Sexuality in the Eighteenth Century* (New York: Columbia University Press, 1999), 75–78.

20. John Ingamells, "Discovering Italy," in *Grand Tour: The Lure of Italy in the Eighteenth Century*, edited by Andrew Wilton and Llaria Bignamini (London: Tate Gallery Publishing, 1996), 21–30, quotation on 26.

21. Alan Bray, "Homosexuality and the Signs of Male Friendship in Elizabethan England," *History Workshop: A Journal of Socialist and Feminist Historians* 29 (1990): 1–19, quotation on 3.

22. Mark D. Jordan, "Sodomy," in *Gay Histories and Cultures: An Encyclopedia*, edited by George E. Haggerty (New York: Garland Publishing, 2000), 830. Jordan also explains that "because *sodomy* is essentially a Christian term, it cannot function easily (if at all) in secular contexts. The history of the category will show how deeply embedded it is in religious speaking and thinking" (828–29). See also Mark D. Jordan, *The Invention of Sodomy in Christian Theology* (Chicago: University of Chicago Press, 1997).

23. I am thinking particularly of Randolph Trumbach, *Heterosexuality and the Third Gender in Enlightenment London*, volume 1 of *Sex and the Gender Revolution*

(Chicago: University of Chicago Press, 1998). Another account of this critical period is Tim Hitchcock's *English Sexualities, 1700–1800* (New York: St. Martin's Press, 1997). In an elegant chapter Hitchcock asks, "Is it surprising, after all, that the century which gave us the debating society and the chapel, in which clubs of all sorts were created, should also give us a homosexual subculture?" (75). If Hitchcock only begins to suggest an answer to this question he also makes it clear that the question is not as simple as it sounds. See also George E. Haggerty, "Heteromachia," *GLQ: A Journal of Lesbian and Gay Studies* 6, no. 3 (2000): 435–50.

24. Haggerty, "Literature and Homosexuality in the Late Eighteenth Century."

25. Ronald Paulson, "Gothic Fiction and the French Revolution," *ELH* 48 (1981): 532–54, quotation on 536.

26. Haggerty, "Literature and Homosexuality in the Late Eighteenth Century."

27. George E. Haggerty, "Beckford's Paederasty," in *Illicit Sex: Identity Politics in Early Modern Culture,* edited by Pat Gill and Tom DiPiero (Athens: University of Georgia Press, 1997), 123–42.

28. Robert Miles, *Ann Radcliffe: The Great Enchantress* (Manchester: Manchester University Press, 1995), 107.

29. E. J. Clery, "Roman Catholicism," in introduction to Ann Radcliffe, *The Italian; or, The Confessional of the Black Penitents,* edited by Frederick Garber and E. J. Clery (1797, repr. New York: Oxford University Press, 1998), xiii, xv, xx, xxi; xxi; see also Sister Mary Muriel Tarr, "Catholicism in Gothic Fiction: A Study of the Nature and Function of Catholic Materials in Gothic Fiction in England (1762–1820)," Ph.D. thesis, Catholic University of America, 1946. Tarr remarks on "deistical attack on 'monkish superstition'" in gothic fiction and "melodramatic sentimentality that revels in 'melancholy pleasure,' 'divine horror,' and 'religious awe'" (121). The latter description best fits the work under consideration here.

30. George E. Haggerty, *Unnatural Affections: Women and Fiction in the Later Eighteenth Century* (Bloomington: Indiana University Press, 1998), 158–65. Clery suggests that Schedoni is not as formulaic a character as some of his predecessors. I agree with that assessment but still feel that the emphasis is maternal rather than paternal in this and Radcliffe's other novels.

31. Regina Maria Roche, *The Children of the Abbey, a Tale,* 4 vols. (London: Printed for William Lane at Minerva Press, Leadenhall Street, 1797), vol. 1, ch. 17, p. 313; further references in the text are to this edition and include volume, chapter, and page numbers.

32. William Henry Ireland, *The Abbess, a Romance,* 4 vols. (London: Printed for Earle and Hemmet, no. 47 Albemarle Street, Piccadilly, 1799), facsimile edition edited by Devendra P. Varma, new introduction by Benjamin Franklin Fisher IV (New York: Arno Press, 1974), vol. 1, ch. 1, p. 3; further references in the text are to this edition and include volume, chapter, and page numbers.

33. For a discussion of this feature of *The Romance of the Forest* (1791), see Haggerty, *Unnatural Affections,* 158–70.

34. For a discussion of the importance of Donatien-Alphonse-François, Marquis de Sade (1740–1814) to the "history of erotic writing," see Stephanie Hammer, "Donatien-Alphonse-François, Marquis de Sade (1740–1814)," in *Gay Histories and Cultures: An Encyclopedia,* edited by George E. Haggerty (New York: Garland Publishing, 2000), 761–62.

Chapter 5: Psychodrama: Hypertheatricality and Sexual Excess on the Gothic Stage

1. Michel Foucault, *The History of Sexuality,* vol. 1: *An Introduction,* translated by Robert Hurley (New York: Vintage-Random House, 1980), 103–5.

2. Horace Walpole, *The Mysterious Mother,* in *The Works of Horatio Walpole, Earl of Orford,* vol. 1, reprinted in *Five Romantic Plays, 1768–1821,* edited by Paul Baines, Edward Burns, et al. (1798, repr. New York: Oxford University Press, 2000), 1–69, further references in the text are to this edition and include act and line numbers. See also *Seven Gothic Dramas, 1789–1825,* edited by Jeffrey N. Cox (Athens: Ohio University Press, 1992), 5, 13–15; and George E. Haggerty, "Walpole's Secrets," in Haggerty, *Men in Love: Masculinity and Sexuality in the Eighteenth Century* (New York: Columbia University Press, 1999), 152–74.

3. Horace Walpole to Robert Jephson (1736–1803), Feb. 24, late Feb. 1775, in Horace Walpole, *The Yale Edition of Horace Walpole's Correspondence,* edited by W. S. Lewis, 48 vols. (New Haven: Yale University Press, 1937–83), 41: 288, 41: 290–91.

4. For a discussion of incest in Otway's play, see Pat Gill, "Pathetic Passions: Incestuous Desire in Plays by Otway and Lee," *The Eighteenth Century: Theory and Interpretation* 39 (Fall 1998): 192–208.

5. Thomas Otway, *Don Carlos, Prince of Spain: A Tragedy,* in *The Complete Works of Thomas Otway,* edited by Montague Summers, 3 vols. (1676, repr. London: Nonesuch, 1926), 1: 100, 3.1; further references in the text are to this edition and include volume, page, act, and scene numbers.

6. The Bible contains no reference to "Sodoms apples," but there is a reference to grapes: "For their vine is of the vine of Sodom, and of the fields of Gomorrah: their grapes are grapes of gall, their clusters are bitter" (Deuteronomy 32:32).

7. Jill Campbell, "'I Am No Giant': Horace Walpole, Heterosexual Incest, and Love among Men," *The Eighteenth Century: Theory and Interpretation* 39 (Fall 1998): 230–60, quotation on 240.

8. Foucault, *The History of Sexuality,* 1: 109, 1: 105.

9. Horace Walpole to George Montagu (1716–71), April 15, 1768, in Walpole, *The Yale Edition of Horace Walpole's Correspondence,* 10: 259–60; see also Paul Baines and Edward Burns, Introduction to *Five Romantic Plays, 1768–1821,* edited by Paul Baines and Edward Burns, Michael Cordner general editor (New York: Oxford University Press, 2000), xiii.

10. Baines and Burns, Introduction to *Five Romatic Plays,* xiii–xiv.

11. Elin Diamond, *"Gestus* and Signature in Aphra Behn's *The Rover," ELH* 56 (1989): 519, 521; see also John Willet, *Brecht on Theatre: The Development of an Aesthetic* (New York: Hill and Wang, 1964), 42.

12. Walpole, *The Yale Edition of Horace Walpole's Correspondence,* 31: 247n.

13. Samuel Taylor Coleridge, *Specimens of the Table Talk of the Late Samuel Coleridge* (London, 1835), 1:154, reprinted in *Horace Walpole: The Critical Heritage,* edited by Peter Sabor (London: Routledge and Kegan Paul, 1987), 148.

14. William Mason (1725–97) to Horace Walpole, Dec. 1, 1772, in Walpole, *The Yale Edition of Horace Walpole's Correspondence,* 28: 54.

15. Sir Horace Mann and Horace Walpole corresponded regularly from the time Walpole visited Italy with Gray in 1739 until Mann's death in 1786. Ibid., 24: 517.

16. Cox, ed., *Seven Gothic Dramas,* 4–5.

17. Ibid., 9–10. for a more detailed description of the gothic stage, see Paul Ranger, *"Terror and Pity Reign in Every Breast": Gothic Drama in the London Patent Theatres, 1750–1820* (London: Society for Theatre Research, 1991), esp. 88–89.

18. Cox, ed., *Seven Gothic Dramas,* 12.

19. Ranger, *"Terror and Pity,"* 51, and "Castle and Cloister," 42–68; Lewis, *The Castle Spectre,* in *Seven Gothic Dramas, 1789–1825,* edited by Jeffrey N. Cox (Athens: Ohio University Press, 1992), 149–224.

20. Ranger discusses this and other uses of incarceration in gothic drama. *"Terror and Pity,"* 49–52.

21. Ranger discusses the role of ghosts on the gothic stage. Ibid., 75–78.

22. Slavoj Žižek, *The Sublime Object of Ideology* (New York: Verso Press, 1989), 120–21, emphasis in the original.

23. For a discussion of the gender rigidity of much later eighteenth-century fiction, see Kim Ian Michasiw, Introduction, in *Zofloya; or, The Moor* (New York: Oxford University Press, 1997), xxvi–xxvii; see also George E. Haggerty, *Unnatural Affections: Women and Fiction in the Later Eighteenth Century* (Bloomington: University of Indiana Press, 1998), 1–20.

24. Cox mentions the review of the printed text by the *Monthly Mirror* (Dec. 1797), see *Seven Gothic Dramas,* 161.

25. Mathew G. Lewis, "To the Reader," in *Seven Gothic Dramas,* edited by Cox, 223.

26. Joseph Roach, *Cities of the Dead: Circum-Atlantic Performance* (New York: Columbia University Press, 1996), 121.

27. Roach, *Cities of the Dead,* 145.

28. Ibid., 153.

29. Joanna Baillie, *De Monfort: A Tragedy,* in *Seven Gothic Dramas,* edited by Jeffrey N. Cox (Athens: Ohio University Press, 1992), 263; 2.2; further references in the text are to this edition and include page, act, and scene numbers.

30. Baines and Burns, Introduction to *Five Romantic Plays,* xxi. For a discussion of the staging of this play, see Ranger, *"Terror and Pity,"* 98–102.

31. Eve Kosofsky Sedgwick, *Between Men: English Literature and Male Homosocial Desire* (New York: Columbia University Press, 25).

32. Cox, ed., *Seven Gothic Dramas,* 54.

33. For a discussion of "forest scenes" in gothic drama, see Ranger, *"Terror and Pity,"* 19–40.

34. Campbell, "'I Am No Giant,'" 247.

35. Stuart Curran, *Shelley's* Cenci: *Scorpions Ringed with Fire* (Princeton: Princeton University Press, 1970), 168, and the chapter entitled "Shelley and the Romantic Stage," 147–82.

36. *Literary Gazette, and Journal of Belles-Lettres, Arts, Sciences, etc.,* April 1, 1820, 209–10; see also Curran, *Shelley's* Cenci, 8–9.

37. Percy Bysshe Shelley, Preface to *The Cenci,* in *Shelley's Poetry and Prose,* edited by Donald H. Reiman and Sharon B. Powers (New York: W. W. Norton, 1977), 239–40; further references in the text are to this edition and include page, act, and scene numbers.

38. Curran, *Shelley's* Cenci, 67.

39. Slavoj Žižek, *For They Know Not What They Do: Enjoyment as a Political Factor* (London: Verso Press, 1991), 134.

40. Žižek, *For They Know Not What They Do,* 134–35.

41. For another perspective on this confrontation see Young-Ok An, "Beatrice's Gaze Revisited: Anatomizing *The Cenci,*" *Criticism* 37 (1996): 27–88. For her, "The Cenci provides a feminist reader with a particularly useful textual reference to investigate not just abominable incidents of paternal tyranny and parricide but much more complex operations of violence, law, and desire that intersect gender issues" (27). By reading Beatrice as a female Prometheus, An exposes a "web of legitimized violence" (36) in which "Beatrice sees herself squarely implicated in the unbreakable chain of oppression" (37).

42. Žižek, *For They Know Not What They Do,* 249.

43. For a discussion of this scene see William Jewett, "Strange Flesh: Shelley and the Performance of Skepticism," *Texas Studies in Literature and Language* 38 (1996): 321–39. Jewett maintains that "throughout her speeches Beatrice attempts to keep the full extent of her suffering at bay by refusing to recognize her identity with the Beatrice who has been raped by her father" (334). This is another way of explaining the uncanny mood that Shelley invokes.

44. Terry Castle, *The Female Thermometer: Eighteenth-Century Culture and the Invention of the Uncanny* (New York: Oxford University Press, 1995), 15.

45. Žižek, *For They Know Not What They Do,* 135.

Chapter 6: "The End of History": Identity and Dissolution in Apocalyptic Gothic

1. Christopher Horrocks, *Baudrillard and the Millennium* (New York: Totem Books, 1999), 14.

2. William Godwin, "Of History and Romance," in *Caleb Williams,* edited by Maurice Hindle (Harmondsworth: Penguin, 1988), 372.

3. Eve Kosofsky Sedgwick, *Between Men: English Literature and Male Homosexual Desire* (New York: Columbia University Press, 1985), 91–92.

4. Slavoj Žižek, *For They Know Not What They Do: Enjoyment as a Political Factor* (New York: Verso Press, 1991): 35–36; also see G. W. F. Hegel, *Philosophy of Right* (New York: Oxford University Press, 1967), 182.

5. James Thompson, "Surveillance in William Godwin's *Caleb Williams,*" in *Gothic Fictions: Prohibition/Transgression,* edited by K. W. Graham (New York: AMS Press, 1989), 173–98, quotation on 179.

6. Thompson, "Surveillance in William Godwin's *Caleb Williams,*" 176–78.

7. For a discussion of the relation between the history of sexuality and the conventional structures of gothic fiction see George E. Haggerty, "Literature and Homosexuality in the Late Eighteenth Century: Walpole, Beckford, and Lewis," *Studies in the Novel* 18 (1986): 341–51.

8. A more complete discussion of the Vere Street scandal appears in chapter 3.

9. Ian Ousby, "'My Servant Caleb': Godwin's *Caleb Williams* and the Political Trials of the 1790's," *University of Toronto Quarterly* 44 (1974): 47–55.

10. William Godwin, *Things as They Are; or, The Adventures of Caleb Williams,* edited by Maurice Hindle (1794, repr. Harmondsworth: Penguin, 1988), 138–39; further references in the text are to this edition.

11. Morton D. Paley, "*The Last Man:* Apocalypse without Millennium," in *The Other Mary Shelley: Beyond Frankenstein,* edited by Audrey A. Fisch, Anne K. Mellor, and Esther H. Schor (New York: Oxford University Press, 1993), 110.

12. Paley, "*The Last Man:* Apocalypse without Millennium," 117.

13. Mary Shelley, *The Last Man* (1826, rpr. Peterborough, Ont.: Broadview Press, 1996), 11; further references in the text are to this edition.

14. Anne McWhir, Introduction to Mary Shelley, *The Last Man* (Peterborough, Ont.: Broadview Press, 1996), xvii–xviii.

15. Barbara Johnson, "*The Last Man,*" in *The Other Mary Shelley: Beyond Frankenstein,* edited by Audrey A. Fisch, Anne K. Mellor, and Esther H. Schor (New York: Oxford University Press, 1993), 260.

16. Paley, "*The Last Man:* Apocalypse without Millennium," 114–15.

17. Audrey A. Fisch, "Plaguing Politics: AIDS, Deconstruction, and *The Last Man,*" in *The Other Mary Shelley: Beyond Frankenstein,* edited by Audrey A. Fisch, Anne K. Mellor, and Esther H. Schor (New York: Oxford University Press, 1993), 270.

18. McWhir, Introduction, xxvii–xix; see also Anne K. Mellor, "Subversive Surfaces: The Limits of Domestic Affection in Mary Shelley's Later Fiction," in *The Other Mary Shelley: Beyond Frankenstein,* edited by Audrey A. Fisch, Anne K. Mellor, and Esther H. Schor (New York: Oxford University Press, 1993), 227.

19. "Global AIDS Epidemic a Picture of Devastation," *Los Angeles Times,* June 28, 2000, A20.

20. Percy Bysshe Shelley, *The Complete Poetical Works of Percy Bysshe Shelley* (Boston: Houghton Mifflin, 1901), 520; see also *Theocritus, Bion, and Moschus,* edited and translated by Andrew Lang (London, 1924), reprinted in *Milton's "Lycidas,"* edited by Scott Elledge (New York: Harper and Row, 1966). For a discussion of the erotics of the elegy see George E. Haggerty, "Desire and Mourning: The Ideology of the Elegy," in *Ideology and Form,* edited by David Richter (Lubbock: Texas Tech University Press, 1999), 184–206.

21. Paley, *"The Last Man:* Apocalypse without Millenium," 110.

22. Robert Louis Stevenson, *Dr. Jekyll and Mr. Hyde,* edited by Emma Letley (1886, repr. New York: Oxford University Press, 1987), 20; further references in the text are to this edition.

23. David Halperin, "Homosexuality," in *Gay Histories and Cultures: An Encyclopedia,* edited by George E. Haggerty (New York: Garland, 2000), 450–52.

24. Eve Kosofsky Sedgwick, *Epistemology of the Closet* (Berkeley: University of California Press, 1990), 172.

25. Graham Balfour, *The Life of Robert Louis Stevenson,* 2 vols. (London: Methuen, 1901), 2: 14; see also Emma Letley, "Explanatory Notes," in *Dr. Jekyll and Mr. Hyde* (New York: Oxford University Press, 1987), 212. The origins of the story are to be found in Stevenson's "A Chapter on Dreams," which is included as an appendix in this edition.

26. For a discussion of Scott's novel in these terms see George E. Haggerty, *Unnatural Affections: Women and Fiction in the Later Eighteenth Century* (Bloomington: Indiana University press, 1998), 88–102.

Chapter 7: "Queer Company": *The Turn of the Screw* and *The Haunting of Hill House*

I would like to thank my colleague Joseph Childers for his comments and suggestions for this chapter.

1. Studies of "The Turn of the Screw" that have informed this discussion include Ronnie Baillie, *The Fantastic Anatomist: A Psychoanalytic Study of Henry James* (Amsterdam-Atlanta: Rodopi Press, 2000), ch. 4, "Autopsy: *The Turn of the Screw"*; Ellis Hansen, "Screwing with Children in Henry James," *GLQ: A Journal of Lesbian and Gay Studies* 9, no. 3 (2003): 367–91; Stanley Renner, "Sexual Hysteria, Physiognomical Bogeymen, and the 'Ghosts' in *The Turn of the Screw,"* *Nineteenth-Century Literature* 43, no. 2 (1988): 175–94; Allan Lloyd Smith, "A Word Kept Back in *The Turn of the Screw,"* *Victorian Literature and Culture,* edited by John Maynard and Adrienne Auslander Munich (New York: AMS Press, 1996): 24: 139–57; and Elton E. Smith, "Pedophiles amidst Looming Portentousness: Henry James's *The Turn of the Screw,"* in *The Haunted Mind: The Supernatural in Victorian Fiction,* edited by Robert Haas and Elton E. Smith (Lanham: Rowman and Littlefield, 1999), 123–30.

2. Henry James, *The Turn of the Screw,* in *The Portable Henry James,* edited by John Auchard (New York: Penguin, 2004), 137–235; further references in the text are to this edition.

3. Of course the reference might also apply to Charlotte Brontë's *Jane Eyre,* but James refers all the way back to Radcliffe herself. Brontë would have provided a more immediate and more accessible reference for James's readers.

4. Claire Kahane, "The Gothic Mirror," in *The Mother Tongue: Essays in Feminist Psychoanalytic Interpretation,* edited by Shirley Nelson Garner, Claire Kahane, and Madelon Springnether (Ithaca: Cornell University Press, 1985), 339.

5. Hansen, "Screwing with Children in Henry James," 372–73.

6. Ibid. In this context see James R. Kincaid, *Child-Loving: The Erotic Child and Victorian Literature* (New York: Routledge, 1994).

7. See especially Hugh Stevens, "Homoeroticism, Identity, and Agency in James's Late Tales," in *Enacting History in Henry James: Narrative, Power, and Ethics,* edited by Gert Buelens (New York: Cambridge University Press, 1997), 126–47. Stevens pays special attention to the force of the term *queer.* "There is, of course," Stevens says, "dispute as to whether 'queer' might have had a homosexual connotation for James at the turn of the century. The *OED* lists 1922 as the first date of this usage, which would, however, almost certainly have enjoyed considerable oral circulation before occurring in writing. It may be that James used 'queer' precisely because its connotation with 'homosexual' is tentative and uncertain. . . . Recent commentators who have argued that 'queer' already had homosexual connotations in the late nineteenth century include Elaine Showalter, in *Sexual Anarchy: Gender and Culture at the Fin de Siècle* (New York: Viking Press, 1990), 111–12; Wayne Koestenbaum, in *Double Talk: The Erotics of Male Literary Collaboration* (New York: Routledge, 1989); and Joseph Bristow, in *Effeminate England: Homoerotic Writing after 1885* (Buckingham: Open University Press, 1995), 145n10. See also Eric Haralson, *Henry James and Queer Modernity* (New York: Cambridge University Press, 2003), 5–8. For Haralson, "One can no more pin down the first instance in which *queer* meant '(a) homosexual' in Anglo-American discourse than one can say 'modernity' commenced on or about December 1910, as in Virginia Woolf's famous formula" (9).

8. Patricia White, "Female Spectator, Lesbian Specter: *The Haunting,*" in *Inside/Out: Lesbian Theories, Gay Theories,* edited by Diana Fuss (New York: Routledge, 1991), 142–72, quotation on 149. The internal reference is to Sigmund Freud, "The Uncanny" (1919), in *Art and Literature,* edited by Albert Dickson (Harmondsworth: Penguin, 1985), 335–76.

9. Mary Ann Doane, *The Desire to Desire: The Woman's Film of the 1940s* (Bloomington: Indiana University Press, 1987), 157.

10. For a succinct summary of this approach see Philip Brett, "Britten's Bad Boys: Male Relations in *The Turn of the Screw,*" *repercussions* 1 (1992): 5–25, reprinted in *Music and Sexuality in Britten: Selected Essays of Philip Brett,* edited by George E. Haggerty (Berkeley: University of California Press, forthcoming).

11. The locus classicus of the danger of such relations is the account to be found in Sheridan Le Fanu's vampire story "Carmilla."

12. Shirley Jackson, *The Haunting of Hill House* (1959, repr. Harmondsworth: Penguin, 1984); further references in the text are to this edition.

13. Although Patricia White's article remains the richest discussion of lesbianism in the film version of the novel, her insights are too genre-specific to be quotable in this context, but I recommend the essay nonetheless. For a discussion of Jackson's attitude toward the novel ("I am always afraid of being alone") see S. T. Joshi, "Shirley Jackson: Domestic Horror," *Studies in Weird Fiction* 14 (1994): 9–28.

14. Julia Kristeva, *Powers of Horror: An Essay on Abjection,* translated by Leon S. Roudiez (New York: Columbia University Press, 1982), 1, see also 90–112 on the figure of death.

15. Michel Foucault, *The History of Sexuality,* vol. 1: *An Introduction,* translated by Robert Hurley (New York: Vintage-Random House, 1980), 103, 104–5.

Chapter 8: "Queerer Knowledge": Lambert Strether and Tom Ripley

1. Patricia Highsmith, *The Talented Mr. Ripley* (1955, repr. New York: Vintage, 1983), 24; further references in the text are to this edition.

2. Henry James, *The Ambassadors,* edited by Harry Levin (1903, repr. Harmondsworth: Penguin, 1986), 418; further references in the text are to this edition.

3. Eve Kosofsky Sedgwick, *Epistemology of the Closet* (Berkeley; University of California Press, 1990), 201.

4. Sedgwick, *Epistemology of the Closet,* 205.

5. "Inversion as a term to describe homosexual desire entered British scientific discourse in 1897, when Havelock Ellis and John Addington Symonds published their book *Sexual Inversion.* The term probably circulated in English thought for at least sometime before that as well, but Ellis and Symonds's book marks its most major and respected articulation as a psychological term." Gregory W. Bredbeck, "Inversion," in *Gay Histories and Cultures,* edited by George E. Haggerty (New York: Garland, 2000), 474.

6. Sedgwick, *Epistemology of the Closet,* 187.

7. Eric Haralson, "Masculinity 'Changed and Queer' in *The Ambassadors,*" in Haralson, *Henry James and Queer Modernity* (New York: Cambridge University Press, 2003), 102–33, quotation on 109. Haralson goes on to argue that because "James structures Strether's quest for a workable sociosexual identity as inseparable from his trials of national identity—his efforts to keep within the bounds of his native culture by expanding those bounds—it is instrumental that Bilham manages to appear 'more American than anybody' while prosecuting a mode of being 'intense' that deviates refreshingly from the usual intensities of American bourgeois masculinity" (119).

8. George E. Haggerty, "Desire and Mourning: The Ideology of the Elegy," in *Ideol-*

ogy and Form in Eighteenth-Century Literature, edited by David H. Richter (Lubbock: Texas Tech University Press, 1999), 185–206.

9. Harry Levin, Introduction to James, *The Ambassadors,* 7; see also F. R. Leavis, *The Great Tradition: George Eliot, Henry James, Joseph Conrad* (Garden City: Doubleday, 1954).

10. Robert Corber, "United States," in *Gay Histories and Cultures,* edited by George E. Haggerty (New York: Garland, 2000), 905.

11. John D'Emilio, *Sexual Politics, Sexual Communities: The Making of a Homosexual Minority in the United States, 1940–1970* (Chicago: University of Chicago Press, 1983), 49.

12. Slavoj Žižek, *The Sublime Object of Ideology* (New York: Verso Press, 1989), 180.

13. For an assessment of the contemporary understanding of the term *camp,* see Susan Sontag, "Notes on Camp," in Sontag, *Against Interpretation and Other Essays* (New York: Farrar, Straus and Giroux, 1966); see also *Camp: Queer Aesthetics and the Performing Self: A Reader,* edited by Fabio Cleto (Edinburgh: Edinburgh University Press, 1999).

14. Kaja Silverman, *Male Subjectivity at the Margins* (New York: Routledge, 1992), 317. Silverman adds that *"The Ego and the Id* encourages us to understand identification not so much as the 'resolution' of desire as its perpetuation within another regime, no longer subject to the same moral restraints" (317). See also Sigmund Freud, *The Ego and the Id* in *The Standard Edition of the Complete Psychological Works of Sigmund Freud,* edited and translated by James Strachey (London: Hogarth Press, 1955) 19: 29.

15. Sedgwick, *Epistemology of the Closet,* 204–7.

16. The *American Heritage Dictionary* defines "queer" as "deviating from the expected norm; strange." The *OED,* similarly, uses words like "strange, odd peculiar, eccentric in appearance or character; also of questionable character, suspicious, dubious."

17. Sedgwick, *Epistemology of the Closet,* 71.

18. Ibid., 73, 75.

19. D'Emilio, *Sexual Politics,* 57.

20. Sigmund Freud, *Three Essays on the Theory of Sexuality,* translated by James Strachey (New York: Basic Books, 1962), 59, 23.

21. D'Emilio, *Sexual Politics,* 58

22. Anthony Minghella, *The Talented Mr. Ripley: A Screenplay* (New York: Hyperion, 1999), 8; further references in the text to the screenplay are to this edition. When the film and the screenplay diverge, it will be noted.

23. Matthew Bell has written that "Hart's habits were as unconventional as his lyrics, and he became both notable and notorious for several of them: cigar smoking, drinking, and cultivating friendships with pimps and gay men." Bell adds that "Hart's witty, intricately rhymed, topical lyrics crystallized an upheaval in the conventions

of song writing for the musical theater; his work spurred the transition from revue-style theatrical music, typified by vaudeville and the *Ziegfeld Follies,* to the modern 'integrated' book musical, realized in *Oklahoma!* (Rodgers/Hammerstein, 1943)." Bell, "Hart, Lorenz," in *Gay Histories and Cultures,* edited by George E. Haggerty (New York: Garland, 2000), 428–29. As D. A. Miller observes, "The historical uniqueness of the Broadway musical among 'the signs' consisted in the fact that it never looked like one." But if the "latent homosexuality" of a character in Tennessee Williams's *Sweet Bird of Youth* can be indicated by his having sung in the chorus for *Oklahoma* in his youth, the sexual motivation of Tom Ripley is encoded in his choice of songs. Miller, *Place for Us: Essay on the Broadway Musical* (Cambridge: Harvard University Press, 1998), 16–17.

24. Dennis Altman, *Homosexual Oppression and Liberation* (1971; rpr. New York: New York University Press, 1993), 98–99.

25. In this they are uncannily similar to the male-male couple Lionel and Adrian, who risk their lives to cross from Italy to Greece at the end of Mary Shelley's *The Last Man* (1826; ch. 6 of this volume). Shelley's novel also ends in a mood of tragic loneliness.

26. A splendid 1960 French film based on this novel, *Plein soleil* (*Purple Noon*), was directed by René Clément and starred Alain Delon. Clément's version downplays the homoerotics of the plot and insists on a more brutally moralistic ending that also undermines Highsmith's insistence that Tom walks away from his crimes. Clément's Tom is trapped by the police as he sunbathes in a secure and self-congratulatory moment. It is an effective ending nonetheless.

27. Minghella, Introduction, *The Talented Mr. Ripley,* xii–xiii.

Chapter 9: Anne Rice and the Queering of Culture

1. Anne Rice, *Memnoch the Devil* (New York: Knopf: 1995), 241; further references in the text are to this edition. The other volumes in *The Vampire Chronicles* include *Interview with the Vampire* (New York: Ballantine, 1977); *The Vampire Lestat* (New York: Ballantine, 1985); *The Queen of the Damned* (New York: Ballantine, 1988); *The Tale of the Body Thief* (New York: Knopf, 1992); and *The Vampire Armand* (New York: Knopf, 1998).

2. Nina Auerbach, *Our Vampires, Ourselves* (Chicago: University of Chicago Press, 1995), 153.

3. Auerbach, *Our Vampires, Ourselves,* 154.

4. Judith Butler, *Bodies That Matter: On the Discursive Limits of Sex* (New York: Routledge, 1993), 223.

5. As Christopher Craft says about *Dracula,* "A swooning desire for an overwhelming penetration and intense aversion to the demonic potency empowered to gratify desire: this is the ambivalence that motivates action and emotion in *Dracula.*" Craft, *Another Kind of Love: Male Homosexual Desire in English Discourse, 1850–1920* (Berkeley: University of California Press, 1994), 73.

6. D. A. Miller discusses a similar arrangement, which he calls the "open secret." He argues that "the fact that the secret is always known—and, in some obscure sense, known to be known—never interferes with the incessant activity of keeping it." For Miller, the resulting paradox "registers the subject's accommodation to a totalizing system that has obliterated the difference he would make—the difference he does make, in the imaginary denial of this system." Miller, *The Novel and the Police* (Berkeley: University of California Press, 1988), 206–7. The material conditions of male-male desire is precisely what this theater gives up in its taunting masquerade.

7. Sue-Ellen Case, "Tracking the Vampire," *differences*, 3, no. 2 (1991): 3.

8. Slavoj Žižek, *The Sublime Object of Ideology* (New York: Verso Press, 1992), 73. Žižek adds, "The symbolic structuring of sexuality implies the lack of a signifier of the sexual relationship, . . . that the sexual relation cannot be symbolized. . . . And to seize the interconnection between the two universalizations, we must simply again apply the proposition 'what was foreclosed from the Symbolic returns in the Real of the symptom': woman does not exist, her signifier is originally foreclosed, and that is why she returns as a symptom of man."

9. I am not saying that the woman and the homosexual are in anything more than an analogous position here. It is important to see this analogy and equally important to distinguish the functions of gender and sexuality in this culture.

10. Žižek, *The Sublime Object of Ideology*, 3.

11. Ibid., 45.

12. Lauren Berlant and Elizabeth Freeman, "Queer Nationality," in *Fear of a Queer Planet: Queer Politics and Social Theory*, edited by Michael Warner (Minneapolis: University of Minnesota Press, 1993), 194–95.

13. Berlant and Freeman, "Queer Politics," 195.

14. All three quotations are from "Foes of Gay Studies at UCR," a report in the *Riverside* (Calif.) *Press Enterprise*, May 22, 1996.

15. AIDS and the sexual transmission of disease and death are topics of concern in various ways in the later volumes of *The Vampire Chronicles*. See the discussion of vampirism in Richard Dyer, "Children of the Night: Vampirism as Homosexuality, Homosexuality as Vampirism," in *Sweet Dreams: Sexuality and Gender in Popular Fiction*, edited by Susannah Radstone (London: Lawrence and Wishart, 1988), 47–72.

16. Eve Kosofsky Sedgwick, *Between Men: English Literature and Male Homosocial Desire* (New York: Columbia University Press, 1985), 25.

17. Sedgwick, *Between Men*, 1–21; see also Gayle Rubin, "The Traffic in Women: Notes toward a Political Economy of Sex," in *Toward an Anthropology of Women*, edited by Rayna Reiter (New York: Random House-Vintage, 1978), 157–210.

18. Craft, *Another Kind of Love*, 89.

Afterword

1. David M. Halperin, "How to Do the History of Male Homosexuality," *GLQ: A Journal of Lesbian and Gay Studies* 6, no. 1 (2000): 87–124, quotation on 110.

2. Elizabeth R. Napier, *The Failure of Gothic: Problems of Disjunction in an Eighteenth-Century Literary Form* (New York: Oxford University Press, 1987).

3. George Rousseau, "Nerves, Spirits, and Fibres: Toward Defining an Age of Sensibility," in *Studies in the Eighteenth Century III,* edited by R. F. Brissenden and J. C. Eade (Toronto: University of Toronto Press, 1976), 153.

Index

GEORGE E. HAGGERTY is professor of English at the University of California, Riverside. His books include *Gothic Fiction/Gothic Form* (1989); *Unnatural Affections: Women and Fiction in the Later Eighteenth Century* (1998); and *Men in Love: Masculinity and Sexuality in the Eighteenth Century* (1999). He has also edited *Professions of Desire: Lesbian and Gay Studies in Literature* (1995) and *Gay Histories and Cultures: An Encyclopedia* (2000). At present he is writing a book on Horace Walpole and editing, with Molly McGarry, *The Blackwell Companion to LGBT/Q Studies.*

The University of Illinois Press
is a founding member of the
Association of American University Presses.

_____

University of Illinois Press
1325 South Oak Street
Champaign, IL 61820-6903
www.press.uillinois.edu

Queer Gothic

Queer Gothic

GEORGE E. HAGGERTY

UNIVERSITY OF ILLINOIS PRESS

Urbana, Chicago, and Springfield

Library of Congress Cataloging-in-Publication Data
Haggerty, George E.
Queer Gothic / George E. Haggerty.
p.   cm.
Includes bibliographical references and index.
ISBN-13: 978-0-252-03108-3 (cloth : alk. paper)
ISBN-10: 0-252-03108-3 (cloth : alk. paper)
ISBN-13: 978-0-252-07353-3 (pbk. : alk. paper)
ISBN-10: 0-252-07353-3 (pbk. : alk. paper)
1. Gothic revival (Literature)—Great Britain.
2. Horror tales, English—History and criticism.
3. Gothic revival (Literature)—United States.
4. Horror tales, American—History and criticism.
5. Homosexuality in literature.
6. Sex in literature.
I. Title.
PR830.T3H254   2006
823'.0872909—dc22   2005035188